D0470257

Get Results with These Guidelines

Achievers share common attitudes and actions, including the fo

- **Set clearly defined goals.** These goals are clear, precise, written objectives with definitive time frames for completion.
- **Respect time.** Organized people monitor every minute, paying equally close attention to how they spend their leisure time and their business time.
- **Write everything down.** Organized people keep their long-term, intermediate, and short-term goals written down where they can see them on a daily basis, and their lists and daily planners are with them at all times.
- **Prioritize.** Always approach tasks in descending order of importance, handling the most important things first and the least important thing last.
- **Focus on the task at hand.** Don't clutter your mind with things that are coming up later or things that you've completed in the past.
- **Study a subject before acting on it.** Judge whether a subject is worthy of your time and attention, and if it is, develop a strategy for approaching the task.
- **Constantly look for ways to improve.** You may be an old dog, but you can always learn a new trick.
- **Delegate.** Recognize the tasks that only you can do, and focus your time on these items. Delegate everything else.
- **Know when to quit.** When you have to abandon a project, move on without any hesitation, guilt, or anxiety.
- **Manage space as well as time.** Maintain an orderly environment where you live and work.
- **Be flexible.** Get pleasure from shuffling tasks and still meeting obligations.

Start Your Business Day on the Right Foot

Here are some great ways to jumpstart your business morning and set the tone for the rest of your busy day.

- Make a good impression with an early phone call.
- Schedule a breakfast meeting.
- Schedule creative writing for the early morning.
- Eliminate yesterday's clutter.
- Glance at yesterday's list.
- Run a quick goal check.
- Scan the news.
- Write thank-you notes.
- Send fan letters.
- Greet everyone you meet with a smile.

Planning Long-Term Objectives

Here's how you coordinate long-term plans so that you stick to them:

1. **Write your long-term objectives on your calendar and keep your calendar in your sight.**

   Whether it's on your desk, in your pocket, or on your kitchen wall, having the calendar visible provides a daily reminder that long-term items need your attention too.

2. **Write your long-term objectives in your planner as constant reminders of what you are striving to achieve.**

   I write "ff" for "fast forward" beside the items in my planner that do not require immediate action but need to be considered for a later time. Whatever annotation works for you, the main objective is for you to commit your long-term projects to your short-term lists in a way that you won't forget them.

3. **Develop a specific list of incremental tasks that leads you toward your long-term objectives.**

   This is the old "eating the elephant one bite at a time" strategy. A project that takes months to achieve certainly requires some work along the way, even if the effort is nothing more than scheduling an hour a week to think about an upcoming event. You can accomplish plenty with advance work, even if a project deadline is months away.

4. **Add those incremental advance-work tasks to your planner and calendar as well.**

   If you're spending time thinking about your long-term project, write "10 a.m. to 11 a.m., *Think about long-term project X*," in your planner.

5. **Give yourself deadlines for every step in the process so that you are constantly under the gun.**

   If each increment is completed on time, the project is likely completed on time as well.

6. **Be ready to adapt to changes along the way.**

   The world today is not the place you thought it would be last year, and the things you predict for next year will probably be wrong. You need to be prepared to adapt your plans and strategies at every juncture.

The IDG Books Worldwide logo is a registered trademark under exclusive license to IDG Books Worldwide, Inc., from International Data Group, Inc. The ...For Dummies logo and For Dummies are trademarks of IDG Books Worldwide, Inc. All other trademarks are the property of their respective owners.

For Dummies™: Bestselling Book Series for Beginners

TM

References for the Rest of Us!™

BESTSELLING BOOK SERIES

Do you find that traditional reference books are overloaded with technical details and advice you'll never use? Do you postpone important life decisions because you just don't want to deal with them? Then our ...*For Dummies*® business and general reference book series is for you.

...*For Dummies* business and general reference books are written for those frustrated and hard-working souls who know they aren't dumb, but find that the myriad of personal and business issues and the accompanying horror stories make them feel helpless. ...*For Dummies* books use a lighthearted approach, a down-to-earth style, and even cartoons and humorous icons to dispel fears and build confidence. Lighthearted but not lightweight, these books are perfect survival guides to solve your everyday personal and business problems.

> *"More than a publishing phenomenon, 'Dummies' is a sign of the times."*
>
> — *The New York Times*

> *"A world of detailed and authoritative information is packed into them..."*
>
> — *U.S. News and World Report*

> *"...you won't go wrong buying them."*
>
> — *Walter Mossberg, Wall Street Journal, on IDG Books' ...For Dummies books*

Already, millions of satisfied readers agree. They have made ...*For Dummies* the #1 introductory level computer book series and a best-selling business book series. They have written asking for more. So, if you're looking for the best and easiest way to learn about business and other general reference topics, look to ...*For Dummies* to give you a helping hand.

IDG BOOKS WORLDWIDE

1/99

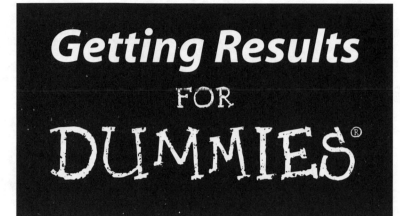

Getting Results FOR DUMMIES®

by Mark H. McCormack

IDG Books Worldwide, Inc.
An International Data Group Company

Foster City, CA ◆ Chicago, IL ◆ Indianapolis, IN ◆ New York, NY

Getting Results For Dummies®

Published by
IDG Books Worldwide, Inc.
An International Data Group Company
919 E. Hillsdale Blvd.
Suite 400
Foster City, CA 94404
www.idgbooks.com (IDG Books Worldwide Web site)
www.dummies.com (Dummies Press Web site)

Library of Congress Catalog Card No.: 99-66333

ISBN: 0-7645-5205-8

Printed in the United States of America

10 9 8 7 6 5 4 3 2 1

1B/QW/RS/ZZ/IN

Distributed in the United States by IDG Books Worldwide, Inc.

Distributed by CDG Books Canada Inc. for Canada; by Transworld Publishers Limited in the United Kingdom; by IDG Norge Books for Norway; by IDG Sweden Books for Sweden; by IDG Books Australia Publishing Corporation Pty. Ltd. for Australia and New Zealand; by TransQuest Publishers Pte Ltd. for Singapore, Malaysia, Thailand, Indonesia, and Hong Kong; by Gotop Information Inc. for Taiwan; by ICG Muse, Inc. for Japan; by Intersoft for South Africa; by Eyrolles for France; by International Thomson Publishing for Germany, Austria and Switzerland; by Distribuidora Cuspide for Argentina; by LR International for Brazil; by Galileo Libros for Chile; by Ediciones ZETA S.C.R. Ltda. for Peru; by WS Computer Publishing Corporation, Inc., for the Philippines; by Contemporanea de Ediciones for Venezuela; by Express Computer Distributors for the Caribbean and West Indies; by Micronesia Media Distributor, Inc. for Micronesia; by Chips Computadoras S.A. de C.V. for Mexico; by Editorial Norma de Panama S.A. for Panama; by American Bookshops for Finland.

For general information on IDG Books Worldwide's books in the U.S., please call our Consumer Customer Service department at 800-762-2974. For reseller information, including discounts and premium sales, please call our Reseller Customer Service department at 800-434-3422.

For information on where to purchase IDG Books Worldwide's books outside the U.S., please contact our International Sales department at 317-596-5530 or fax 317-596-5692.

For consumer information on foreign language translations, please contact our Customer Service department at 1-800-434-3422, fax 317-596-5692, or e-mail rights@idgbooks.com.

For information on licensing foreign or domestic rights, please phone +1-650-655-3109.

For sales inquiries and special prices for bulk quantities, please contact our Sales department at 650-655-3200 or write to the address above.

For information on using IDG Books Worldwide's books in the classroom or for ordering examination copies, please contact our Educational Sales department at 800-434-2086 or fax 317-596-5499.

For press review copies, author interviews, or other publicity information, please contact our Public Relations department at 650-655-3000 or fax 650-655-3299.

For authorization to photocopy items for corporate, personal, or educational use, please contact Copyright Clearance Center, 222 Rosewood Drive, Danvers, MA 01923, or fax 978-750-4470.

 is a registered trademark under exclusive license to IDG Books Worldwide, Inc. from International Data Group, Inc.

About the Author

Mark McCormack is the founder of International Management Group, a multi-million dollar worldwide corporation that is a consultant to 50 Fortune 500 companies. His books include *What They Still Don't Teach You at Harvard Business School* and *The World of Professional Golf.*

ABOUT IDG BOOKS WORLDWIDE

Welcome to the world of IDG Books Worldwide.

IDG Books Worldwide, Inc., is a subsidiary of International Data Group, the world's largest publisher of computer-related information and the leading global provider of information services on information technology. IDG was founded more than 30 years ago by Patrick J. McGovern and now employs more than 9,000 people worldwide. IDG publishes more than 290 computer publications in over 75 countries. More than 90 million people read one or more IDG publications each month.

Launched in 1990, IDG Books Worldwide is today the #1 publisher of best-selling computer books in the United States. We are proud to have received eight awards from the Computer Press Association in recognition of editorial excellence and three from Computer Currents' First Annual Readers' Choice Awards. Our best-selling ...For Dummies® series has more than 50 million copies in print with translations in 31 languages. IDG Books Worldwide, through a joint venture with IDG's Hi-Tech Beijing, became the first U.S. publisher to publish a computer book in the People's Republic of China. In record time, IDG Books Worldwide has become the first choice for millions of readers around the world who want to learn how to better manage their businesses.

Our mission is simple: Every one of our books is designed to bring extra value and skill-building instructions to the reader. Our books are written by experts who understand and care about our readers. The knowledge base of our editorial staff comes from years of experience in publishing, education, and journalism — experience we use to produce books to carry us into the new millennium. In short, we care about books, so we attract the best people. We devote special attention to details such as audience, interior design, use of icons, and illustrations. And because we use an efficient process of authoring, editing, and desktop publishing our books electronically, we can spend more time ensuring superior content and less time on the technicalities of making books.

You can count on our commitment to deliver high-quality books at competitive prices on topics you want to read about. At IDG Books Worldwide, we continue in the IDG tradition of delivering quality for more than 30 years. You'll find no better book on a subject than one from IDG Books Worldwide.

John Kilcullen
Chairman and CEO
IDG Books Worldwide, Inc.

Steven Berkowitz
President and Publisher
IDG Books Worldwide, Inc.

Eighth Annual Computer Press Awards ≥1992

Ninth Annual Computer Press Awards ≥1993

Tenth Annual Computer Press Awards ≥1994

Eleventh Annual Computer Press Awards ≥1995

IDG is the world's leading IT media, research and exposition company. Founded in 1964, IDG had 1997 revenues of $2.05 billion and has more than 9,000 employees worldwide. IDG offers the widest range of media options that reach IT buyers in 75 countries representing 95% of worldwide IT spending. IDG's diverse product and services portfolio spans six key areas including print publishing, online publishing, expositions and conferences, market research, education and training, and global marketing services. More than 90 million people read one or more of IDG's 290 magazines and newspapers, including IDG's leading global brands — Computerworld, PC World, Network World, Macworld and the Channel World family of publications. IDG Books Worldwide is one of the fastest-growing computer book publishers in the world, with more than 700 titles in 36 languages. The "...For Dummies®" series alone has more than 50 million copies in print. IDG offers online users the largest network of technology-specific Web sites around the world through IDG.net (http://www.idg.net), which comprises more than 225 targeted Web sites in 55 countries worldwide. International Data Corporation (IDC) is the world's largest provider of information technology data, analysis and consulting, with research centers in over 41 countries and more than 400 research analysts worldwide. IDG World Expo is a leading producer of more than 168 globally branded conferences and expositions in 35 countries including E3 (Electronic Entertainment Expo), Macworld Expo, ComNet, Windows World Expo, ICE (Internet Commerce Expo), Agenda, DEMO, and Spotlight. IDG's training subsidiary, ExecuTrain, is the world's largest computer training company, with more than 230 locations worldwide and 785 training courses. IDG Marketing Services helps industry-leading IT companies build international brand recognition by developing global integrated marketing programs via IDG's print, online and exposition products worldwide. Further information about the company can be found at www.idg.com.   1/24/99

Author's Acknowledgments

I would like to thank Steve Eubanks and Mark Reiter for their support and assistance.

Publisher's Acknowledgments

We're proud of this book; please register your comments through our IDG Books Worldwide Online Registration Form located at http://my2cents.dummies.com.

Some of the people who helped bring this book to market include the following:

Acquisitions, Editorial, and Media Development

Project Editors: Tim Gallan, Tere Drenth

Senior Acquisitions Editor: Mark Butler

Copy Editors: Corey Dalton, Donna Fredrick

General Reviewer: Mark Reiter

Editorial Assistant: Carol Strickland

Acquisitions Coordinator: Lisa Roule

Editorial Managers: Seta K. Frantz, Pamela Mourouzis

Production

Project Coordinator: Emily Perkins

Layout and Graphics: Joe Bucki, Kate Jenkins, Barry Offringa, Tracy Oliver, Jill Piscitelli, Doug Rollison, Janet Seib, Brian Torwelle, Maggie Ubertini, Erin Zeltner

Proofreaders: Laura Albert, John Greenough, Nancy Reinhardt, Marianne Santy

Indexer: Anne Leach

General and Administrative

IDG Books Worldwide, Inc.: John Kilcullen, CEO; Steven Berkowitz, President and Publisher

IDG Books Technology Publishing Group: Richard Swadley, Senior Vice President and Publisher; Walter Bruce III, Vice President and Associate Publisher; Joseph Wikert, Associate Publisher; Mary Bednarek, Branded Product Development Director; Mary Corder, Editorial Director; Barry Pruett, Publishing Manager; Michelle Baxter, Publishing Manager

IDG Books Consumer Publishing Group: Roland Elgey, Senior Vice President and Publisher; Kathleen A. Welton, Vice President and Publisher; Kevin Thornton, Acquisitions Manager; Kristin A. Cocks, Editorial Director

IDG Books Internet Publishing Group: Brenda McLaughlin, Senior Vice President and Publisher; Diane Graves Steele, Vice President and Associate Publisher; Sofia Marchant, Online Marketing Manager

IDG Books Production for Dummies Press: Debbie Stailey, Associate Director of Production; Cindy L. Phipps, Manager of Project Coordination, Production Proofreading, and Indexing; Tony Augsburger, Manager of Prepress, Reprints, and Systems; Laura Carpenter, Production Control Manager; Shelley Lea, Supervisor of Graphics and Design; Debbie J. Gates, Production Systems Specialist; Robert Springer, Supervisor of Proofreading; Kathie Schutte, Production Supervisor

Dummies Packaging and Book Design: Patty Page, Manager, Promotions Marketing

◆

The publisher would like to give special thanks to Patrick J. McGovern, without whom this book would not have been possible.

◆

Contents at a Glance

Cartoons at a Glance

By Rich Tennant

page 5

page 33

page 129

page 197

page 221

Fax: 978-546-7747
E-mail: richtennant@the5thwave.com
World Wide Web: www.the5thwave.com

Table of Contents

Introduction

● ●

*E*veryone wants to get better results. Who hasn't heard (or said), "Gee, I wish I could . . ." or "Why can't I . . . "? For most people, chaos and confusion permeate every day life, creating a great deal of stress and a lot of unnecessary anxieties. Taking control seems daunting. The classic response is, "I wish I could get more done, but there are just so many things going on, and I'm pulled in so many different directions by so many different people that my schedule is out of my control." If you've ever uttered those words or thought that way, this book is for you. This book can keep you from being overwhelmed or out of control, and help you accomplish all of your personal and business goals.

Becoming more organized in your work, your home, and your everyday life not only makes you more efficient and productive, it frees your mind of anxiety and changes your life for the better. Rather than being scattered and overwhelmed, you can be happier, and perhaps healthier. Relationships at home and at work will improve as other people notice your promptness, and the control you display over your life will bring you both joy and a sense of accomplishment. The more organized you are, the more manageable your home, your business, and your life become. And who doesn't want that?

At some point, everyone has felt the panic that disorganization brings: the racing heartbeat as you sit in traffic while a meeting you're supposed to attend gets underway; the breathless apologies you utter to friends as you arrive late for an engagement; the anger you heap on yourself when you forget a task, a phone call, or even an item at the grocery store. The reactions are natural, even reasonable. They are also unhealthy. Your blood pressure and heart rate go up, your patience goes down, your mind races, and before you know it you're driving faster and more recklessly than normal, you're rude to strangers, and your day is, for all practical purposes, ruined. The dominos begin to fall as you let one disorganized fiasco spill over and contaminate other activities you have planned. Before you know it, the day is over and you're exhausted. Your schedule has been hectic, but you have little to show for your efforts. You're tired, but you have no sense of closure; no satisfaction that comes from completing your goals. You're anxious, and in some cases you take that open-ended anxiety to bed with you. Sleep is fitful, if it comes at all, and in no time the next day is upon you, and the cycle starts again.

It doesn't have to be that way. Contrary to what some people believe, achievers aren't born organized and prompt. It isn't genetic, nor is it a divinely inspired talent. Organization and time-management are learned traits; habits that can become just as natural as tying your shoes or brushing your teeth. There are no magic formulas, no pills or drugs to take, and no hypnosis or meditations. Just a few simple principals coupled with tasks that can be practiced and mastered.

Once you apply the principals outlined in this book, expect to:

- ✔ Have more time for your family and for leisure activities
- ✔ Develop a reputation as someone who respects the time and goals of others
- ✔ Accomplish more than you ever thought possible
- ✔ Effectively use the resources at your disposal without becoming overwhelmed
- ✔ Lower or even eliminate anxiety
- ✔ Exert more control over your life
- ✔ Become more successful in business and personal relationships

How to Use This Book

You can find many different methods for getting results as there are achievers. In this book, you get a healthy dose of my results-oriented philosophies and tactics, but I've also included anecdotes from business leaders, sports figures, and politicians with whom I'm acquainted. These stories further reinforce the importance of creating and maintaining a strong organizational structure.

You can skim through the topics that interest you, or you can read the book straight through. Even if you do read it completely, however, keep it nearby after you're finished with it to use as a reference. Finding out how to get results is like taking up a new sport — you probably won't be an expert at first. Achieving results requires practice, patience, and fine-tuning along the way. Keeping this book near your desk or on your nightstand for quick reference improves your chances of success.

I also suggest that you keep a stack of note cards (3 x 5 or smaller) nearby so that you can jot down some of the more salient points in this text and keep them available for easy reference. These note cards can act as reminders that you are in control of your time and space — and ultimately, the results you achieve.

How This Book Is Organized

I've divided this book into five parts, with each part containing four or more chapters. The table of contents provides a more detailed breakdown of each chapter.

Part I: Getting Results in Any Arena

This part outlines the rudiments of getting results, including prioritizing your tasks, establishing a plan, avoiding becoming disorganized, visualizing your objectives, focusing on details, worrying less, committing to the process, and becoming disciplined in your approach. In short, this part is your starting block — achieving results is the finish line.

Part II: Getting Organized

This part provides you with a measuring stick and a roadmap to help you reach your own organizational goals. You find out what being organized can do for you — and for your results. This part dispels the myths and misconceptions about organized people while outlining the hallmarks of highly organized individuals from all walks of life. You discover how to master paperwork and data using low-tech tools, unclutter your life by using only the most productive high-tech gadgets, use the Internet and e-mail to streamline your day, create storage solutions that really work, and find ways to organize your home and money.

Part III: Time Is on Your Side

No matter how rich or poor you are, how many employees you have, or how many resources you have at your disposal, you're limited by one constant factor: time. Everyone has 24 hours in a day — no more and no less. Managing and maximizing those hours is critical if you are to achieve results. This part shows you how to maximize your time.

Part IV: The Finer Points

One of the greatest traits that achievers possess is their ability to make their results look easy. Just like professional athletes who make the most difficult and mind-boggling feats look fluid and effortless, the results-oriented have mastered the subtleties and nuances of getting results and makes it seem natural. What do they know that you don't? This part shares the subtle details.

Part V: The Part of Tens

In this part, I've put together an assembly of tips, keys, drills, and traits that help you achieve better results. You could spend a lot of time in this part! Even though the reading is light and easy, the principals are critical to your success.

Icons Used in This Book

Throughout this book, I've used *icons* — little pictures out in the margins — to highlight critical information. Here's how to translate those icons:

This icon points to tips that directly help you achieve better results.

These are points that you should commit to memory or perhaps transfer to note cards for easy future reference.

If you don't pay attention to the points denoted here, trouble will eventually find you!

These true stories from my years as an entrepreneur and international sports manager provide real-world examples — examples of what to do or what not to do — that help you get results.

Where to Go from Here

You are holding this book because you want to be get better results in your career and in your life. Each minute you spend reading this text should move you closer to that goal. If, for some reason, you become distracted by outside influences, put this book down, tend the matter before you, and start reading again only when you can focus on the information here. But keep those distractions to a minimum. If you find that you don't have time to read the chapters in this book that apply to your situation — that too many people require too many things for you to finish — park yourself in a room, lock the door, and turn the page. For your own well-being, you need to embark on the journey toward achievement.

Part I

Getting Results in Any Arena

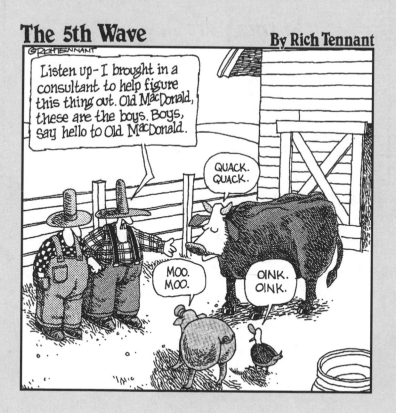

In this part . . .

This part outlines the fundamentals of getting results. From visualizing your objectives to prioritizing to establishing a plan and following through, the chapters in this part help you master the traits that are consistent in all achievers. And along the way, I give you an array of real-world examples that can help you see what others have done as they've achieved remarkable results.

Chapter 1

The Basics of Getting Results

The basics of results-oriented activities are simple. If you are to get better results, you must prioritize every action and activity you undertake, you must compartmentalize everything you do in order to remain focused on the task at hand, and you must maximize your time and energy to move toward your goals. None of these three basic steps is any more or less important than the other two, but taking them one at a time and in order is critical.

Mastering Your Priorities

Before any organized action can be taken, you must have a list of priorities. Here's how:

1. **Stop reading, take out a note card, and list the things you need to accomplish within the next three or four hours.**

   If you're like me, your list includes making a few phone calls, reading some material (hopefully, a few more chapters in this book), perhaps attending a meeting or two, completing some administrative tasks, and maybe blocking some time for recreational or leisure activities.

   No doubt the list is pretty full (probably too full given the block of time allotted).

2. **Go back through your list and put a number by each item to denote order of importance.**

   Number one should be the most important thing that you hope to accomplish during the allotted time, number two the second most important, and so on. This ranking takes a little more time than writing the list, because you may view reading the paper and calling one of your work colleagues as equally important tasks. Still, you should weigh all of the variables, and then assign priorities.

3. **Cut the list in half.**

   This is the hard part. There's no way you're going to do everything on your list in the time you've allotted. You aren't going to complete some of the things, or you are going to finish them late. Even worse, you may try to squeeze a task into a time ill-suited for it, and as a result, either perform very poorly or be more concerned with rushing the task than focusing on doing the job well. By cutting the list in half, you not only give yourself plenty of time to accomplish everything that you've set out to do, you force yourself to reexamine your priorities and move what's really important to the top of the list.

If you're in a meeting or having a conversation with someone, make sure that you prioritize the important items you want to accomplish during the meeting, and try to get to those items as quickly as possible. Too often you're hoping to pitch an idea or broach a particular subject, but, rather than jumping right into the topic, you ask about the person's family, her golf game, or how her stock portfolio is doing. That's fine if you have plenty of time for the person to recount every shot she hit during last Saturday's round, but few people have that luxury. If you have a one-hour meeting with someone, and you have three things to discuss in that one-hour period, you better not waste time chatting about unrelated issues.

Be prepared to adjust your schedule if a high-priority item comes up while you're in the middle of a lower-priority project. Sometimes adjusting is easy. If you're reading the paper and one of your children comes in with a bloody nose, you put the paper down and attend to the child. The paper may be a morning priority, but your child's health overrides it. Plenty of times, however, your choices aren't so clear. Imagine that you're on the phone with someone from your office who wants to go over "a few items." You know, however, that doing so will cause you to be late for another call with an important client. What do you do? Unfortunately, most people don't do the right thing. Instead of asking the office colleague to postpone the conversation, most people sit, listen, and even prolong the call by asking for more details — all while an important client is waiting. I assume that these people think cutting off a co-worker is rude, when actually the rudest (and dumbest) thing to do is leave a client wondering why you can't seem to call him on time.

Prioritizing for a hole-in-one

Usually you want to make your top priority the first item on your agenda, but there are times when doing so isn't the wisest course of action. After years of dealing with Arnold Palmer's schedule, I knew that if I really wanted him to attend a meeting, I should make it the fourth or fifth item on our agenda. I sequenced my items like this because I knew that when Arnold came home from traveling the tour, he would reject the first three offers I brought to him — no matter how good they were.

I would say, "Arnold, company X would like you to test some new irons they've developed," and he would say, "Mark, I just got in off the road and I'm exhausted. I really don't want to do anything."

So I would say, "Okay, well the folks at sports magazine Y would like to come over and shoot a pictorial," and he would say, "No, Mark, I'm exhausted. I don't want to do anything."

This dialogue would go on for a few more minutes until, finally, Arnold would start feeling sorry for me. When I caught the first note of pity in his voice, I would spring the top priority item on him, and he would agree. This method was a little sneaky — and certainly not the most conventional way to prioritize a meeting — but it worked. Finding a similar technique for inserting your top priorities in the right place could help you reach your goals.

Putting a Task in the Right Compartment

Whether you are organizing your desk so items can be easily found or structuring your day so you can focus on the task before you, compartmentalization is the second step to getting results.

After you establish your priorities (for a day, an hour, or a particular meeting or project), *compartmentalization* means focusing on each individual item without letting any one activity encroach upon the timing and effectiveness of any other. For example, if I complete an intense meeting in which I had a vocal disagreement with someone, I can't let my feelings carry over into my next meeting or call. That would be unfair to the next person I encounter. For example, if I snap at my secretary, I'm giving her the impression that I'm angry or upset about something she's done. The same is true if my wife calls right after I have a testy meeting. Unless I'm able to compartmentalize, I may be rude or short with her, which would be unfair.

Compartmentalizing is easier said than done. Turning your emotions on and off like a spigot is difficult (sometimes impossible), and everyone has a tendency to let emotions about one thing bleed over into other situations. However, you can take several steps to maximize your compartmentalization:

- ✔ **Write down every action you plan to take.** After you've committed your priorities to paper, you can free your mind of worry and anticipation.

- ✔ **Cross items off your list.** You get a feeling of accomplishment when you take the time to mark through a completed item. Whether the outcome of the task, meeting, or call was to your liking, crossing the item off your list lifts a burden from your mind.

- ✔ **Think in terms of the present.** If you can't do anything about a particular matter until hours, days, or even weeks later, cluttering your mind with that item is a monumental waste of space. By focusing on the here and now, you accomplish more, and carry over less.

If you find that you're having trouble compartmentalizing your time and activities, transfer the current item on your schedule to a note card and keep that note card in sight while you perform the assigned task. If your mind begins to wander, or if you feel yourself injecting emotions from a previous task into the current one, just glance at the note card to remind yourself of your current focus. Hopefully, this snaps you back to the matter at hand and frees your mind of clutter. When you complete the task, rip up the note card and throw it away. This action is more dramatic than crossing an item off a list. Actually throwing the card away (both literally and figuratively) allows you to move ahead.

Naps aren't just for kindergartners

I take naps. As an early riser who often makes a dozen or more overseas calls before 6:00 a.m., I often build nap times into my schedule so I can remain fresh throughout the day, even if my wife and I are entertaining well into the evening. A lot of people don't understand my napping habit, and even more wonder how someone as busy as I am can take a couple of hours out of the day to fall asleep.

In fact, finding the time is easy. I condition myself by writing down specific times for my naps, and I rarely let anything interrupt or distract me when nap time rolls around. If my nap is scheduled between 2:00 and 3:30 in the afternoon, I make sure that I finish all other business by 1:45 so that I can be in the bed and asleep by 2:00. No matter how contentious the day has been, when I cross off the last item prior to my nap, I am ready and able to sleep, simply because napping is the next item on my agenda. I have compartmentalized my mind, and I don't allow anything to disrupt my nap time.

Too often, if a person discovers that I'm napping, her first thought is "Gee, that person must not have anything to do if he can while away the day in bed." Exactly the opposite is true. The most productive people regularly schedule rest into their days — and they don't let anything interrupt those times. You may be well served to join them.

Maximizing Every Moment

After you prioritize and compartmentalize your time and activities in order to focus on each task, you need to maximize your day and the space around you. The best way to describe maximization is to think of your day as a trip to the grocery store. If you're out of milk, you have several options as part of your trip:

- ✔ You can go to the store and just buy milk, getting in and out as quickly as possible.

- ✔ You can go to the store to buy milk, but while you're there you can walk through every aisle, maybe making a few purchases along the way, and maybe not.

- ✔ You can maximize your trip to the store by creating a list of everything you need, and using the opportunity to pick up all the items in one, highly productive trip.

Option three makes the most sense, but people don't often carry that same logic over to their business dealings or other aspects of their lives.

Periodically, I examine the travel records of our senior people to learn where they are traveling, and what they are doing while on these trips. During one such examination, I discovered that one of our executives had made several trips from Cleveland to California within a few weeks. When I questioned this executive about these trips, he listed the reasons — the meetings he attended and so forth. I quickly discovered that, although all his reasons were valid, he could have scheduled all the meetings around one extended trip rather than several quick jaunts across the country.

Also, I realized that this person had flown across the country for one meeting without putting anything else on his agenda. As a result, a trip that could have included meeting several clients, following up on other business, helping out his colleagues who may have needed something done in California, or hustling new business, ended up accomplishing only one thing. He went to a store (on the other side of the United States) and only bought one gallon of milk.

In real estate, maximizing is known as *highest and best use* — a phrase used to describe the most economically efficient use of a particular piece of land. For example, a gas station situated on beachfront property near Monterey, California, would not be considered the highest and best use of that acreage, nor would a pig farm in a bustling downtown area. The land has more value than the assets currently on it.

Time also has a highest and best use — something of which I constantly remind our clients and the companies with whom we do business. If someone wants Tiger Woods to attend a luncheon a week before the U.S. Open, for example, the answer is most likely no. The highest and best use of Tiger's time during that week is to prepare for a major championship, no matter how important the business luncheon is.

In order to maximize your time and improve your results, you need to constantly ask yourself whether what you are currently undertaking is the highest and best use of your time. If it isn't, stop what you're doing, adjust your priorities, and maximize the time you have left.

Many people often spend their days scurrying from place to place, completing tasks without ever stopping to analyze the cost of the time they're spending. If, for example, an executive were to take an hour out of the middle of her day to go home and mow her lawn, that hour has a value. The executive could be making calls, conducting meetings, generating business, and probably creating more income than the $20 it would cost her to have a neighborhood kid mow her lawn after school. The highest and best use of her mid-day hour is in the office, not at home behind a lawn mower.

Put a dollar value on every minute of your day and, before embarking on any activity, ask yourself whether the results you hope to accomplish are worth the amount of time (in dollars) that you have to spend.

Chapter 2

Eating the Elephant One Bite at a Time

- -

In This Chapter

▶ Overcoming overwhelming situations

▶ Establishing the right plan

▶ Executing, correcting, and executing again

- -

The title of this chapter comes from a conversation I had with the great Scottish golfer, Colin Montgomerie. Our discussion centered on how Montgomerie prepares himself for golf's four major championships. Colin's opinion (and I wholeheartedly concur) was that, in order to avoid being overwhelmed by the pressure and added hoopla surrounding the majors, a player must focus on each individual shot and psychologically remove himself from his surroundings. Golfers who are competitive at the highest levels in the greatest championships must maintain the ability to break their games into manageable increments — one shot, one hole at a time.

In describing this idea to me, Colin said, "You can eat an elephant. It will take you seven million bites, but it can be done."

There is a great lesson in that statement. Overwhelming tasks are only overwhelming when you look at them in their totality. The first step toward managing the seemingly unmanageable — cleaning up the apparently insurmountable mess; writing the daunting proposal coming due; taking charge of the out-of-control schedule — is to break each task into smaller increments. By focusing on the small part instead of the large whole, your tasks seem easier and your anxiety is certainly lower.

Getting a Handle on Overwhelming Situations

Suppose that you need to clean and organize the messiest room in your home or office. If the task seems overwhelming, begin by breaking it down into manageable pieces. As a first step in that process, shield your eyes with your hands so you can only see the three square feet of the room next to the door. You can certainly clean up that small area. Then shift your vision to another three-foot area. Surely you can clean up that small section, too. Repeat this process as many times as needed until you have completely cleaned the room. Perhaps your manageable bites are bigger than a three-foot-square area, or maybe they are smaller. Whatever size bite you choose, if you focus solely on that area, you conquer the toughest tasks.

You can do the same thing with your time. Every day has 1,440 minutes. Assuming that you need 8 hours (or 480 minutes) of sleep, you're left with 960 minutes in which to complete all the tasks you set for yourself in a given day. Of course, thinking in one-minute increments is difficult for anyone — reading this page has probably taken you more than one minute — but you can divide your day into manageable bites of between 15 and 30 minutes. View a task that's likely to take an hour as consuming four 15-minute time increments. A half-hour task takes two bites.

Here's how two sports greats manage overwhelming situations.

- **Tennis bites:** I once asked Martina Navratilova how she elevated her game to new levels for major championships such as Wimbledon and the U.S. Open. What she said surprised me at the time.

  "Mark, I try not to think about where I am or what circumstance I'm in," she said. "If I'm serving for match point at Wimbledon, I try to pretend I'm at an indoor match in Athens. I want to forget where I am and what the shot means, and simply focus on executing."

  By taking herself out of the moment and focusing on the manageable bite, Navratilova was able to execute critical shots, thus becoming one of the greatest champions in the history of women's tennis.

- **Eight points a quarter:** When Michael Jordan retired from the NBA in 1999, he did so with an astonishing average of 31.5 points per game — an NBA record. In addition to being an incredible testament to Jordan's skill as a basketball superstar, the record is a great indicator of his mental drive and determination. No matter who the opponent or what incarnation of the Chicago Bulls were on the floor, Jordan got his 32 points every night for 13 years.

When he was asked how he could maintain such astonishing consistency at such a high level for such an extended period of time, Jordan answered, "I simplified it a few years ago. Thirty-two points a game is just eight points a quarter. I figure I can get eight points a quarter in some kind of way during the course of a game."

Averaging 32 points a game for a season is a daunting, seemingly unreachable goal; doing so for over a decade is unthinkable. Jordan managed this feat by breaking the points down into what he deemed a manageable bite: eight points a quarter.

Developing a Manageable Plan

Contrary to what you might think, there is no "right" amount of planning when managing an event or working on a project. Of course, you can plan yourself into oblivion and never get around to actually doing anything. Conversely, you can start reacting to whatever is thrown your way without any plan at all. Both will achieve the same bad results.

Some rules to remember for effective planning include:

- ✔ Don't insist on 100 percent when 90 percent will do nicely.
- ✔ Always strive for at least 90 percent.
- ✔ Don't get detoured onto the side streets.
- ✔ If you do find yourself on a side street, return to the main path as quickly as possible.

When in Japan . . .

I once had lunch with Mr. Yoshiaki Tsutsumi (the chairman of Kokudo Keikaku Co. Ltd. and one of the richest men in the world), whom I had met in 1970 while in Japan. After several years of swapping Christmas cards, I asked my staff to set up a meeting. We soon confirmed a date and time for a Japanese associate and me to venture to one of Mr. Tsutsumi's hotels in Tokyo.

Within days of confirming the lunch meeting, things got interesting. Representatives from Mr. Tsutsumi's office called my secretary and requested the license number of the vehicle we would be driving to the hotel. We then received another call informing us that the walk from the curb to the hotel lounge where we were to meet Mr. Tsutsumi would take six minutes, and that we should plan our arrival accordingly.

When we arrived at the hotel the doorman greeted us by name (obviously tipped off by our license plate) and no fewer than six other employees greeted us by name during the six-minute walk to the lounge. The personalization was a nice touch, and the meal was exceptional.

When Betsy and I eat dinner alone at home, our plan consists of going to the refrigerator and throwing together some leftovers. When we're having guests over for dinner, we plan a little more thoroughly. If we're hoping to make a big first impression on an important client or customer, we pull out all the stops, planning everything from the wine that's served to the seating to where the salt and pepper shakers are placed on the table. I may even ask my secretary to call our guests' offices to find out what kind of food they like or dislike, and to ask if they have any allergies or other problems. I've even phoned to find out what sort of drinks my incoming guests prefer, so I can have their favorites on hand when they arrive.

When I serve lunch as part of a meeting, on the other hand, and I don't want the proceedings to drag into the late afternoon, I tell the staff to put the first course on the table ten minutes after everyone has received a pre-lunch drink. This prompt delivery moves the lunch along, and sends a signal to everyone that I intend for the meeting to be swift. Such subtleties in planning are important if you want to avoid being distracted.

You can apply the same logic to other planning, as well. Like most chief executives, I have neither the time nor the inclination to read 50-page proposals, no matter how glossy and expensive they might be. Nor am I likely to spend much time sitting through high-tech digital presentations. I need five succinct paragraphs. If those paragraphs capture my attention, I might read an additional two pages. Not that I'm out of touch with my own business — quite the opposite — but as an involved executive, I need encapsulated information. If you spend thousands of dollars and hundreds of hours developing a flashy proposal, you may find that it isn't necessary, and might never be seen by the decision-maker.

The three-minute proposal

Back when the now infamous John Delorean ran the Pontiac division of General Motors, I had the opportunity to pitch a proposal for Pontiac to sponsor a sport. John and I were attending a party together, and I said, "John, how you would like to own a sport?"

He asked, "Which one?" and I said, "Skiing. Or more specifically, professional downhill and slalom racing." John asked a few questions about how such a deal would work, and I explained, in general terms, the mechanics of Pontiac sponsoring downhill skiing. After about three minutes of discussion, Delorean said, "I

think we'll do that. Let's get together and work out the details."

Within months we had a deal. Had I assigned the task of pitching this proposal to some of the other executives in our company, we might still be preparing a voluminous presentation complete with slides, CDs, and thousands of lines of data. I understood that Delorean didn't want or need a flashy and expensive presentation. As a result, we developed a successful relationship with Pontiac based on a three-minute conversation at a party.

Resolving to Execute, Correct, and Execute Again

Tom Peters (a Palo Alto, California, management consultant and author) said that most American companies would be better off if they adhered to a "ready, fire, aim," strategy instead of the "ready, aim, aim, aim, aim, aim, fire" strategy. In many ways I agree with that assessment, but I add my own addendum. Most people, whether at home or in business, would be better served by a strategy of "ready, fire, aim a little closer, and fire again."

You shouldn't be afraid to execute a plan sooner rather than later, as long as you're prepared to evaluate your errors, make corrections, and re-execute.

Clutter — whether in your house, your office, your schedule, or your brain — is nothing more than postponed decision making. Taking action quickly and decisively removes the clutter. Whether or not making swift decisions moves you closer to your goals depends on your ability to correct yourself along the way.

Get started. Make a plan for your week, for your day, and for the next hour, and quickly begin executing to get results. You can eat Colin Montgomerie's elephant as long as you take the beast one bite at a time.

Chapter 3

The Toughest Space to Harness: The Six Inches between Your Ears

In This Chapter
▶ Structuring your thoughts so you can manage your time and space
▶ Visualizing your objectives
▶ Focusing on the details
▶ Worrying less to achieve more
▶ Interrupting yourself

Disorganization, missed opportunities, missed appointments, chronic lateness, and feelings of being overwhelmed are all symptoms of the same affliction: A lack of mental organization and discipline. Mental organization is not to be confused with I.Q. or brainpower. I'm not suggesting that you have to be smart, or even well-educated, to get results. What I am suggesting is that before you can manage projects, you have to harness your thoughts.

Mental organization goes well beyond just conceptualizing or visualizing (although both conceptualizing and visualizing are important). Waking up in the morning and saying to yourself, "Okay, today I have to make ten phone calls, attend three meetings, and be home for little Johnny's piano recital," does not constitute mental organization. Those appointments should already be committed to paper so you *don't* have to expend any mental energy on them. Mental organization means focusing on the tasks at hand and trusting that your short-term objectives move you toward your longer-term goals.

Being Mentally Organized Isn't Brain Surgery

The number of people who assume that being mentally organized requires squashing, or at least stifling, creativity astonishes me. The objection comes down to the old left-brain, right-brain argument: The results-oriented person must be the button-down bean-counter who thrives on structure and who never created anything unique in her life, and the free-spirited artist or genius can't be encumbered by the boundaries of discipline. These stereotypes lead to myths such as the "absent-minded professor" or the "flighty, bohemian artist," and those who strive to be organized at home and at work are classified as "plodding," and "uncreative." These labels are hooey of the highest magnitude.

Getting results is not left-brain or right-brain dominated. In fact, the most successful actors, actresses, artists, authors, and musicians are extremely structured people. They understand that in order to excel in their crafts they must structure their surroundings and be organized and disciplined in their thinking and actions. Mental discipline and organization frees their minds for more creative pursuits.

In addition to managing athletes, our company represents a number of the finest musicians, artists, and authors in the world including Itzhak Perlman, Jose Carrera, Dame Kiri Te Kanawa, and Pat Conroy, among others. Amazingly enough, the clients in our music and literary division are, as a group, more structured than the athletes, models, and executives we represent. Kiri Te Kanawa, the great soprano, is an incredibly disciplined woman who goes to great lengths to ensure that her concerts are perfect in every detail. From the lighting, to the acoustics, to the size and shape of the stages, to the colors of her clothing, no detail is too small for Kiri. She is the epitome of organization while also being recognized as one of the most creative artists in her field.

If You Can't See Where You're Going, Chances Are Good You Won't Get There

The first step in organizing your brain is to visualize your objectives. Where do you want to be? In what area do you want to achieve better results? Can you see your goal in your mind? If you can't answer all of these questions, you need to exercise your imagination and come up with some very distinct organizational goals.

These goals must be:

- ✔ Specific and detailed
- ✔ Within your control
- ✔ Compatible with your character
- ✔ On a schedule

Writing goals down

I've always said that a goal isn't a goal until you write it down. Committing a goal to writing makes it real. The action also requires putting something that could be extremely personal on paper — a tough task for some, but necessary nonetheless. Until you write a goal down, it's nothing more than a fantasy or a wish.

NASA's changing goals

Although an institution, not an individual, NASA provides one of the best examples of both specific and nonspecific goals and the results affected by each. In the 1960s, at the organization's peak, NASA had one very specific goal, articulated by John F. Kennedy: "Put a man on the moon by the end of the decade and return him safely to Earth." This goal was the rallying cry, the vision, and ultimately the mission of thousands of scientists, engineers, administrators, and astronauts. The entire nation latched onto the vision, because it was specific, attainable, on a definitive schedule, and soul-stirring. As a result, thousands of people from hundreds of disciplines came together and accomplished one of the greatest feats in history: a man on the moon.

Contrast that with the debacle NASA went through in the 1990s with the Hubble Telescope. Designed to be a giant magnifying glass in Earth's lower orbit, the Hubble Telescope was supposed to provide astronomers with a broader view of deep space. However, as the Hubble project was gaining momentum, NASA's vision changed. Rather than rallying around a clearly defined goal like the one articulated in the 1960s, NASA's objective in the 1990s became to deploy the Hubble Telescope as cheaply and efficiently as possible. Costs were cut, tests were overlooked, and the focus shifted from the mission to the expense ledger. As a result, the Hubble was deployed with an embarrassing and costly flaw. An out-of-focus lens made the orbiting telescope virtually useless. The mistake was like giving a nearsighted man the wrong prescription glasses — but these spectacles cost U.S. taxpayers over a billion dollars.

Ultimately the problems with the Hubble Telescope were corrected, but NASA's credibility could not be repaired. Had the institution that put a man on the moon in 1969 become inept? Not at all. NASA simply lost its vision (quite literally, in this case), which made all other actions irrelevant.

After you put the goal down on paper, the pressure is on. Action is required. You are committed to either success or failure — to either reaching your goal or falling short. The second you write the goal down on paper, you place your credibility on the line, if only with yourself.

Specifying your goals

Because establishing your goals is so important, you should put a great deal of time and mental effort into the process. The more specific your vision, the more likely you are to organize yourself around it. For example, if your goal is "To increase business," you have nothing on which to develop an organizational strategy. The statement is too vague, and the time frame is open-ended.

If, however, you say, "I want to increase my personal contribution to revenues by 30 percent in the next 18 months," then you have begun to shape your vision. You have defined clear goals and set the time frame.

McCORMACK MEMORIES

Visualizing success

Professional athletes are exceptionally adept at visualization. I remember Arnold Palmer telling me he never tees off in a tournament without first playing the course in his mind. He executes each shot perfectly in his imagination before walking onto the first tee. By the time he reaches the third or fourth hole, he has already played the hole in his mind, so all that's left to do is execute what he has already visualized. This sort of positive reinforcement gives Arnold an advantage before striking the first shot of any tournament.

Perhaps the best visualizer I've met in recent years is Tiger Woods. In addition to being one of the most talented and creative golfers I've seen in 50 years, Tiger is one of those unique individuals to whom goal-setting comes naturally. When he was a junior golfer, he set very specific objectives for himself and timetables in which to complete each task. He taped a list of golfing records (most belonging to Jack Nicklaus) to the back of his door and, as he racked up amateur victories, he methodically crossed the records off as if they were his personal things-to-do list.

Talent can't be overlooked when analyzing athletes as gifted as Tiger Woods and Arnold Palmer. Perhaps just as important to their overall successes, however, are the visions these athletes set for their careers and the structured way in which they approach their goals. As they were winning championships, electrifying galleries, and setting unprecedented records, neither man was the least bit surprised. They visualized their accomplishments in advance. When the records fell, all they did was cross them off their lists.

McCORMACK MEMORIES

Realistic dreaming

Sometimes the vision of your goal may be stirring, but the actual mechanics of accomplishing the task are too daunting, too expensive, or completely out of your control. In addition to client representation, our company also owns and/or represents a number of sporting events around the world, including the World Match Play (Golf) Championship in London and the Indianapolis 500. Several years ago, one of our executives floated the idea of a New York Grand Prix. The idea caught fire around our office and soon everyone was talking about how great seeing Indy cars speeding through vacant Manhattan streets would be. We soon convinced ourselves that the New York Grand Prix could be the biggest sporting event in the number one market in the world.

At the same time the grand prix proposal was captivating the imagination of our senior executives, another member of our staff suggested that we create a traveling figure skating tour called Stars on Ice. We represented a number of world-class figure skaters that, unfortunately,

had very few options for displaying their talents after they retired from Olympic competition. In fact, with the exception of the Ice Capades and a couple of silly traveling companies that required skaters to dress up in Smurf costumes, world-class figure skating had no outlet.

Obviously, the skating idea didn't have the sex appeal and sizzle of the New York Grand Prix. Most of our executives smiled, nodded, and put the Stars on Ice idea on hold. Years later, because of timing, community ordinances, civic groups, politicians, and other factions over which we had no control, the New York Grand Prix idea was scrapped. Discover Card Stars on Ice, on the other hand, became one of IMG's most recognized and profitable ventures.

The vision of Stars on Ice might not have caught on right away, but, because we controlled most of the variables, Stars on Ice became a reality and the much grander New York Grand Prix became a wonderful idea with no chance of getting off the ground.

TIP

The goal is still a little fuzzy, though. You can do better. What elements of revenue are within your control? What stirs your soul and gets you excited? What can you wrap your character around and get enthused by? Once you answer these questions you can hone your vision even further. The end result could be something like, "My goal is to close three of the ten projects I am currently working on in order to increase my contribution to company revenues by 30 percent in the next 18 months. I also want to contact ten new people in the next year and develop relationships that will lead to long-term future business." Now you have something you can sink your teeth into. You have set the goal, clearly defined the vision, and established a reasonable time frame and end result. From this point, you can break your goal into manageable bites, focusing on each step needed to close the three deals, and establishing a detailed strategy for how you will spend your time and resources on each. The organizational process becomes easy because the vision is clearly defined.

Hone In on the Task at Hand

Have you ever been so engrossed in reading a book or an article that you completely shut out the world around you? Have you ever been so enthralled with a story that your imagination took over and you forgot you were reading? If your answer is yes (and I suspect most of you have experienced that suspension of disbelief at some point), then you have experienced the kind of mental focus needed to be an achiever. You must have an extraordinary amount of discipline to go through your day without letting your mind wander. But, just as you can't wait to get to the next page of your good book, when you apply this same intense focus to your daily list, you realize an enormous sense of accomplishment after you complete each task.

Put yourself on a deadline with each task you undertake and keep applying pressure. In the beginning, I suggest that you purchase a stopwatch (an inexpensive one) and put yourself on the clock as you start each task on your list. Meeting your time limits is challenging at first. You find yourself feeling anxious as conversations with colleagues drag on longer than your allotted time and the stopwatch continues to tick. This pressure heightens your awareness of time wasted each day on unproductive conversations and activities. You also become more creative in cutting conversations short and eliminating distractions from your day.

If you're like most people, you tend to focus on those things that offer the most satisfying rewards. Based on this assumption, employers base bonuses and compensation structures on goals they want to see completed. Unfortunately, a lot of mundane tasks with no immediate rewards must also be tended to on a daily basis. One way to mentally gear yourself up for those tasks is to assign a reward to yourself for each task you complete within a specified time frame. For example, if you finish cleaning your office and sorting through all the papers in your in-box by 5:00, you allow yourself to go to the golf course or indulge in an after-work social activity you would otherwise skip.

Be careful, though. You don't want to set the bar too low or fudge on the rewards. If you are one minute past your deadline, you must have enough discipline to deny yourself the reward, otherwise the exercise is useless. If, however, you are honest enough with yourself to stick to your guns and you set your deadlines realistically high, this drill improves your ability to focus and minimize distractions.

McCORMACK MEMORIES

Ignore the distractions

One of my business acquaintances is the editor of a monthly magazine in New York. His sole responsibilities are to edit one section of the magazine and write a thousand-word column every month. Simple enough. Yet, he spends at least one weekend a month slaving over his computer at home, writing his column.

After several months of witnessing this pattern, I asked him, "Do you enjoy giving up your weekends to write your column?"

He said he hated it.

"Then why not write it during the week?"

His response was all too typical of the unfocused executive. "I'm too busy having meetings, going out to lunch, talking on the phone, and pushing paper to get any work done," he quipped.

Other things always attempt to divert our attention away from the tasks that need to be done. But the achiever is able to put those distractions aside.

You Have Enough to Do Without Worrying

Many years ago an elderly gentleman told me, "Worrying is like sitting in a rocking chair. It's something to do, but it doesn't get you anywhere." That might be an exaggeration, but some version of that axiom is certainly true. Too much worrying can not only disrupt your concentration and detract from your efficiency, but it can also harm your health. High blood pressure and certain heart conditions have been attributed to stress — one of the side effects of worrying.

I'm a positive-thinking person, but also a worrier. When I receive bad news I immediately try to counterbalance it with good news so I can come away feeling positive and not carry my worry with me throughout the day. Fortunately, I've now reached a position in my life and career where the things that worry me are much different than they were 30 years ago. When I was a burgeoning young entrepreneur, I often felt my time was not my own. If Arnold Palmer, Jack Nicklaus, or Gary Player (my first three clients) needed me at an obscure hour, I got on an airplane and traveled to them. As time went on and my company grew, I was able to delegate a large number of those responsibilities and thus take control of my schedule.

Today, I worry about time and become annoyed if anything disrupts my schedule. If someone is late or early for a meeting or a flight is late or canceled, I worry about how these disruptions are going to affect the rest of the items I hope to accomplish that day. My colleagues tell me I should be happy with my worries, because the issues that annoy me are minor in the overall scheme of things. They are probably right.

When worrying becomes a distraction, you need to act on the worry. Too often people allow their worries to encroach into other areas of their lives, which leads to poor performance and the addition of new worries. If a situation is so critical that you are consumed with worry, change your schedule in order to deal with the worrisome item. Rearranging your day may disrupt an otherwise carefully orchestrated schedule, but a little reshuffling is better than letting your worries carry over into other unrelated events and activities.

Don't Interrupt Me — I Interrupt Myself Enough for Both of Us

All interruptions are self-inflicted: You either let the interruptions happen or you don't.

Often, managers have an open door policy. They even insist that the doors to their offices be open at all times — an admirable stance that shows employees that the boss is accessible. Unfortunately, such a setup also invites interruptions. If everyone believes that you are available at all times, you are.

How you deal with incoming phone calls is another indicator of how much control you have over your own agenda. If you accept every call that comes in, your schedule is at the mercy of anyone in the world who has your phone number. Taking control of when and how you accept phone calls is critical to your time and perhaps to your sanity.

I have always said that I would rather make calls than take calls. By returning someone's call or scheduling a call at a predetermined time, I control when a conversation takes place and usually how long it lasts. If, for example, I am calling a client about a personal matter — say a divorce or other highly charged situation — a call may last half an hour or longer, so I schedule it toward the end of the day. If the conversation runs a little longer than expected, it doesn't throw the rest of my day behind. I make short calls early, usually starting between 4:30 and 5:00 a.m. with calls to Europe, and making early calls to employees and clients with whom I can conduct my business quickly.

Being able to control my schedule is wonderful, but wasn't always so easy. For many years, I took calls from Arnold, Gary, and Jack whenever the phone rang. Talking to them was my job. Soon, however, I learned that if I called them at specified times I could not only initiate the conversation, but I could get any issues they might want to discuss out of the way on my time schedule. Arnold was an early riser, so I always called him first, then Gary, and then Jack. The calls made me appear to be a wonderfully conscientious manager (which I was) but also allowed me to control my time and eliminate phone interruptions from my three biggest clients.

I learned that the best way to avoid phone interruptions was to initiate the calls on my schedule. You will be stunned by how much time you save if you employ that same strategy.

One worrier is enough

As I was preparing for an overseas trip, I asked one of my associates to keep an eye on a pet project of mine that I had assigned to one of our executives. I knew that the executive in question had a lot of other items on his plate and I was worried that he would not give the project the time and attention I thought it needed. There was even some fear on my part that he would forget about the project completely.

My associate gave me some incredible insight on my worries about this project. She said, "You don't have to get excited about this project, because he (the executive in charge of it) is excited about it. What you have to worry about are the things that don't excite him."

That pearl of wisdom stuck with me, and, after some rumination, I modified it slightly and the phrase became the McCormack Rule of Worrying, which is, "You don't need two people worrying about the same thing at the same company (or in the same household). One is enough."

Chapter 4

Taking the Leap

· ·

In This Chapter

▶ Honing the craft of getting results

▶ Shortening your learning curve

▶ Committing to the process and being disciplined enough to make your plan succeed

· ·

*T*he road to getting results begins with realizing that achieving is an ongoing process that evolves over time. Like honing any new skill, you must start slowly, gradually becoming comfortable with each new step in the process.

I can't give you a magic potion or step-by-step formula for getting results. A fair amount of your education will be trial and error. There are, however, some key points — some absolutes — that you should write down on your note cards and, eventually, commit to memory. This chapter takes a look at those principles.

Getting Results Isn't a Talent — It's a Craft

Too often I hear people say things like, "I would love to get better results, but I just don't have the ability in me." These people assume that achieving great results is a God-given talent — a product of good genes and natural ability. Nothing could be further from the truth.

You don't have to be gifted to get positive results. Getting results is a learned craft, not a talent, and can be taught, practiced, and perfected over time.

Anyone willing and committed can become better at getting results. Whether you need to clean out your closet, manage a complicated project, or complete the 12 tasks of Hercules, the process is the same for everyone. First and foremost, you have to believe that you can get great results, and you have to take control of your life and your surroundings.

Managing the overwhelming

Right after she won two major championships (including the U.S. Open) in her rookie year and was voted Female Athlete of the Year by the Associated Press, our company signed South Korean golf sensation Se Ri Pak as a client. Se Ri quickly became the hottest female athlete in the world, and the demands on her time were overwhelming. Like a lot of young, well-meaning athletes, Se Ri didn't want to disappoint anyone, so she tried to accommodate as many people as she could — traveling to corporate outings, answering media requests, posing for photographs, and enduring an exhausting schedule. Her time was not her own.

But that situation didn't last long. By the end of her rookie season, Se Ri realized that she had to take charge of her life if she intended to reach her goals in golf. As a result, she developed a personal organizational plan that accommodated as many requests as she could comfortably manage without infringing on her practice or playing time, and without running herself ragged. Not everyone has been accommodated, but Se Ri has done her best and has taken charge of her life.

The Learning Curve

Just because you don't have a team of professional managers at your disposal doesn't mean that you have to handle every item that comes your way.

Your learning curve will improve dramatically if you let go of certain things that either

- ✔ No longer require your personal attention
- ✔ Take away from higher priority items on your list

Although much has been written in the media about the handshake deal that I entered into with my first client, Arnold Palmer, in the late 1950s, the deal itself was based on filling a simple need. While chatting in his office one day about the various projects we might consider together, Arnold pointed to a large stack of mail on his desk and said, "Mark, I wish there was somebody who could take care of all this for me. That's what I really need. I spend so much time answering mail when I'm home that I barely have time left for golf."

A light bulb went off in my head, and I spent the better part of that night sorting through Arnold's mail. When he got up the next morning, I presented him with several piles of mail: one that required his immediate attention, one he could review in his leisure time, one he might want to read but didn't require his personal attention, and one (junk mail) to throw away.

Arnold couldn't have been happier. This was the start of a 40-year business relationship and a life-long personal friendship. Had I not taken the initiative, Arnold probably would have never delegated the task of going through his mail to someone else, even though sorting it himself clearly wasn't the best use of his time.

You may not have a manager staying up all night sorting your mail, but you certainly have plenty of tasks that you can pass along to others.

Do the first things first

Any item that tops your priority list deserves to be handled first, unless you have time-constraint reasons for delaying action. You should always take care of the most important items before the ancillary items, even if doing so means changing or disrupting your regular routine.

If you have a family emergency, disrupting your routine is simple. A trip to the emergency room always comes before vacuuming the living room carpet. Less urgent items, however, require a little more thought. If you must choose between calling a friend on her birthday or going through your standard routine of sorting the mail and reading the paper, you may consider foregoing your standard way of doing things to pick up the phone (if you value your friend's feelings).

At the end of each day, take inventory of the things you accomplished, and the things you wanted to do but didn't complete. Then check where both the complete and incomplete items fall on your priority list. You may be surprised by how many high-priority items on your list don't get done, while you easily finish items much further down the list.

Practice makes perfect

Just like everything in life, the more you practice working toward results, the more proficient you become. At first the practice is laborious, and you experience some frustration when you don't see the instant results you had hoped for. But just like the beginning golfer has to hit a seemingly endless stream of practice balls before he feels marginally proficient, you must practice the basic fundamentals of achieving results if you want your project or task to end successfully.

Write everything down. Get into the habit of writing down every single activity you need to accomplish in a day, no matter how small or rudimentary the task. Mark the items off the list after they're completed. In some cases, writing the task down may take longer than the action itself. But writing everything down is one of the only ways to condition yourself to making lists and focusing on the tasks you have before you.

Like most goals in life, getting results in your project requires discipline and commitment. If you are not accustomed to writing lists, planning ahead, cleaning up, or handling details, simply claiming you don't have these skills in you is much easier than making a commitment to change your behavior. If you're committed, you must devote yourself to learning and perfecting the craft of achieving great results — and you must not waver from that commitment. Remaining devoted is the only way to ultimately succeed.

Part II
Getting Organized

The 5th Wave   By Rich Tennant

"The new technology has really helped me get organized. I keep my project reports under the PC, budgets under my laptop and memos under my pager."

In this part . . .

Getting organized is the first step in getting results. In this part, I discuss the value of organizing your personal surroundings, project data, mail, technological gadgets, and money — and look at the cost of being disorganized. From the paper you touch to the way you organize your personal space to the strategy you employ when returning phone calls, developing a simple organizational system is critical to your success. This part shows you how.

This part also looks at technological advances in the way people communicate and conduct business. For the well-organized person, these new advancements offer more creative ways to accomplish numerous tasks in shorter periods of time. For the disorganized person, however, the dream is a nightmare. This part takes a look at the full gamut of tools and toys in today's information marketplace, and shows you how to make organized use of modern conveniences.

Chapter 5

The Value of Being Organized

*O*rganization and disorganization are not quantifiable absolutes. For example, you may know someone who keeps his office immaculately organized with not a single scrap of paper out of place. On the other hand, this person has trouble getting to meetings on time or promptly returning phone calls. In one respect (the housekeeping of his office) this person is considered organized, but in another (time and task management) he is considered less organized or even disorganized. Is he an organized or disorganized person? Certainly the people in the meetings and the ones sitting by their phones waiting for him to call believe one thing, while those who only see this man in his office have an entirely different opinion.

Although I seriously question the man's priorities, the truth is that both opinions are accurate. He is both organized and disorganized. His desk, his chair, and the space in his office are his priorities; therefore he keeps those areas organized. Meetings, phone calls, and interaction with others are obviously not as important to him, so he is disorganized (and rude) in those areas.

You can think of organization as a continuum. At one end sits the completely disorganized person — the one with piles of paper on her desk, and who lives with her personal belongings strewn about or piled in corners throughout her cluttered home. She is always late, always harried, and has a reputation for being absent-minded. Chances are good that this person hasn't reached her full career potential. The excuses she uses include: "Hey, it's my own special system. I know where everything is." Or, "I don't want to be a neat freak. Those people are weird." Or, even better, "It's not my fault. My boss keeps piling things on me, and I can't seem to catch up." This person is the epitome of all things disorganized.

On the other extreme of the organization continuum is the organizational freak — the person who has mapped out every minute of every day for the next year of his life. His surroundings are immaculate. He knows the exact location of everything in his office and home, and nothing is ever out of place. This person has never been late, never missed returning a phone call, never let a pile accumulate on his desk, and never worn unmatched socks. Nothing is ever impetuous with this person. He jealously guards his time and his surroundings, and manages the clock better than an NFL quarterback. He is a classic overachiever who has probably been labeled obsessive at some point in his life. This man has taken organization to an extreme.

Ninety-nine percent of people fall between these two extremes. Unfortunately, too many people relate more to the disorganized example than with the organized one. In order to change your place on the continuum, you have to ask yourself a few questions:

- ✔ Where am I on the organizational continuum?
- ✔ Where do I want to be on the continuum?
- ✔ How am I going to get there?

Draw a horizontal line on a note card. On the left end of the line write down the traits of the completely disorganized person. At the other end, write a description of the fanatically organized person. Next, place a mark on the line to denote where you think that you currently fall in the organizational continuum and list a few of your weakest and strongest organizational traits. Now draw a star at the point on the line where you want to be and list your organizational goals. Keep this card with you as a constant reminder. As you progress through the steps outlined in this book, add additional marks on your note card to denote your progress.

What Does It Cost to Be Organized?

"Gee, I would love to organize my office, but I can't afford matching bookshelves and filing cabinets, so I'll just sit in this mess until my cash flow improves."

Believe it or not, one of the most common (and outrageous) excuses for remaining in a state of disorganization is the perceived cost associated with cleaning up. This goes back to the premise that being disorganized must be someone or something else's fault — there must be a barrier to entry that keeps the disorganized person in such a flummoxed state. The easiest culprit is money. "I'm not organized because I can't afford all the accoutrements. I don't have a secretary. I can't afford a computer or electronic planner. My house isn't big enough." And on and on it goes.

Watch tools!

My personal organizational system consists of a yellow legal pad and a pen (total cost: $2.99). Each page in the legal pad represents a day. I draw a vertical line down the center of each page. On the left half of the page I write down the names and numbers of people I need to call that particular day. The things I need to do go on the right side of the line. Along the left margin I write times during the day when I plan to attend to each task. As I complete each activity, I draw a line through it. If the call or activity requires follow-up at a later time, I simply turn to the appropriate page and make a follow-up note. Tasks that don't get completed are transferred to the next page (or the next day) in my pad.

I've been using this system for 40 years, and built an international company that employs over 2,000 people in 40 different countries with it. Granted, when I first started this system legal pads cost a nickel, but in the grand scheme of things my investment in an organizational system has been pretty nominal for the results it has yielded.

Opportunities lost

There is a tremendous opportunity cost associated with remaining disorganized. Every misplaced message or task left unaccomplished has a cost. Sometimes the cost can be a diminished reputation. You become known as someone who doesn't return phone calls (inconsiderate) or someone who is consistently late to meetings (undependable). These labels can tarnish your business and personal relationships.

The cleanliness of your office speaks volumes to your co-workers and clients. A cluttered desk piled with scribbled notes and backlogged files screams disorganization. How can a client entrust you with his business if you can't be trusted to handle the items currently on your desk? And how can a co-worker rely on you if you have proven yourself unreliable in other, seemingly innocuous situations? The answer is simple: They can't.

Because the disorganized person is constantly reacting to what others are throwing his way, he has very little time to proactively go after more business. He is constantly on the defensive. Meanwhile, the organized individual handles his schedule in such a way that he has time to make new contacts, develop new relationships, and expand his horizons on all fronts.

Following is a list of rules that, if followed, can get you on your way to being more organized and efficient:

- ✔ If cost is an obstacle to getting organized, change your approach.
- ✔ A pen, a legal pad, and a plan are all you need to start getting organized.

✔ There are costs associated with every disorganized action you take. Being late for one meeting or forgetting to return one phone call sends a signal — one which will cost you greatly in the long run.

✔ Organized people are proactive and seize opportunities. Disorganized people are reactive and can never climb out of their self-dug hole.

The value of time

Time is money. You've, no doubt, heard that expression. You have probably said it a few times yourself. But too many people never really take the opportunity to put a dollar value on their time. Of course, hourly employees have some notion of what their time is worth to their employer (and if you have ever paid hourly rates to an attorney you know the value some people place on their precious minutes). However, most people have no idea what their time is actually worth.

McCORMACK MEMORIES

Being proactive about proactivity

Sometimes being proactive must be mandated. I expect the senior sales executives at my company, International Management Group (IMG) to meet five new people a year. That might not sound too difficult, but many of our executives claim that they don't have the time or the opportunity to meet five people in 52 weeks! It's a sad but true part of any business; people develop cliques and breaking out of their routines to explore new horizons is difficult for them. Unfortunately, the more senior the executive, the less likely she is to broaden her contact base. The most senior people find that going through their files and relying on old contacts is much easier than making new ones.

Because of that propensity, I have made the five-person contact mandatory. Additionally, I require our senior people to report on their five new people and explain how the contacts can be developed into future business.

When I first instituted this mandate, the hue and cry among IMG's executives was deafening.

There was no way they could meet and develop five new relationships, they said. They had more work coming out of their existing contacts than they could handle. The mandate was unreasonable! So I tested my theory by going back through my own contact lists over the past 20 years. What I found was eye-opening.

The contacts that accounted for 90 percent of my business 20 years ago, only accounted for 50 percent of my business ten years later. Those same contacts represent less than 20 percent of my business today. Each year, I found that the new names replaced the old in terms of the amount of business generated. My list today looks nothing like my list from 20 years ago, or ten years ago, or even five years ago. Because of my proactive approach to meeting new people and developing new contacts, I'm sure that a good portion of my business five years from now will come from people whom I've yet to meet.

I have a friend who takes great pride in his ability to travel around the world at minimal expense. He will negotiate airfares and hotel rates with great tenacity, and, as a result, he always gets the best prices. Unfortunately, his trips sometimes require him to take two extra layovers and stay an additional night in a particular city. Often he flies into one city, rents a car, and drives several hundred miles to his ultimate destination because of the money he saves over flying directly to his city of choice. Sometimes that course of action makes sense, but other times I question whether my friend has examined the time he wastes sitting in airports, driving rental cars, and staying extra nights in hotels — all to save a few dollars on airfare. Saving money is wonderful, but giving up control of your schedule to do so might not be worth the trade-off in the long run.

Just as you value your own time, you must respect the value of other people's time as well. Being late for a meeting, dinner engagement, or appointment is not only rude, it also tells the person with whom you are dealing that you believe his time is worthless.

Because I own my company, I have the luxury of calling internal meetings at times that are convenient for me. I'm the boss, so my employees usually bend their schedules to accommodate me. Sometimes, however, employees can be too accommodating. Recently, I asked a senior executive with my company to name a convenient time when I could call him at home on the weekend. He said what I assume he thought I wanted to hear, which was, "Mark, you can call me any time. I'll be available whenever you want."

While wonderfully accommodating, his answer was not at all what I wanted to hear. By leaving the time frame open-ended, this employee risked the chance that I would call while he was eating dinner, playing with his children, taking a nap, or any number of activities that might distract him from the discussion we needed to have. I would have preferred he tell me that he would be available between 6:00 and 8:00 p.m. on Saturday evening. I would have been able to mark that time on my schedule knowing he would not be distracted during our talk. His time has value, and I would have felt much better had he recognized that fact and responded accordingly.

Likewise, you must demand that others respect the time you grant them. Recently, I scheduled a routine doctor's visit for 7:00 a.m. on a Friday morning. When I made the appointment, the receptionist requested that I arrive 15 minutes early to fill out the necessary paperwork. I did as asked, showing up promptly at 6:45 and filling out forms before my 7:00 a.m. appointment. When 7:45 rolled around and I was still in the waiting room, I asked the receptionist if there was a problem.

"No," she said. "You're next."

"I should have been the first," I responded. "When was the first appointment scheduled?"

"Seven o'clock."

"And what time was I scheduled to be here?"

After a slight hesitation, the receptionist said, "The doctor will see you now, Mr. McCormack."

I'm sure everyone has had a similar experience. I only share this story because it so perfectly illustrates the utter disrespect some people have for the time of others. My appointment went well, but the chances of me returning to that particular physician are slim. He lost my respect by "telling" me he thought my time was worthless.

Conversely, I'm almost as annoyed by the person who is 30 minutes early for an appointment as I am by the person who is 30 minutes late. Even when the person arriving early assures me that he doesn't mind waiting, I know his time has some value, and I don't like having him waste his time even though I'm on schedule and he is early. It's silly, but I obviously worry more about the value of this person's time than he does.

What Being Organized Means

Perhaps the key element that separates the well-organized from the disorganized is this: Organized people know their limitations. In a classic Clint Eastwood western, the villain says, "A man's got to know his limitations." Predictably, the villain in the movie underestimates Eastwood's powers as a hero, resulting in a shoot-'em-up in which Eastwood emerges the victor. Of course, that's a movie. In truth, the villain was exactly right: A person does need to know her limitations if she is to maximize her time and resources.

My wife, Betsy, will often schedule a trip to the mall at 10:00 a.m. and a meeting at our house at 11:00. I know the timeframe is impossibly short because the mall is a 20-minute drive from our house. Travel-time alone on her trip is 40 minutes. More often than not, parking takes approximately 10 minutes, getting to the store (if she's walking fast) eats up another five, and (in a best-case scenario) picking up the item she wants, paying for it, and getting back to the car takes another 20 minutes. The minimum time for a trip to the mall can be calculated at an hour and 15 minutes. Throw in a packed parking lot, a slow checkout line, and a minute or two of browsing, and the trip becomes an hour and a half or longer. Yet, Betsy believes that she can make it home in an hour. Her assertion is unrealistic, even illogical, but she fervently believes it, because she doesn't completely appreciate her limitations.

I, however, go overboard in the opposite direction. If I have to go to the mall to pick up an item, I call ahead and make sure that the item is readily available. Because I know the travel time to the mall and I can anticipate the time it will take to park my car and walk to the store, sometimes I inform the store

I will be there in 30 minutes. If the store does its job, my package should be waiting for me when I arrive, and I should be pulling my car back into my driveway an hour and ten minutes after leaving home. Even with my meticulous plan, the trip has still taken over an hour. There is no way I would schedule another meeting based on the assumption that I would be back home in under an hour. Traffic could be heavy, or the salesperson might ignore my request and be on the phone when I arrive. Any number of variables beyond my control could disrupt my trip. Therefore, I always err on the safe side, scheduling my next appointment an hour and a half or more after my trip to the mall. If everything runs perfectly, I arrive home 30 minutes before my next meeting, and have time to make a call or two, or go over the agenda for the next meeting. None of my time is wasted, because I have planned my schedule based on limitations I know exist.

On the other hand, I might schedule six internal meetings between 7:00 a.m. and 11:00 a.m. — an unreasonable number for most people. But before embarking on such an aggressive plan, I know how long each meeting is going to last and insist on keeping the agendas very tight. That strategy doesn't mean that someone isn't going to approach me after one of the meetings and ask to discuss his life and all the problems therein, but, rather than disrupt my tight schedule, I will set up another time and place to sit down with that person. The six-meeting schedule is workable only if I set the agenda and keep things moving. Any deviation from the program and everything falls apart.

The disorganized person schedules six meetings for the same four-hour period, but fails to formalize the agendas or set time limits, so she likely never makes it to the third, fourth, fifth, or sixth meeting. The first two meetings eat away her entire morning and become little more than glorified encounter groups where little gets accomplished. The remaining meetings are either rescheduled, or forgotten all together.

By the same token, a disorganized person plans to make phone calls from his car between meetings only to discover that the battery on his cell phone is dead, or that he is in an area where the reception is too poor to speak to anyone. The organized person hires a driver to transport her between meetings so she can make calls, take notes, and read while in transit. She also makes sure that the phones are fully charged and that a strong cell covers the driving route so cell phone reception won't be interrupted.

The disorganized person plans to attend his son's 7:00 baseball game, but "emergencies" at the office keep him late most nights. The organized person puts a high priority on her son's game, and isn't distracted from her schedule by the demands of others. When problems arise at work, she neatly fits them into her schedule to be dealt with at a predetermined time in the future. By writing the items on her list and placing a realistic resolution time on each item, this person is not only able to attend her son's game, but can enjoy it without worry or anxiety.

An organized person is:

- ✔ Time sensitive and realistic about what he can accomplish in a given block of time.
- ✔ Space sensitive, realizing that everything has a place, even if that place is the trash can.
- ✔ Aware of the demands on her time, and careful not to over-promise.
- ✔ Disciplined in sticking to his organizational system, whatever that system might be.
- ✔ Confident and focused on her goals.
- ✔ Able to leave work-related problems at work because they are written down and assigned a time to be handled in the future.

An organized person is not:

- ✔ Better equipped or surrounded by staff and resources that are out of reach for most ordinary citizens.
- ✔ Humorless and so obsessed by his schedule and surroundings that one out-of-place scrap of paper throws him into a tizzy.
- ✔ Necessarily smarter, or more talented than you are.

Why you're probably not as organized as you think

Humans have a marvelous knack for deluding themselves. Whether the topic is physical appearance, health, or talent, many people have inflated opinions when self-evaluating. I find this particularly true in sports. People believe themselves to be great golfers, tennis players, and coaches when, in fact, they are average (or below) on all counts. The same principle holds true in organizing. Everyone believes herself to be organized, because the alternative is to be disorganized and unproductive — no one wants to admit that.

Keep a record of how often you are late for meetings or with deadlines, and jot down the reasons you believe that you fell behind schedule. Also, jot down a list of items you have misplaced over the course of the last month. Put both lists aside. Then, in a few weeks, come back to them and try to objectively evaluate whether or not you were being honest with yourself. A little distance can open your eyes to your own organizational shortcomings.

Chronic lateness denial syndrome

I have a friend (and longtime client), who plays women's professional golf, with whom I meet at least once a quarter. During a recent visit to California, we scheduled a dinner in Beverly Hills. At 8:00 p.m., the time our dinner was to begin, she called from her car to say that she was running late.

"I'll be there in twenty minutes," she said.

Her comment prompted me to ask where she was. When she gave me her location and told me what traffic was like, I said, "You probably won't be here for another hour. Why don't I change the reservations?" She hesitated, but I was insistent, and she finally acquiesced to the new schedule while continuing to insist that she would only be a few minutes late.

An hour later she strolled into the restaurant, apologizing profusely and insisting that this incident was highly unusual. She is never, ever late, she said. I found her comment amusing because my experiences have shown her to be between 15 and 30 minutes late for *everything.* Even while sitting in Los Angeles traffic, she was still convinced she could make it to the restaurant in 20 minutes when I knew the more likely (and ultimately accurate scenario) put her there in an hour.

I have found these situations to be a theme with my friend. She consistently over-schedules, becomes flustered when she falls behind, but continues to insist that she is never late for anything.

A dose of reality would help this person and a lot of others like her.

Honesty is the best policy — especially with yourself

No one intends to over-schedule or run late, but the problems that most people experience are based on self-delusion and unintentional dishonesty. If people took the time to assign realistic times to the tasks they want to complete, they would realize that their schedules are unworkable.

I recently had a lunch meeting scheduled in New York with a business associate (a man) who ended up being almost a full hour late for the meeting. Of course, he apologized and said that he was tied up with a couple of errands he had to run on the other side of town. His explanation prompted me to ask what his morning schedule looked like.

When he listed all the things he hoped to accomplish, I was shocked. In addition to a mid-morning meeting on the other side of the city, he had scheduled several other stops before our lunch. There was no way he was ever going to meet me on time, and, if this man had been honest with himself (and with me), we could have rescheduled. He could have finished his tasks without worry, and I would have certainly felt better about his ability to organize.

How organized are you?

Take the following couple of tests and check out the grading system that comes after them.

A personality test

1. Do you know what you will be doing at 10:37 tomorrow morning?

2. Could you find your car keys inside of one minute?

3. Do you have an organizational tool (a day planner, a legal pad, or a series of notes) at your side at all times?

4. Of the calls you know you will make, do you know whom you will call first tomorrow?

5. Are your most important business and personal phone numbers written down in one place?

6. Do you have meals with your family around a table at least three times a week?

7. Is over half your closet floor visible without moving or removing anything?

8. If you were to be hit by a truck and killed this afternoon, would your family know all the necessary critical information, and could they find all the documentation needed to survive the loss?

9. Do you have a will?

10. Have you scheduled your next physical examination with a doctor?

11. Has your garage been organized in the last six months?

An organizational quiz

12. Has a bill collector called your home or office in the last two years?

13. Have you ever forgotten a family member's birthday or your anniversary?

14. Are there any unread newspapers or magazines lying around your house or office?

15. Have you been late for a meeting, dinner, or appointment in the last two weeks?

16. Are all the storage spaces in your home full?

17. Have you misplaced or had trouble finding an important document in the past month?

18. Were you interrupted more than twice today?

19. **Have you gone to the market without a list more than once in the last month?**

20. **Have you had a disagreement or discussion with your spouse or a family member in the last month that centered around information you hadn't shared with anyone?**

Grading

In questions 1-11, give yourself five points for every "yes," and in questions 12-20, give yourself five points for every "no."

If you scored:

- ✔ **90 or above:** You are an exceptionally well-organized person who has little trouble completing tasks. In addition to being successful in your chosen field, you are more likely to be healthier and happier than many people your age and in your profession.

- ✔ **80 to 90:** You have good organization systems in place, and you adhere to those systems most of the time. A little fine-tuning and you could elevate yourself to new heights in your career and personal life.

- ✔ **70 to 80:** Face it, you're disorganized. Try as you might, circumstances tend to overwhelm you and you are often at the mercy of others. Make a commitment to change your life immediately by applying the systems outlined here.

- ✔ **Under 70:** You need help, and you need it quickly. Life must be a constant struggle, with strained relationships at work and home. The answer to your chaos could start with something as simple as a pen and a notepad, but you *must* make a personal commitment in order to improve.

What Being Organized Doesn't Mean

The idea of "being organized" brings with it all sorts of misconceptions. This section helps deflate those myths.

The "uptight personality" myth

I can't help but chuckle when I hear someone say, "People who are organized are way too uptight," or "I don't want to be organized because I'd rather stop and smell the roses." Actually, organization relieves tension; therefore, by being more organized you are better equipped to smell the roses than if you are always running late or sorting through the latest mess in your home or office.

The fun-loving organizer

One of the most organized athletes I've ever known is a young professional golfer named Justin Leonard. In fact, some might call him obsessive. Not only does Leonard organize his schedule to the minute, he even organizes his closet by day of the week. Monday's outfit is always perfectly coordinated and neatly hung on the left side of the closet with Tuesday's ensemble immediately to its right and so on. His pants are always perfectly pressed, and his shoes are polished and neatly aligned in the closet beneath his hanging clothes.

Justin also keeps his mail organized, dividing it into distinct piles according to priority and sorting through each piece until he has either answered it, filed it, or placed it aside for future action.

When he practices golf, he has a distinct routine beginning with short iron shots and working through the rest of the clubs in his bag with great precision. He plays the same way. When he emerged from the scoring trailer after having

just won the 1998 Player's Championship, Justin methodically removed the extra tees from his pocket and poured them into his golf bag. Then he removed his golf glove and placed it in a re-sealable plastic bag before unzipping another compartment in the bag and retrieving his watch, wallet, and other belongings. All Leonard's movements were very systematic and regimented, even though he'd just won $720,000 and one of the most prestigious non-major championships on the PGA Tour.

Given that information, many of you might peg Justin Leonard as an uptight patrician with no sense of humor and no time for fun and frivolity. If so, you couldn't be more wrong. Leonard is one of the more fun-filled personalities on the PGA Tour — a man who is never without a joke, and who is the life of the party at almost every function he attends. He enjoys life and never takes himself too seriously. In short, he is the antithesis of the uptight personality while being one of the most organized men in professional sports.

The "chained to your day planner" myth

Another often-repeated fallacy is that organized people are somehow bound to their schedules like prisoners. The disorganized person who says, "I don't want to be held captive by a predetermined schedule," sums up this myth. The disorganized masses need their freedom — or so they claim. To them, having a written organizational system means the death of flexibility and spontaneity. Organized people, they argue, are shackled to their daily planners with no room for modification.

Nothing could be further from the truth. Because I write everything down and have set times in which to accomplish certain tasks, I am able to enjoy leisure activities without worrying about the next meeting or the proposal that's coming up in a few days. I am also in charge of my day and my surroundings. If Tiger Woods were in town and wanted to play a round of golf, I could adjust my schedule, maneuver a few activities around, and play golf with Tiger without feeling guilty or unproductive — a luxury the disorganized person can never fully appreciate.

The "inflexible ogre" myth

Despite what seems to be conventional wisdom, organized people are neither mean nor inflexible. They simply understand the value of their time and space, and they do their best to conform to the guidelines they have set for themselves. Some of the nicest and most accommodating people I know are also the most organized.

No one in professional sports is known more for his openness and accessibility than Arnold Palmer. A big part of Arnold's charm and charisma is due to his unfailing friendliness and willingness to accommodate others. He always seems to make time for those around him — from a youngster standing along the gallery ropes for an autograph to one of the many corporate sponsors Arnold has been aligned with over the years. Yet Arnold is incredibly organized, keeping his finger on the pulse of numerous business ventures while continuing to compete on the golf course. He is a great example of someone who is flexible while remaining organized. And, during his almost 50-year career, no one has ever called Arnold Palmer an ogre.

Planning to not worry

During a recent golf game with a business associate, my fellow competitor was obviously not enjoying the round, and his mind seemed a million miles away.

"What's wrong?" I asked. "You seem preoccupied."

He shook his head and said, "It's this meeting I have next week. I really have no business being out here with something that important coming up."

When I pressed him on exactly what he would be doing if he were back in his office, I discovered (as I had suspected) that everything my friend needed to do to prepare for the meeting had already been done. His presence in the office wouldn't move him or his company an inch closer to the goals of next week's meeting. But he couldn't convince himself. He kept fretting over the details, so much so that he couldn't enjoy a simple round of golf.

Had my friend been more confident in his organizational system, he would have checked his daily planner and known the details were covered. Not only would he have been freed from the prison of his day planner, he would have certainly scored better on the golf course.

Transitions — the shorter, the better?

I hate transition times — the times between the ending of one engagement and the beginning of another. Nothing frustrates me more than ending a meeting and then idly chatting for an additional fifteen minutes while I walk someone to the door. Usually the only thing accomplished during those times is an agreement to meet or speak again at some vague time in the future. The rest of the time is, in my view, wasted.

My wife is mortified by my attitude. She believes that cutting these transitions short is rude and that I am often insensitive to the signals and nuances people give out during those times. In some respects she is probably right. But I also believe that being late to your next appointment is ruder than cutting a transition short.

Am I an ogre? Even Betsy wouldn't go that far, but there is probably a happy medium between her open-ended transitions and my abrupt endings.

The "obsessive-compulsive" myth

Obsessive-compulsive disorder is a serious psychological problem that affects millions of people. This disorder is also a label wrongly given to people who are simply meticulous and regimented in their personal organization. Idiosyncrasies, no matter how silly they may seem, do not make someone obsessive or compulsive.

Quirks have meaning

I have an acquaintance who seems perfectly normal in every respect — except when it comes to the way dishes are aligned in his dishwasher. As silly as it sounds, this man will excuse himself from a dinner party (even if it's being catered) to make sure that the dishes — in particular the silver — have been placed in the dishwasher to his specifications. He even has instructions posted throughout the kitchen detailing how the dishwasher is to be packed. This behavior is a curious quirk that has earned him unwanted attention.

Many of his friends have labeled the man obsessive, some going so far as to suggest that he might have a mild psychological disorder. I never, for a minute, believed that he had a psychological problem. So I asked him why he was so insistent on his dishwasher procedures.

"When I was a kid, I reached into a dishwasher and accidentally jammed the prong of a fork under my fingernail. It was one of the most painful things I had happen to me as a child, and I've never forgotten it. Since then, I've insisted that people loading the dishwasher place all forks with the prongs down and all knives with the handles up. That way I don't have to worry about someone having a similar accident."

His explanation made perfect sense. The answer, it turned out, was simple.

Chapter 6

Learning to Love Low-Tech

· ·

In This Chapter

▶ Finding your organizational system and sticking with it

▶ Ensuring that your system achieves the results you want

▶ Rediscovering the power of paper and pen

▶ Becoming proactive

▶ Organizing your personal space

· ·

*I*n Chapter 5, I discuss my personal organizational system. The legal pad is never outside my reach and I write everything down in one place, assigning days and times when I plan to take care of various tasks. That system has worked for me for years, and I've grown a successful company with it. That doesn't mean, however, that my system works for you.

A vast and highly competitive industry has evolved around helping people become better organized. Companies offer daily runners, personal planners, daytime systems, calendars, wall units, computers, and a gallery of pocket gizmos all designed to help you organize your time and space. Naturally, each system has its benefits and drawbacks.

Of course, I have a bias toward my personal system, because it's mine and it has worked so well for so many years. The legal pad and note card system I use provides several advantages:

✓ **It's easy.** I never have to learn any techno-wizardry to implement my system. I've been able to read and write since I was about six years old, so I've possessed the skills to run my system for over 60 years.

✓ **It's cheap.** Legal pads and note cards are still a relative bargain on the open market, and they are available at almost every corner store.

✓ **It's timeless.** I've never had to upgrade hardware, software, or buy new inserts. The system is the same today as it was 40 years ago.

✓ **It works.** If something demonstrably better came along, I would try it. Nothing has, and I doubt anything will in the future.

That is not to say that the personal planner industry is a rip-off. Plenty of fine, time-tested systems are available on the market. However, before you run out and purchase a system of any kind to help you get organized, you need to absorb what I discuss in the next section.

Everybody Has a Personal Organizational System

Your system might be good or it might be horrid, but don't be deceived; you do have a system for being organized (or disorganized). Your office or home might be in a shambles. If that is the case, whether you want to admit it or not, your system consists of living in a mess. The reason you're reading this book is not because you don't already have an organizational system; you're reading the book because you want to *change* the one you have.

In order to develop a new, more effective organizational system, you must first:

- ✔ Identify the system that's right for you.
- ✔ Simplify the system so that it isn't a burden.
- ✔ Codify the system so that it truly becomes your own.

Whether you're managing your day based on a scattered series of notes plastered on your office wall or you're working from a sophisticated (and no doubt expensive) system you purchased from your credit card company, all organizational systems need to meet certain basic requirements in order to be effective. Your organizational system must:

- ✔ **Insist that you write everything down.** If you're relying on your memory, your system is doomed to failure. No matter how bright you are, memories fail, time escapes you, and things slip your mind on a daily basis. If you only write down half the things you need to do, your system is only 50 percent effective. If 75 percent of the items in your day make it to your list, your system operates at 75 percent efficiency. Whatever system you choose, it must force you to write everything down if it is to be 100 percent effective.

- ✔ **Be convenient.** The number of people who rely on preprinted desktop calendars or stationary units (such as computers) shocks me. What do these people do when they aren't in their offices? My system goes with me everywhere. It's at my bedside when I go to sleep at night, and it's with me throughout the day. Because I constantly travel and maintain three primary offices and staffs on two different continents, any system that isn't portable and convenient won't work for me. I suspect that, although most of you probably don't travel the number of miles I do in a year, you spend more time away from your desk than you do sitting behind it. Your organizational system is no good if you're in one city and it's in another.

✔ **Be easy to read and understand.** Remember that the organizational system is *your personal* system, not a treatise or a novel you plan to submit for publication. No one else needs to understand your notes or system. If someone picked up my legal pad, not only would she have no idea what I planned to do in a given day, she would probably question whether English was my first language. Because no one else sees what I put on my list, I abbreviate everywhere I can, and I write quickly (and often illegibly). Despite what some of my staff think, I'm not using code in order to keep anything secret. I just don't want to waste time perfectly maintaining my system when I could be spending that time accomplishing the things on my list.

✔ **Deal in manageable increments of time.** I'm amused when I see the popular year-at-a-glance calendars hanging in offices around the country. Because of the amount of traveling I do, the number of people I meet, the calls I make, the meetings I chair, and the entertainment events I host, my year-at-a-glance would take up a good part of a Times Square billboard. Although most people would look at my schedule and think that it's out of control, I am able to manage my time because my system focuses on one day. One page in my legal pad represents one day's activities. I can manage that. If I were to list everything I have scheduled in a month or even a week, the volume of tasks would seem overwhelming. I can handle more activities, because I focus on a manageable increment of time: one day.

✔ **Let you download information.** Although "downloading" is now primarily used as computer jargon, it isn't a high-tech term. My system of downloading information is simple: If, at the end of my day, there are unfinished items on my list, I simply transfer the items to the next page (or the next day) in my legal pad. I don't have to worry about unfinished items falling through the cracks, because I know I've transferred them to another time.

✔ **Reward you for being organized.** My reward comes when I cross an item off my list. I get a sense of accomplishment when I mark through a task. Not only am I reminded that I am working, but that I am accomplishing something as well. Maybe you need more of a stimulus than just a sense of closure, but whatever rewards you set for yourself, make sure that your organizational system supports the rewards as well as the tasks you are completing.

In with the good, out with the bad

I know an executive who uses a color-coded organizational system in his office to handle paperwork. According to him, "The big question I face each day is: How do I divide my energies between the good news and the bad news so that I deal effectively with the money-losers, but don't spend too much time on them — and get so depressed — that I forget about the money-makers?"

His creative solution to the problem was to have all his paperwork — letters, messages, memos, and other documents — placed in either red or green files. Red is for bad news, green is for good. He spends no more than an hour a day going through the red files, and then focuses the remainder of his day on the green (or good) files.

"You can't believe what an emotional boost I get out of seeing a thin red file on my desk each morning," he told me. "It's reassuring to know that within an hour, my red file will be out of my life and sitting on someone else's desk."

A Quill and Parchment Still Get the Job Done

Technology is advancing more rapidly than any of us ever dreamed possible. Twenty years ago, the personal computer was a novelty — something less than 5 percent of the population found important enough to own. A decade ago, the fax machine was innovative, and portable computers were the size of medium-sized suitcases. No one outside academia had ever heard of the Internet, and electronic mail and computer conferencing were science fiction. Not only are all these technological advances now upon us, some of them are already becoming obsolete as newer, faster, broader-sweeping innovations are developed and taken to market every day.

In this day and age, my suggestion that the best way to achieve and maintain a personal organizational system is to break out a pen and paper might seem a bit old-fashioned, but I still believe it to be true.

The traditional paper and pen method has a number of advantages over more high tech forms of organizing your appointments, including

- **Convenience:** No matter where you are, you can always find a pen and paper.
- **Ease:** No batteries, surge suppressers, or floppy disks are required.

Newer isn't always better

One morning as I checked my legal pad, I noticed that I had made a note to call an old friend. It was his birthday — a fact I would never have remembered without the benefit of my pad.

When I mentioned the birthday to my secretary, she winced and said, "I'm sure I have that in my computer, but I haven't been able to boot it up this morning."

That left me wondering how she would manage if the power went out, or if her hard drive crashed, or if a virus invaded her computer. I don't have to worry about any of those problems with my system.

The more complicated the machine, the more things can go wrong. Computers are invaluable tools, but as this illustration proves, nothing beats a pen and a piece of paper when it comes to keeping simple things simple.

✔ **Usability:** Computers are great tools, but organization is about lists — things-to-do lists, people-to-call lists, projects-to-be-completed lists — and you can manage lists more easily on paper than with complicated machinery. Although having the latest gadget might be cool or fun, part of being organized is simplifying. Paper and pen are about as simple as you can get.

Make Your List as Proactive as Possible

All of us must react to situations and the demands of others at certain times. If Arnold Palmer needs to speak to me, I always adjust my schedule to accommodate his request. Of course, after 40 years, I know Arnold would never interrupt my day without just cause. If he says that he needs to speak to me right away, I know the conversation must be important. With few exceptions, however, my list is proactive. I initiate at least twice as many activities as I react to. Of course, because I own my company, I have the luxury of delegating to my staff, so I have control over what I do and do not add to my list.

No matter what your professional status, however, you should make a conscious effort to make your lists more proactive. Here are a few tips to help you:

- Before adding an item to your things-to-do list, ask yourself if completing the item moves you closer to any of your short- or long-term goals. If the answer is no, reconsider the action.

- For every item you put on your list that is reactionary (cleaning up a crisis, responding to an urgent request, and so forth) fit an additional proactive item somewhere into your schedule. Or, to invert Newton's Third Law, for every reaction, you should create an equal and opposite action.

- Change your mindset so you never think that you've run out of things to do. There are always proactive projects you can add to your daily list.

Making Space

Organizing your space, whether in your home, office, a conference center, or a hotel room, is just as important as organizing your time and tasks. But just as you should spend very little time assembling your list and the majority of your time actually attending to the tasks of the day, the key to effectively organizing your space is efficiency. I've seen countless business people spend

The curse of the in-box mentality

An executive friend of mine spoke with me recently about a problem he was having with a subordinate. In addition to being chronically late with assignments, the subordinate constantly left loose ends for others to clean up, and never reached his full potential. I asked my friend what he thought was wrong with this man.

"He has an "In" box mentality," the executive said.

"What do you mean?" I asked.

"Just look at his desk," he said. "The "In" box is always full, and the "Out" box is empty. He doesn't have an agenda of his own. He's so busy reacting to the memos and other stuff that lands in his box that he spends all his time reacting to other people's agendas. He's not pursuing anything proactive."

According to this executive, an "In" box mentality is bad, because it means that the employee has no original ideas of his own. An "Out" box mentality — where the "Out" box is full of original ideas being shipped to others — is a good thing in this executive's view. He believes that "Out" box thinkers project their own agendas and control their destinies. In a lot of ways, he's right. Original, proactive thinking is the lifeblood of any business and it is imperative to the personal growth of any professional. Of course, detailed follow-up or "In" box thinking is also important in order to get things done. Without proactive thinkers, however, there would be nothing in anyone's "In" box, so it is the "Out" box people who blaze new trails.

hours organizing their offices only to spend the same number of hours organizing it again a month later. The art of this process is simple: Space is only organized when it makes your life more convenient. Answer these questions to discover whether your space is truly organized:

- ✔ Are the things you touch most within easy reach?
- ✔ Have you touched every item in your personal space within the last year?
- ✔ Have you "organized" the same space more than once in the last six months?
- ✔ Are there any piles in your space?

If you answered "yes" to the first two questions and "no" to the last two, you have a good grip on the space around you. If you answered "no" to either of the first two questions and "yes" to either of the last two, you need to spend time thinking about how you use space, and what you need to change to use your space more effectively.

Horses for courses

The heading for this section is an expression in the world of horse racing. Certain horses are favored on certain tracks because of length, texture, angles, and other variables in the track that give advantage to one horse over another. I use "horses for courses" to mean that all space has a highest and best use. For example, I wouldn't invite a group of executives to a dinner party and serve the meal around my kitchen table. Although it's a fine dining area for my family, the space is inappropriate for a more formal function.

Before you make any decisions about space, you must first determine how the space is to be used, and what sort of impression you want to make on those who see it.

Police interrogation rooms are intentionally stark and cold because the goal of the rooms is to make the person being interrogated uncomfortable with her surroundings. Hospitals, on the other hand, go out of their way to make their private rooms as warm as possible because they hope to alleviate a patient's anxieties. These are extreme examples, but remember them when you plan a meeting or a social gathering. Every space provokes a feeling. Your job is to figure out what feeling you want people entering your space to experience.

If I'm spending one night in a hotel and the chance of my making any phone calls is slim, my prerequisite on where the bedside phone is located isn't as important. I might not bring the request up at all. Because I consider how I'm going to use a particular space first, I am able to organize that space with relative ease.

The rules for organizing personal space

A number of guidelines can help you better organize your personal space, including

- If your space seems disorganized to you, it looks twice as disorganized to everyone else.

- You never get a second chance to make a first impression. Your space *is* your first impression.

- Every space provokes a feeling from the person entering it. Being cognizant of what people feel in your space will help you change it for the better.

- The same space may have different requirements, depending on how it is used.

Low-Tech Organizational Test

Time to test your mastery of the low-tech skills you need to press forward and get organized. Remember the answers to these questions as you structure your own personal organizational system.

1. My most important phone numbers are with me at all times.

True.

False.

Phone logic

Because I travel so often, I am very particular about the size and setup of my hotel rooms. In addition to having a desk with a phone, I always insist that the bedside phone be located on my left side.

Some hotel managers find my request peculiar, but my reasoning is quite logical; if I'm lying in bed, I want to be able to hold the phone in my left hand and listen in my left ear, leaving my right hand free to take notes.

If the phone is on the right side of the bed, the cord gets tangled under my chin and I have difficulty writing. The request is simple, but it makes my hotel stays much more convenient.

---

2. If someone approaches me while I am away from my home or office and asks me to make a call or follow up on a task, I will:

> Check my notepad to see when I can accommodate the request and give the person an answer on the spot.

> Make a note to myself on a piece of paper and tell the person I will get back to them after I get home or in my office.

> Make a mental note to follow up once I return home, and then hope I remember the request by the time I go to bed.

3. My things-to-do list for tomorrow consists:

> Completely of assignments given to me by others.

> Of projects I have initiated.

> Of a balanced blend of proactive and reactive assignments.

> Of nothing. I don't have a things-to-do list for tomorrow.

4. I always have enough chairs in my office for the meetings I call.

> True.

> False.

5. Before I invite someone into my home for the first time, I will:

> Consider my objectives and orchestrate the visit so as to maximize this person's good feelings while in my space.

> Make a cursory cleaning of my home so as not to embarrass myself.

> Do nothing. This is my home and should be accepted as my personal space.

6. When I host an out-of-the-office business function, I always:

> Check the list of attendees to ensure that their needs are accommodated in the space where the function will be held.

> Make a preliminary visit to the site and go through the details of the function with an on-site coordinator.

> Call to make sure that the room is available.

> Let someone else handle the details.

The correct responses to these questions depend largely upon your personal goals and your ability to be honest in your own self-evaluation. Return to this test as you advance in your organizational maturity and see how your answers change over time. The most important thing to take away from this test, however, is the fact that none of your answers required you to plug in a machine or use anything more complicated than a pencil, paper, and a telephone. Once that concept sinks in, using more advanced organizational tools is easy.

Chapter 7

The Perils of Paperwork and Data

*O*ne of the most perilous aspects of getting organized is figuring out what to do with all the paper and data that comes into your life. Even for the most organized and efficient individuals, the sheer volume of paper, reports, and information — from junk mail to memos, personal letters to newspapers — can be overwhelming. Because paper and data tend to accumulate, you *must* have a system in place to attack this information, and you must be diligent in sticking to that system if you are ever to dig out from under your personal mountain of pulp.

You Can't Read Everything

I love golf. In addition to playing competitively through my college days and actually qualifying one year for the U.S. Open, I started my company, in part, because of my love for golf and my desire to be around the game. In addition, every year since 1966, I have published a book entitled *The World of Professional Golf,* which chronicles professional golf events around the world.

Even though I love golf (and it still represents a substantial portion of my business), reading every golf publication, golf book, or golf story written in a year is impossible. I can't even read all the memos that come out of the golf department of my company, much less the 10,000 golf books written or the hundreds of publications circulated on a daily, weekly, or monthly basis. If I did nothing else during my day but read golf material, I still wouldn't have enough time.

As a result, I narrowed my reading to a few salient magazines and newspapers dealing with those areas of golf in which I have a particular interest. Also, my staff prepares a weekly report — with summaries and results of tournaments from around the world — so that I can stay abreast of the game without being overwhelmed by mountains of paper.

If I have to be that selective about a subject I love as dearly as the game of golf, you should also be mindful of the material you allow yourself to peruse. Unless an item fits into your schedule and moves you closer to your personal goals, sometimes it is better left unread.

When I first started my company, I insisted on reading every memorandum, seeing every letter, and getting a copy of every bill that came through our doors. Today, such papers would fill the Superdome in a year. I quickly realized that I was either going to have to cut back on my reading and trust my people to handle their own correspondence, or spend my entire life reading. Letting go was tough, but I really had no choice. If I was going to grow my company and retain my sanity, I had to decide which papers I would see and which documents could be handled by others.

At present, I still read a half-dozen newspapers every day and enjoy receiving personal correspondence from friends. Other than those two exceptions, however, I insist on seeing only correspondence pertaining to internal disputes between two or more of our employees, or files detailing problems with clients. Because I am a lawyer as well as the owner of the company, I read every paper related to any lawsuits that we might be involved in or any documents that might place us in legal jeopardy. The only other documents I occasionally review are expense reports from 20 or so employees whom, I suspect, might be going overboard on travel and entertainment expenses. On every other subject, I receive prepared summaries. Still, all these papers make for a pretty healthy dose of reading material, but nothing compared to the volume of paper that goes through our company every day.

As difficult as cutting back on my policy of reading everything was, it was even more difficult for me to accept that the people around me were in the same boat. Just as I can't read everything, the people I trust can't read everything that comes their way either. They, too, must prioritize, summarize, skim, and delegate.

For years I have kept every letter, every memo, and every note I've ever written in what I call my "chron files," short for "chronicle" or from the Latin word meaning "time." Copies of these files are given to Betsy and my children so they have an on-going historical record of what I write. Obviously, these files have become voluminous, so now my secretary writes a synopsis of each document she copies. Rather than pouring through forty or more pages, Betsy can quickly scan the synopsis page and determine which documents she needs to read and which can be stored for review at a later time.

The trick has been to make sure that someone reads and attends to everything. Ensuring that nothing of value slips between the cracks is a battle I fight regularly and one I will continue to wage as long as I remain an active chairman in my company.

Four Options for Your Paperwork

When a piece of paper comes into your possession, you have four options. You can

- Act on it.
- File it away to be acted on at a later time.
- Delegate it to others for action.
- Take the boldest action possible and toss it!

I use mail as an example, although the same principles apply to memos or couriered documents. When my mail arrives, I adjourn to my office, go through the stack, and make six distinct piles. The first pile goes to my Cleveland secretary. Some of the items are self-explanatory, but I often attach a self-adhesive note to each letter with instructions on how and to whom the letter or document is to be delegated. The second and third piles are for my New York secretary and my London secretary, respectively, and I apply self-adhesive-note instructions to the documents in those piles as well. The fourth pile is for Betsy, my wife, and the fifth pile contains the items I need to read. I discuss the sixth pile in the following section.

Once I segregate the mail into these distinct piles I break my "to read" pile into two sub-piles: one for business reading and one for leisure reading. The business pile takes precedence, so I make another pass through that mail and arrange it so the most important documents are on top of the pile, and the least pressing items are at the bottom of the stack.

After going through this process (which takes less time than it probably took you to read about it), I attack my business pile with one mission in mind: Touch the mail as few times as possible and handle each item as quickly and efficiently as I can. When I dive into the reading pile my objective is to handle each piece of mail one time. Sometimes doing so is impossible, but, by setting the "one touch" goal as my ultimate objective, I enter the process with a get-in-and-get-out mindset.

If, for example, I receive a letter from Brenda Blumberg (one of my oldest and dearest friends from South Africa), I answer it as promptly as I can. That doesn't mean that I drop everything and write Brenda a letter on the spot. What I do is make a note in my pad (which, of course, I have by my side) to write a follow-up letter to Brenda at a predetermined time in the future. Then

I am free to either put Brenda's original letter in one of the piles for my secretaries, or I might place it in a personal correspondence file in my office. Either way, I have acted on this piece of mail, even though my action has been to defer follow-up until a later time.

A notice from one of our senior executives announcing his plans to leave the company, however, would be handled much differently. In that case, I would most likely stop everything and attend to the letter. The rest of the day's mail would have to wait. Chances are good that I would have to reschedule some other activities I had planned, but the resignation of a key employee is a piece of mail that requires my immediate attention and action.

If, however, I receive a thank-you note from one of the clients or customers we entertained at Wimbledon or the World Match Play Championship, I read the note, but no follow-up is required (immediately or in the future). Because I want to keep the letter, I file it away in an "incoming correspondence" file. This action eliminates it from my list of things to touch, but places the letter where I can find it again if needed.

After I have finished my business pile, I may or may not attack my "leisure reading" pile right away. When I decide to get to the leisure reading, however, I approach it in much the same way I did my business reading. I skim through the stack, placing the item I am most interested in on the top, and the items I am least interested in on the bottom. Then I read through each item and put it in a file for future action, act on it immediately, or simply file it as needing no further action. Using this procedure, I handle every item in an efficient manner, touching each piece of mail as few times as possible to achieve maximum results.

What about the sixth pile?

I make three piles I set aside for various secretaries, the pile for my wife, and my "to read" pile (which I later subdivide into business and leisure reading). I also make a sixth pile — it's trash. During my first pass through the mail, I make sure that a trash can is within easy reach, and I pour a great many documents into the can as I am sorting and making piles.

A lot of items don't get to the envelope-opening process. Obviously, junk mail is easy to pitch (although recognizing the stuff at first glance is getting tricky). Anything that starts out with "You Could Already Be A Winner!" or is addressed "Dear Occupant" doesn't get opened, but the sneakier marketers (or more savvy marketers, depending on your perspective) have become very adept at disguising junk mail. Items that look like checks, invoices, or wedding invitations often catch my attention, but once I realize these items are nothing more than cleverly packaged junk, I throw them away.

The midnight paper bandit

Lou Wasserman, the former chairman of the entertainment conglomerate MCA, once told me that he liked to walk through the offices at MCA after everyone had gone home and throw away all the papers left sitting on desks. He took the approach that, if a document isn't worth handling before leaving the office for the day, it isn't worth handling at all.

Although Wasserman's method was certainly a radical way to get his point across, he was admired and respected for his principles — one of which was quick, decisive action. He believed in answering all correspondence on the day it was received, and that nothing should be left on your desk after you turned out the light and closed the door.

Imagine what would happen if Lou Wasserman came into your home, and you will probably increase your efficiency when dealing with paper.

Tossing other kinds of mail isn't so easy, however. For years I made a habit of reading and answering all the resumes that crossed my desk. I felt flattered that these people would want to work for my company, and I also felt an obligation as chairman to acknowledge my receipt of these resumes. I have changed that philosophy, however. Because computers enable applicants to churn out thousands of resumes, each looking just as professionally printed as the first, I no longer answer any letter or resume that states, "If you need an executive with my abilities, please contact me at ____." After years of laboriously answering every resume, one fact finally dawned on me: If an applicant doesn't even have enough initiative to pick up the phone and follow up with a call after sending me her resume, I shouldn't waste my time reading or responding to her information. These types of resumes now get recycled.

I also throw away most of the letters that pitch new ideas for sporting events. Not that I think we have a monopoly on good ideas for future events or sporting affiliations, but the sheer volume of letters I receive (with ideas ranging from Arctic golf to competitive bungie jumping) makes responding to every one an impossibility. Most of the time I read the letters, and, if the idea is intriguing enough, pass the letter along to someone else in the company. Still, 90 percent of the time those letters get recycled.

After years of honing my skill in picking out junk mail, I now throw away a much larger stack of mail every day than I place in any of the other five piles. You would be well served to do likewise.

The boldest move you can make when you sort through paper is to increase the number of items you pitch into the circular recycling file. In order words, if in doubt, throw it out.

In order to avoid being consumed by a mountain of paper, establish some rules for handling paper quickly and efficiently. This list isn't comprehensive, but your personal set of rules should certainly include the following:

- Designate one spot in your home or office for handling paper, and only deal with mail and other documents when you are physically in that spot. Setting aside this special area keeps your paperwork from encroaching on other activities and other areas of your life.

- Try to touch each piece of paper one time and one time only.

- If you can't touch a paper only once, make sure that you never touch the same piece of paper more than twice.

- If you touch a paper more than twice, it had better be one of the most important documents in your possession. Otherwise, you are wasting your time and being ruled by a paper tiger.

- Keep files in alphabetical order and segregated between business and personal.

- Make sure that your files are convenient, but not out in the open or strewn about.

- The first time you touch a piece of paper, do something with it — even if the "something" is filing it away for future action.

- Double the amount of paper you throw away.

Pretend that you're moving

I have a friend who sells his home and moves every five years, whether he needs to or not. In addition to being fairly savvy about real estate and making a substantial profit each time he changes addresses, this man says, "Everybody should move twice a decade just to have a thorough throwing away."

What makes this statement slightly humorous is the grain of truth he has obviously found. Every time I moved from one home to another, I came across things I couldn't believe I still owned.

Invariably, I threw away a lot of items that didn't warrant being packed up and moved. You have probably had similar experiences, as well.

It shouldn't require something as radical as selling your house for you to reevaluate the worthiness of all your stuff — particularly the paper — that has accumulated over the years. Perhaps now is the time for a "thorough throwing away" — whether or not the moving trucks are parked in your driveway.

The world needs more confetti

You don't have to work in a high-security government installation to need a paper shredder. In fact, if you aren't shredding the dozens of credit card applications you receive every month, you are leaving yourself open to a huge risk. Millions of dollars are swindled each year, and thousands of innocent citizens have faced long-term credit nightmares because of paper theft. With a social security number and an address (both of which can be found in your garbage if you aren't careful), criminals can wreak havoc with your life, sometimes putting you on a credit blacklist that takes years to clear up.

Shredding documents doesn't completely protect you from the perils of fraud, but doing so is certainly a good start. Shredding also protects others with whom you correspond. A friend might feel more comfortable sending a personal letter if he is aware of your vigorous shredding practices.

The only disadvantage to shredding is that, once shredded, a document is gone forever — not a bad thing if your goal is to de-clutter your life and eliminate your problems with paper.

Storage solutions for sensitive documents

Certain documents need special attention, whether or not you touch them regularly. Your homeowner's insurance policy, for example, isn't something you're likely to keep by your nightstand, but you should keep it stored in a convenient and safe place for easy access. The same holds true for your life insurance policy, deeds or titles to any property you own, your will, important legal documents, and sensitive financial information. You might not touch these items for years, but you must keep them safely stored.

To ensure your safety and the protection of your most sensitive documents, consider

- ✔ Purchasing a fireproof safe or filing cabinet. These are expensive, but the protection they provide is well worth the price.

- ✔ Leasing a safety deposit box from a local bank. You can't put an entire file cabinet into it, but for your most sensitive and valuable items nothing beats a dual-key safety deposit box.

- ✔ Duplicating important documents and keeping copies in several locations. This option may be a little more complicated than simply sticking an original document in a fireproof safe, but having back-up copies in several different places is certainly a viable alternative.

> ✔ Telling someone you trust where your documents have been stored. I can't imagine anything worse than passing away unexpectedly without Betsy or my children knowing where to find all the important documents they would need.

No matter how technical our society becomes, you never eliminate paper from your life, nor increase your options for handling it. The chairman of a Fortune 500 company has the same options when handling paper as the homemaker organizing the family budget. The only difference is volume.

Garbage In . . .

Decisions today aren't hampered by a lack of data, but rather it is an over-abundance of data — some good, but mostly useless — that floods your home, television, phone, and computer screen on an almost daily basis, that fuels disorganization, and hampers decision-making.

For example, our company represents the licensing and marketing rights to the Wimbledon name and logo. At the time we structured that arrangement, no one understood how the name of a tennis tournament held in Wimbledon, England, could be marketed and transformed into a worldwide brand. I understood the value of the name, however, and we were able to capitalize on that brand recognition.

Part of our job in maintaining the integrity of the brand is to monitor the use of the name Wimbledon. As easy as that may sound, the task has become almost impossible to manage. A simple Internet search of Wimbledon produces over 150,000 hits, including everything from London travel guides to a Pete Sampras Fan Club link. Almost none of the information has any bearing on our marketing arrangement with the All England Club and the Wimbledon Committee, but we still have to check it out. This is a classic and all-too-familiar example of how easy it is to become bogged down in a data glut.

Data overload isn't unique to the business world, however. If you live in Cleveland and your kids want to adopt a golden retriever puppy, the most logical place to begin your search is the local Golden Retriever Rescue Club. However, Internet searches on the subject regularly produce between 170,000 and 200,000 documents about the Golden Retriever Rescue Club of Cleveland, Ohio. Unless you or your kids have 40 or so hours to kill, it would be impossible to review all the information relating to the puppy world.

So what can you do? How can you cut through the clutter and obtain the data you need without wasting a great deal of time and energy? The following sections show you how.

Clarifying what you really want

Determine how much data you want or need. That task isn't always as easy as it initially sounds. If, for example, I want to know how much money our company is spending on long-distance telephone service, depending on how I make my request I may get one number (the total amount spent on long distance calls from all phones in all offices around the world) or I could get 1,000 or more lines of detail complete with methodologies, trends, and breakdowns by office, country, city, department, or individual. If I'm not specific in my request, I may even receive a comparative analysis of long-distance charges between departments with historical references to show how much more or less we are spending on long distance this year over last. In fact, one simple question — "Hey, how much are we spending on long distance?" — could result in a 50+-page glossy report complete with color charts and graphs.

As ridiculous as this scenario sounds, it is a real-world example of how access to too much data can get out of hand. The sections that follow give examples of the best way to avoid this data overload.

Ask better questions!

Here are some examples of well-meaning questions, the results they produced, and some alternative questions that may have resulted in more precise answers.

Wrong way:

> Q: What is our company's current payroll burden?

> A: A 92-page listing of all full-time, part-time, and independent contract employees, along with the median income of each, the highest and lowest salaries, the benefit packages offered, a summary from the payroll registry, and a pie chart showing payroll as a percentage of total expenditures.

Right way:

> Q: I'm examining some new tax laws, and I need to know the average monthly amount we are paying in pre-tax salaries (no benefits) in all our U.S. operations. I don't need a breakdown right now, just one number.

> A: One number.

Wrong way:

> Q: Where should I go to buy a computer?

> A: 1,000 pages of reference and advertising material listing everything from system mainframes to pocket PCs.

Right way:

Q: What local stores have the best prices and most reliable service for desktop PCs with 3 gigs of memory, high-resolution monitors, state-of-the-art CD drives, and Pentium III processors?

A: A list of six to twelve retailers in close proximity to your home or office.

Wrong way:

Q: If I relocate to Orlando, where should I live?

A: Over 30,000 residential listings in the greater Orlando metropolitan area ranging from a $30,000 mobile home to a $16 million estate with frequent updates from hundreds of real estate agents interested in making you their customer.

Right way:

Q: I'm considering a move to the greater Orlando area. Because I have small children, I need to live near the best schools, in a low-crime area with easy access to shopping and dining. My price range is the low $300,000s and I would prefer a quiet cul-de-sac in a planned residential community.

A: A healthy 100 or so listings, but manageable.

Wrong way:

Q: How should I invest my money?

A: Over 10,000 books and over 1,000,000 Internet sites willing to answer (and help you by taking your money away).

Right way:

Q: I have $350,000 in employee stock options that are going to roll over in six months when I retire. My investment goals are conservative, and I want low capital risk. What is the largest and most reputable financial planning institution that specializes in small to mid-sized retirement plans?

A: A list of 20 to 50 reputable investment firms.

Know what you want before you ask

Whether you are searching the Internet, pouring through your local library, or requesting data from your employees, co-workers, or family members, it is important that your requests are specific. A vague question always produces a broad-sweeping answer. The more precise you can be in your requests (even if you are the one who ultimately does the research), the more likely you are to get usable data.

If possible, convey your motivations to whomever is helping you search for data. By letting your researcher in on your ultimate goals, you stand a much better chance of getting the right information. Notice in the "Right way" scenarios, each question was prefaced with a setup or brief explanation of why the person asking the question needed the data. This little bit of insight was the difference between getting broad, unmanageable answers, and getting concise, usable data.

Remember the reason you need the data

Data falls into three distinct categories:

- Need-to-know data
- Nice-to-know data
- Useless data

Obviously, need-to-know data is the most important. This is the information you must have in order to make informed choices and take intelligent action. It is the income projection you need before committing yourself to a project, or the flight information you need before departing on a trip. Sometimes the data is right at your fingertips, and other times it is frustratingly illusive, but regardless of how easy or how difficult it is to find, need-to-know data is the information you need most.

Nice-to-know data can range from the baseball box scores to the five-day weather forecast. It won't kill you not to find it, but you may feel better about life if you have the data at your disposal.

Useless data is just that: useless. It doesn't help you make short- or long-term decisions, nor do you find it particularly interesting. Unfortunately, this is the data that often seems most prevalent in today's media-rich communications environment. It is a pitfall of the information age that as more sources for information become available, those outlets are filled with contrite, trivial, and ultimately useless information that has no redeeming social value. You might win a Trivial Pursuit game by knowing who styles Tom Hanks's hair, or how far it is from the Earth to the sun (in kilometers), but other than that the data serves no purpose other than to confuse and clutter.

One of the primary flaws of disorganized people is their inability to differentiate between the three types of data. The disorganized person confuses nice-to-know information with need-to-know information, and he spends entirely too much time sorting through and humming over useless information.

- **Tests for categorizing data:** In order to avoid the data trap and use data as part of your overall organizational plan, you need to discipline yourself in determining which data you review. Whenever you come into contact with data, ask yourself the following questions:

- **Does this information deal with my most immediate concerns?** If your answer is yes, then the data falls into the need-to-know category. If the data deals with an issue that you may eventually address but one that isn't on your short-term agenda, it falls into the nice-to-know category, and if you couldn't care less, it is useless.

- **Am I better equipped to make a decision because of this data?** Again, if the answer is yes, then it is information that you need to know. If the answer is no, the information is either a nice little respite you should file away for future reference, or it is worthless and a waste of your time.

- **Have I saved time or wasted time with this data?** If you are able to take decisive action as a result of the data, then you are obviously saving time and future anxiety. If you aren't able to do much after you examine the data and you gain no joy from it, then it has been a waste of your precious time.

- **Did the information lead me to future positive action?** Sometimes a nugget of data may come your way that has no immediate use, but steers you in a positive direction for the future. In that case, the data is definitely need to know, even though you didn't act on it the day you received it. These tidbits are rare, but they are always worth pursuing.

- **Did I ask for this information?** The best way to judge certain data is by whether or not you asked for it. Obviously, if one of your children has been in an altercation at school, that is information you need to know (even if you have forgotten to tell the child's teachers to contact you when such situations arise). As for other information, however, the "Did I ask for this?" test is a fairly good measure of the priority you should place on data.

✔ **The back-end first theory:** When I ask for data within our company, I usually want no more than one page of information, even though I may follow up later with a more detailed request. I call this the back-end first theory. I would rather start at the bottom line or the back-end of data and work my way back through the details as I need them. For example, if I want to know how much we are spending each year on courier services, I want to start at the back-end with one number. From there I can get a summary of how much is being spent in each office, or how the number is broken down by department or by month. However, by knowing the bottom line first, I can control how much detail I choose to undertake. It may be none, and it may be several pages of spreadsheet information. Either way, I control the data, because I start at the back-end and work my way forward.

> ✔ **Bad data is worse than no data at all:** If there is anything worse than receiving mountains of useless data, it's receiving concise data that is inaccurate. The reason bad data is worse than no data is because with no data you are less likely to act until you have the information you need. Having bad information means that you are likely to make a decision based on flawed assumptions, often leading to dire consequences.

Selecting software

Most personal computers systems these days come with a standard Microsoft business software package already installed or ready to install, and for most small business people or most households, that package (along with an Internet service package) is sufficient for 90 percent of the things you may need. After that, the sky is the limit.

Because many of our clients are well-known professional athletes, I have become somewhat familiar with the video game market, only because so many of the games now license the names and images of our clients. The graphics of these games are amazing, and when I watch people playing them I am stunned by how far this industry has progressed over the last decade. Still, video games, CD-making software, flight simulators, and other novelty software probably won't make you more organized, nor will they save you much time or improve your efficiency.

Same words, different meanings

One of the biggest problems I have had with information is the lack of understanding that often occurs between information systems managers and the rest of the people within the company. That communication disparity was evidenced recently when our company spent a small fortune implementing a sophisticated software program to capture income and monitor cash flow. Unfortunately, the process took much longer than expected because the information systems department understood the programming, but had very little expertise in how our company generated income. The managers and executives who were responsible for generating income knew nothing about sophisticated projection models. I had better luck getting our Japanese office communicating with our Cleveland office, even though most of the people in those offices spoke two different languages.

After the system was finally up and running, I received my first report and immediately noticed a problem. A line item that showed substantial income in 1999 showed a zero balance for the year 2000. I knew this particular piece of business would generate more income in 2000 than it did in 1999.

When I asked about the problem I was told, "No one in the I.S. department understood that this business was ongoing, but all the project managers assumed that it was common knowledge."

Garbage in, garbage out — but in this case it was awfully expensive garbage.

When you select software for your home or office, be mindful of one rule:

> If it saves you time and moves you closer to your goals, buy it. If it distracts you from your goals and wastes your time, trash it.

This rule applies to home-business software as well as some of the new Internet-specific programs available. While looking through a "Household Budgeting" program (a piece of software I assumed would help a homemaker balance the family checkbook, store recipes, and keep track of grocery lists), I found a general ledger icon, a spreadsheet function, and a pop-up screen asking if I wanted to calculate accumulated depreciation. Maybe some homemakers need a depreciation schedule on their living room suite, but I found this feature to be overkill, and a monumental waste of time and computer memory.

After you have made a decision on which software you want to purchase, IDG Books Worldwide, Inc. probably has a book that can walk you through it. With those books as a reference, anyone could figure it out.

Doing the balancing act

As with most decisions you have to make in your newly organized life, the amount of data you receive and the way you respond to it evolves over time. If you are constantly mindful of the pitfalls, and diligently do your best to keep the process simple, you stand a better-than-average chance of using data effectively. Without that mindset, however, the information monster may consume you, and the rest of your organizational efforts will have been for naught.

Chapter 8

How Much Stuff Do You Really Need?

1 have an acquaintance who insists on being one of the first to own the latest and greatest technological advancement, even if the item has no redeeming value to his business or personal life. When laptop computers first hit the market, he bought one of the first models even though he rarely traveled more then 100 miles from his home or office. Every year he buys the latest electronic pocket organizer, and he has more features on his cell phone than any human could possibly need.

During a recent meeting he showed me his latest gadget, a combination digital pager, phone, and computer that could page him anywhere on the planet while allowing him to send and receive e-mail and make phone calls to any of the 500 preprogrammed numbers in the phone's database.

When I asked him how many names he currently had programmed into the phone he said about 50. Although I thought that the number was probably an exaggeration, I asked him how many times he had referenced his phone's database. The answer didn't surprise me, but it was telling.

He said, "I've only used it a few times — maybe a dozen, tops. I'm usually in my office, so I can check my Rolodex, but it's nice to know that if I'm on the road I have this digital option if I need it."

This man is one of thousands who finds it necessary to be on the cutting edge of technology. Even though he and many others couldn't possibly use the advancements at their fingertips, they are compelled to own the latest and greatest gadgets because of the "nice to have" options these marvels of ingenuity provide. For this man, and for many others just like him, the phones, computers, pagers, pocket organizers, and many other high-tech items he purchases are toys. They are cool, and he feels cool and cutting edge by owning them, but as far as being necessary or even productive tools, these items don't come close to being worth the expense.

On the other side of that coin, I have a friend and fellow entrepreneur who adamantly refuses to enter the technological age. In his words, "They lost me when they did away with rotary phones."

Even though he travels almost 200 days a year, this man refuses to purchase a laptop computer or a cell phone. Part of this refusal is stubbornness, but I also believe a good part of his reluctance to advance into the late 20th century stems from a fear of appearing inept. By his standards, his own grand-children are technological wizards, surfing the Web and sending video e-mails, but he wouldn't know how to log onto the most basic computer system. He would never admit it, but I believe my friend refuses to learn the basic functions of today's technology because he doesn't want to appear ignorant, or worse yet, out of touch.

For years this man was able to get away with shunning technology. Several years ago it was still acceptable not to have an e-mail address, or be unavail-able because of travel. However, as the techno-curve shortened and a major-ity of people became Internet and cell phone active, those excuses became less acceptable, and my friend found himself falling behind the times. His cus-tomers found it untenable that he could not be contacted when he was out of the office, and not being able to send and receive electronic correspondence dampened his ability to grow the business.

As a result, my friend has spent more money bringing assistants along on busi-ness trips, phoning his office from locations around the world, and hiring addi-tional people who are technically literate than he would have ever spent had he simply learned a few basics and taken advantage of technology. For him, technology is a tool that could help improve his business if he chose to use it.

The perfect balance is somewhere between these two examples.

Identifying Techno-Tools

An old adage says that you don't need to know how a fine Swiss watch works in order to tell the time. That saying perfectly illustrates the trap most people fall into when they use high-tech instruments, worrying about *how* a piece of equipment functions instead of realizing *what* it can (or can't) do for you.

For example, one of the newest innovations being offered in automobiles today is the *Global Positioning System* or *GPS*. By bouncing radio signals off satellites, a GPS can track the location of your vehicle and interface that information with a series of grids to determine which road you are on and how far you are from your intended destination. Depending on the sophistication of your system, your car may be able to provide directions while you are driving. You simply program your destination into the car's computer, and a voice tells you where you are, how long it should take to arrive, and when and where to make the correct turns. GPS is a marvelous advancement and a great example of how far computer technology has come in the last decade.

Unfortunately, as wonderful as the *how* is, *what* it can do for you isn't that simple. Unless you travel a great deal by car or have difficulty finding your way around your hometown, the system is an expensive luxury that offers little benefit. For me it would be virtually useless. I know my way around Orlando fairly well, and when I am in New York, London, Cleveland, Paris, or any other city where I am conducting business, I either hire a driver or take a cab. A global positioning system to tell me how to get from my home to the grocery would be a neat toy, but a complete waste of money from a practical standpoint.

However, if I traveled by car from city to city, or if I spent a great deal of time in my car traveling to customers in various regions, the GPS would be an invaluable tool. Not only would I not have to carry an endless supply of maps, but I could properly schedule my day with accurate travel-time calculations, and the system would eliminate any anxieties I may have about getting lost. I could focus on my next meeting without worry. The car wouldn't let me miss a turn.

How the system works is unchanged in both the examples I give earlier, but *what* it can do for the user is quite different. In my case, the GPS would be a neat but expensive toy, and in the case of the frequent car traveler, it would be an invaluable tool. In both cases, however, how the system works is irrelevant to the end results.

Distinguishing Tools from Toys

To determine how a particular piece of equipment may better your life and to avoid the pitfalls of falsely rationalizing the purchase of a toy, you may want to ask yourself some important questions.

How frequently will you use the item?

Be honest. It's easy to convince yourself that you may use that neat new gadget every day, but the world is littered with stationary bikes and in-home exercise equipment that have become little more than glorified coat racks. In order to determine how frequently you may use an item, you must be specific. When would you have used it yesterday? The day before? How and when will you use it tomorrow? How will it fit into your travel schedule?

These are all questions that relate to frequency, and ones you should answer before purchasing a new piece of equipment.

How much time are you wasting by not having this item?

This is a different question than "How much time will I save by buying this item?" By framing the question in the negative, you must seriously evaluate how much time you are currently wasting, not convince yourself of the time you may save. Convincing yourself of the time you save may be a lie waiting to happen, but figuring out how much time you're wasting without the item is grounded in today's reality. If you can honestly pinpoint the exact hours or minutes that you waste each day because you do not own a particular piece of equipment, then you can make a serious and studious buying decision.

How much money are you losing by not owning the item?

Again, the answer to this question requires specifics. It is easy to assume that you are losing countless potential income because you don't have the most sophisticated computer system on the planet, but unless you can quantify a specific loss, you may be basing your buying decision on an unsubstantiated and often ill-informed guess.

What is the learning curve for this item?

How quickly can you master the skills needed to make this item really useful? If you don't know, you shouldn't buy it.

Which features are critical and which are cool?

You may consider a cell phone a critical business tool, but do you really need the 500-number programming feature? Or the video game option? Or the e-mail link? These are all neat items, but they tend to cloud your judgment. If you only need a basic phone, that's all you should purchase. Leave the bells and whistles at the circus.

Are you buying for today or next year?

It's amazing how many people buy a computer system that exceeds their current needs with the expectation that they may "grow into it" in a few years. The only problem with that logic is the rapid change in the computer industry. A few years from now, the system you thought you would grow into may be completely outdated. When making a purchasing decision, buy for today and let next year take care of itself. Plenty of innovative marketers are worrying about the future for you.

Is this item increasing efficiency or simply creating more work?

I have never purchased a computer system, be it a series of interoffice PCs or a mainframe system complete with sophisticated software, that someone didn't say, "This is going to cut back on manpower and save the company money." I chuckle out loud when confronted with that statement now because I know from years of experience that no computer system has ever diminished manpower. If anything, new systems mean new people (usually *more* people) to input data, analyze results, and fix whatever problems may arise. Systems may run more efficiently if you purchase a particular item, but be careful. More likely than not, all you may do is create more work churning more data, and build in a longer workday for yourself and for others.

Do you have the infrastructure to handle this new item?

Whether it's space in your home or office, a proper power source, or the brainpower to handle whatever it is you're buying, your results depend on how prepared you are for the new item in question. Without the proper infrastructure, you are wasting your money and your time.

Can you afford the item?

This is another question where honesty in your answer is paramount. You may have no trouble justifying the expense of the item you want to purchase (most bad purchases are always worth the expense at the time), but you must also consider the other things you could do with the money that you're about to spend. Whether paying yourself a bonus, hiring another staff member, buying a new chair for your desk or a new lamp for your table, or simply putting some additional money in your mutual fund, you have options. The money you may spend on this item isn't idle.

To ensure that you've considered all these options, make a list of ten things that you could purchase if you don't buy the item you are considering. If it's worth foregoing all ten alternatives, you may be making a wise purchase.

What are the alternatives to this item?

Rarely are you faced with only one option when you make a buying decision. Whether you're considering a nontechnical purchase such as a new Rolodex or a high-tech laptop complete with built-in modem, sound system, and enough memory to download the New York Public Library, you always have more than one brand, more than one price point, more than one feature, and more than one alternative when making a decision. You should examine all of your options before you decide whether or not to spend your money.

What Works and What Wastes Your Time

In order for a gadget to fit into your organizational plan, it must pass several tests:

- **Is it more efficient than what you have now?** My pen and notepad are pretty darned efficient. In order for something to beat that test, it must be fast, easy, convenient, and portable — a tall order for any electronic device.

- **Does it reward you for completing tasks on time?** You can't draw a line through an item on an electronic pocket planner, unless you have one of those electronic notepads with a magic pen, which strikes me as a bit silly. Why not opt for a conventional pad and paper? Unless your electronic reminder sends out smiley-faced icons or plays *God Save the Queen* after you complete each task, you need to consider how your gadget rewards you.

- **Will you have more or less freedom by using it?** Remember, the sole purpose for getting organized is to accomplish more tasks in less time. Unless your electronic system frees you from the burdens that have you down now, it's not worth the expense.

Computers are a given

In the late 1970s, the only people who owned personal computers were hobbyists who programmed the new contraptions to run their electric train sets. Without a personal computer today, you are a decade or more behind the rest of the business world. You don't have to own the latest, greatest, most

Lost in technology

Before departing on a trip to a city I had never visited, I thought it would be a good idea to get directions from the airport to the hotel where I would be staying. I asked my assistant if she would get the directions for me. Several minutes later as I was passing through the outer office, I noticed a small crowd gathered around my assistant's desk starring at her computer screen.

"What's going on?" I asked.

"Oh, we're getting the directions to your hotel," my assistant said.

I assumed that task had already been completed, so I asked how she and the six gathered spectators were accomplishing this feat.

"The hotel's Web site has directions from each of their properties to various landmarks. We're trying to access the hotel where you're staying so we can print a map from the airport."

I nodded at this and returned to my office where I picked up the phone and dialed the toll free number for the hotel chain. After speaking to a helpful customer service representative, I was given detailed directions to my hotel, complete with some local information on what traffic should be like at the time of my arrival.

When I returned to the outer office, my assistant looked up and said, "We've found it! It will only be a second and we will have a map printed for you."

I didn't have the heart to tell her not to waste her time.

---

powerful giga-driven supercomputer, but you do need a reasonably up-to-date system with Internet capabilities and standard business software. To be without that technology is to put yourself behind the organizational eight ball, especially in business.

Cell phones are a must

As much as I may seem like an old fuddy-duddy with no use for modern conveniences, I certainly understand and appreciate when an innovation becomes a mainstream necessity. Cell phones have reached that status. Not only can they free you from worrying about missing a call, but they have become a safety staple.

Because of the low cost and convenience of cellular phones, a majority of middle-class working individuals own at least one. Not only has this changed the way we think about space, it has heightened our expectations. We expect to reach a plumber if we have an emergency, because we assume that the plumber has a pager and a cell phone on his tool belt. Ten years ago such an assumption would have been laughable. Now we expect this unlimited access.

Our collective patience runs thin when our calls are not returned promptly, even when we know someone is traveling or spending time out of the office, because we expect people to be reachable. A standard response to the line, "I'm sorry, he's out of the office right now," has become, "Well, could you have him paged," or "Please give me his cell phone number." In today's fast-paced world, unreachable is unacceptable.

Digital versus analog

For the time being, all cellular systems operate off of a series of land-based cellular antennas that capture radio waves from cellular phones and feed them into cable or telephone land lines. Satellite phones, which operate by bouncing signals off of satellites much like Global Positioning Systems, are also available, but for a few years at least, the costs of these systems may remain limiting, and the quality of the conversations is suspect. It takes a while to bounce a radio wave off a satellite, which means that you notice palpable delays in satellite phone conversations.

For the time being, the most advanced (and most practical system) is digital cellular phone service. While still relying on land-based antennas, digital reception is clearer and more powerful because of the increased frequency of the digital sound wave. Most analog systems operate in an 800 to 1,000 megahertz range, and digital waves can be as high as 2,500 megahertz.

Returning calls

Back in the 50s and 60s, Lyndon Johnson became one of the most powerful and influential politicians in American history, much to the surprise of those who knew him personally. Johnson was not a very polished man. He didn't speak well, nor was he attractive, charming, or overly inspiring. His earthy and sometimes crude behavior became legendary, and after he became president the White House staff was visibly uncomfortable with the unrefined mannerisms of their commander in chief.

Johnson did have one policy that served him well as a congressman, a senator, a vice president, and a president, however. He insisted that all phone calls be returned and all letters be answered the same day they arrived. No matter how many staff members it took, the sun never set on an unreturned phone call or an unanswered letter in Lyndon Johnson's office. This policy, as simple as it was, helped propel one of the rawest figures in American politics into one of history's most memorable figures.

Today that level of service is expected in both business and social life. An unreturned phone call today is never due to uncontrollable circumstances. It's a shun. You are intentionally ignoring someone if you do not return a phone call the day it was received, and if you don't believe it, just ask the person whose call didn't get returned. Cell phones and pagers have heightened the expectations that calls will be returned, not in days, but within hours or even minutes. Because of these new expectations, it is important that you establish personal policies on when you return calls and what message you send to those who are waiting for you to call back.

Digital systems are also safer. All sound waves can be intercepted, but a digital wave consists of nothing but numbers (ones and zeros), and an analog sound wave carries an actual conversation. Anyone intercepting your analog wave can hear your entire conversation (as Newt Gingrich can attest), but anyone who intercepts a digital signal can hear nothing but a computer squeal. Digital sound waves can also carry data in addition to voice. This capability allows you to check and send written messages (like e-mail) from your digital phone — a feature unavailable on an analog system.

Voice mail

This feature is always tricky. I hate leaving a voice mail message, because I never know when the person may retrieve the message. It beats the alternative, however, which is to have a phone go unanswered or get a message that "The cellular customer you have called has traveled outside the service area."

Pitfalls of technology

Reliability is still the biggest downfall of any of the electronic devises on the market today. Because cell phones rely on antennas and batteries, there are times and places when your phone may fail. In remote areas where no cells are available, your phone is useless, just as it is when the battery dies.

That is why a cell phone must always be viewed as a convenience. After it becomes a crutch, you are in trouble, because these systems can fail at the most inopportune times. Unless you expect that failure and have organized a contingency plan, you aren't really organized at all

If the biggest pitfall of cellular technology is reliability, the second biggest pitfall is accessibility. Before you turn your cellular phone on, you have to ask yourself one simple question: "Am I prepared for this thing to ring?" If the phone is turned on, you have to be ready for it to chirp, beep, or sing at any moment because you're at the mercy of anyone who has your cell phone number.

For the organized person that is no problem. The phone is off (or set for voice mail) most of the time. She only turns it on when she is making calls or expecting calls. She may keep it on when driving, simply because that's a down time in which she can accomplish one task (driving to her destination) while attending to another (speaking to a caller on the phone). Even that scenario is suspect, however, because cell phones have now surpassed alcohol as the leading cause of highway accidents.

The disorganized person is insecure with the cell phone, believing that it is his obligation to keep it on and be available to anyone at any time. You have certainly seen him: the man at the dinner table with the cell phone to his ear, chatting away while his dinner guests look at everything else in the restaurant but him; or the spectator at a tennis match or a golf tournament who stands as close to the action as possible so when the cell phone rings it causes maximum disruption. These people may mean well, but their insecurity with being "out of touch" or "unavailable" won't let them do the right thing and turn the darn phone off.

Using an assistant effectively

Even though most of my company's senior executives have assistants in their offices to field, re-route, and return phone calls (if for no other reason than to apologize and say that the executive won't be able to phone in today), there are still instances when a call from a client or important customer doesn't get returned on the day it was received. In most cases the executive who didn't return the call gets an earful. No matter how valid his excuses, the fact that he didn't return a client phone call is a slap in the face to the client, and our clients are not bashful about letting us know when they feel slighted.

That's why all our top-level assistants are trained to communicate the whereabouts of their bosses to anyone who is attempting to reach them. If, for example, I am in Hong Kong when a call comes in, the time difference alone is enough to prohibit me from returning the call. But my assistant handles situations like this by simply telling the caller the truth.

"I'm sorry, Mr. McCormack is out of the country and won't be calling in for the remainder of the day. Is there anything I can do for you, or can someone else in the office help?"

This sort of front-end openness eliminates a mountain of future problems, because the caller understands he isn't being slighted or ignored. I'm out of the country in another time zone and therefore unreachable. The caller's expectations are tempered by the savvy honesty of a well-trained assistant.

However, I understand and appreciate how voice mail can act as a practical alternative to an assistant. Many modern cellular phones also function as pagers. If the phone is set on the paging mode, the caller is transferred into voice mail and your phone beeps, chirps, sings, or vibrates to let you know you have received a message. If the caller has simply keyed in his phone number, that number will appear on your phone's display screen. If he has left a voice message, that message can be retrieved at your convenience. This function allows you to screen your calls, return calls at your convenience, and avoid taking a call that may disrupt other activities you are in the process of accomplishing. In short, it is a feature I highly recommend, even though I personally hate leaving voice mail messages.

You can soften my hatred (and, I suspect, the hatred of others) with your voice mail greeting. Cute, comic messages are not only passé, they are interminably annoying. An acquaintance of mine works with rock and roll musicians, and he sometimes gets a rock star to record his voice mail greeting. I assume that he does this to be cute or cool, but even if I know who Lenny Kravitz is, the fact that he recorded this man's outgoing message doesn't impress me in the least. If anything I find it distracting.

The best voice mail greetings are the ones recorded at the beginning of every day. "Hi, you've reached Mark McCormack. It's Tuesday and I will be traveling most of the day, so if you have an urgent need, please call my office at (phone number) and ask for my assistant. Otherwise, leave your name, number, and a brief message and someone will get back to you soon."

In this example, I temper expectations and offer alternatives. The caller still may be annoyed that he cannot reach me personally, but at least I present him with several options, and he won't spend the rest of the day wondering what I'm doing and fuming over why I haven't returned his call.

The most frustrating and unacceptable voice mail setups are the ones that don't allow you to transfer to a real person. If I am calling the president of a company, I am just as likely to reach an automated voice mail system as I am a receptionist. Unfortunately, after punching the appropriate numbers and queuing my way through to the president's office, there is a good chance that I will end up in his assistant's voice mail with no where to go but back to the automated menu. This is the seventh layer of voice mail purgatory. If your system allows this to happen, it needs to be changed. It is also frustrating to be forced into voice mail when making overseas calls. Time changes and travel schedules are such that you never know when someone may retrieve a voice mail message, so even if you leave a time to call back, you can never be sure whether the person you are trying to reach received the message. The best voice mail systems always give you an out. Especially if you are making an important business call during normal business hours, there should be a way for you to speak to a live human being.

Call forwarding

Another convenient feature that has become a double-edged sword is call forwarding, a standard accessory that forwards incoming calls to another number. If you're leaving home but expecting a call from your spouse, you can simply activate the call-forwarding feature on your home phone and send incoming calls to your mobile number.

The pitfall in this feature, once again, comes from people's expectations. Callers expect you to answer your phone these days, even if you are not home or out of your office. All you had to do was forward your calls to your cell phone, and a lot of people can't understand why you may not choose that option.

A built-in address book

Athough I still believe nothing beats a good old fashioned pen and pad for making lists, sticking to schedules, and remaining organized, the newest cellular phones offer many Palm Pilot-type features that can be extremely useful, especially if you are traveling. The most convenient is the Rolodex feature. No matter how detailed your notepad may be, it's impossible to carry hundreds of hand-written phone numbers with you. It would take too much time to transfer these numbers into your notepad, and even if you could, why would you want to? The odds of needing one phone number out of the hundreds you have in your Rolodex are so small that it makes the effort of carrying them around seem silly. You can program the numbers into a Palm Pilot or a cellular phone, however, and have them at your disposal no matter where you are.

Be careful, however. If you rarely initiate calls from your cell phone, or if you spend most of your day with your Rolodex by your side, this feature isn't for you. It may seem intoxicating, but there is no reason for you to spend the money or take the time to program hundreds of addresses and phone numbers into a phone or a Palm Pilot if you have that information sitting next to you on your desk. It's cool being on the cutting edge, but sometimes it's not worth the price or the effort.

An even more enticing feature offered in some models is Samsung's "Smart Speak" technology. This bit of digital magic allows you to ask your phone to dial a number. For example, rather than looking up one of the pre-programmed numbers in my Palm Pilot, with Smart Speak, I simply say, "Dial John Q. Public at his office in New York," and the phone dials the number automatically. In addition to being voice activated, this feature also has voice identification security. My phone can be programmed to recognize and respond to only my voice, and your phone would only respond to your voice. This feature is extremely convenient when calling someone from your car, where looking up a number can be hazardous to your health. Other than that, however, the technology is still much too expensive for the benefits it offers. If prices continue to fall (as they have done with all innovations in these areas), this feature would be well worth adding to your system.

When to turn it off

There is a time and a place for everything. Your cell phone should be in the off position at these times and places:

- ✔ **Any meeting.** Whether social or business, having the phone ring while engaging someone else is disruptive and rude. Turning it off saves embarrassment for everyone, especially you.

- ✔ **Any event that demands quiet.** A golf tournament, tennis match, concert, play, speech, or any other venue that demands quiet and decorum is no place for a cell phone.

- ✔ **Any time you are in the middle of something else.** Whether you're laboring over an important project or giving your kids their baths, the cell phone is an interruption from time you have set aside to get other things accomplished.

Mobile phones and pagers are wonderful things with endless features. They can be lifesavers if you are stranded on the side of the road and timesavers if you are running behind in your schedule. They can also be rude, obtrusive, and obnoxious. You are responsible for controlling these tools. If you don't, they will most certainly end up controlling you.

Everything else is up to you

Use your discretion (and hopefully your good judgment) to purchase what-ever future gadget you believe may help you in your quest to become more organized. If you have answered all the questions outlined in this chapter and you feel comfortable that a certain piece of equipment fits into your organizational plan, then by all means buy it.

But don't fall victim to the idea that owning it makes you better. You either have organization in your bloodstream or you don't. No miracle of science or technology can change you.

Understanding Techno-Speak

Information technology is growing and changing so rapidly that if someone were to attempt to own the latest and greatest versions of every high-tech innovation that came along, no time would be left for work or play. He would spend all day downloading software and upgrading systems, never actually using any of the new stuff he found so necessary to buy in the first place.

Too many people are caught in some version of that trap. Because they don't completely understand the technological changes taking place (and who really does?), they believe that the best strategy is to simply "keep up" by buying the latest and greatest technological breakthroughs regardless of cost or benefit. Some of this compulsion is the old "keeping up with the Jones" syndrome. A neighbor — or in the case of business, a neighboring or competing company — may purchase a new piece of technology, and all at once the same piece of equipment becomes a much higher priority for you or your company. Falling behind would be unacceptable. Even though you have no idea how to use whatever it is you are about to spend a fortune purchasing, you believe the purchase is worth it to remain on the cutting edge.

Keeping up with the times

I don't know a single CEO who hasn't spent too much money attempting to stay on the cutting edge of technology. In most cases, the CEO doesn't understand today's cyber-rich environment, so he trusts others inside his company to steer him in the right direction. Unfortunately, the underlings aren't spending their own money, and they recognize that the boss is clueless when it comes to computers, so they behave like kids in a candy shop, spending company funds on the grandest information-gathering gadgets money can buy.

A good part of that impulsiveness stems from a generation gap. Most CEOs are over 50 years old, which means that they were probably in their 30s before they ever logged onto a computer. Most Internet users and almost all information managers are under the age of 40. That ten-year gap isn't as relevant in other areas, but when trying to understand technology, a decade is a chasm few can bridge.

Consider that college graduates entering the workforce today were born after the Shah fled into exile and Iranian militants took hostages in the U.S. embassy. Today's new graduates have never owned a turntable or a vinyl record, and they have no idea where they were at the time Ronald Reagan was shot. To them, the Dodgers have always been in Los Angeles, and there was never a day that football wasn't played indoors. Today's incoming workforce has never lived a day without the personal computer. They are younger than the original Apple II, and most have never known anything but a Windows- or Mac-based operating system. Keying DOS commands onto a monochrome screen is as foreign to them as the quill and inkwell are to older generations.

They are, however, the skilled players in today's techno-driven world. Their knowledge and expertise has made them an invaluable part of the business environment. In the business world, they are the information managers — the young people wearing jeans who command more respect than do some senior-level executives. Unfortunately, the culture of fast-paced, high-tech innovation is moving so quickly that this new breed of expert has little time for the "old guys" who don't know how to configure a networking wizard through the serial port. Therein lies the problem. Most CEOs are the "old guys."

Getting the experts working for you, not against you

In the Academy Award winning movie *Philadelphia,* Denzel Washington plays an attorney representing a man who was wrongfully dismissed from his job because he has AIDS. Several times during the courtroom drama, Washington's character asks the defendants to explain their position. At interrogatories and at trial, when the answers didn't meet his standards of acceptability, he would say, "I don't understand. Please explain it to me like I'm 5 years old."

If you truly want to get the experts working for you and not against you, make that line your mantra. Repeat after me: "I don't understand. Please explain it to me like I'm 5 years old."

You may be shocked to find out how much respect you earn when you admit that you don't understand all the nuances of technology. You may also be amazed at the number of experts who rally to your side because you have asked for their assistance. The one thing I found out about information managers is that they love to share their knowledge. If you ask them how a particular number was derived, they may launch into an explanation that vastly exceeds the question you asked. They can't help it. It's in their nature.

You have to be willing to listen, however, and you have to be prepared to ask seemingly silly follow-up questions. If a term is thrown out that you don't understand, stop the conversation immediately and ask for clarification — just like a 5-year-old kid. If you still don't understand the answer, put your teacher on the hot seat. As the boss or the customer, you are entitled to an explanation you can understand and use. If the person you are asking can't provide that explanation in simple language, find someone else who can.

Reading high-tech people

It isn't imperative that you understand everything there is to know about software, hardware, networks, and everything in-between, but you do need to know how to read the experts in those fields. Some information and data managers are trustworthy, always shoot information to you straight, and go out of their way to keep you properly (but not overly) informed — then there are the others. You know who they are — the fast-talking, impatient gurus who are always too busy to stop and explain exactly what they are doing, or the doomsday prognosticators who are forever predicting the end of the world if you don't spend all your hard-earned dollars on a new package of goodies. A data manager who lies to you because he knows he can is the worst one of all.

You may never be able to learn the intricacies of your expensive and cutting-edge technical operations, but you can do a few things to ensure that your supports staff is trustworthy and looking out for your best interests.

Where two or three are gathered, there's bound to be a dispute

One of the best ways to find out how your data managers and M.I.S. team operate is to put several members of the support team in a room and ask them to solve a problem in your presence. You may not understand any part of the discussion, but you will figure out a great deal by watching your people interact with each other in a pressure situation. Individually, they may each be able to pull the wool over your eyes, but after their peers confront them, the ones who know their stuff always shine through.

You are also bound to find out more by listening to your experts debate a problem than you ever would if you had asked each expert individually. Their impassioned arguments say a lot about whose side they are really on.

Fool me once, shame on you; fool me twice . . .

There is no excuse for trusting someone who has betrayed you in the past. That is not to say that you should never forgive a mistake. We're all human, even those of us who spend our days staring at computer screens and churning out data, and we all make mistakes. Whether or not I may trust you after a mistake depends in large part on the circumstance and on your willingness to acknowledge the mistake and your attempt to make amends. If you have been honest and the mistake was simply an unfortunate lapse, certainly you deserve a second chance. But rarely do I give you a third chance, nor may many other CEOs I know. In baseball you get three strikes, but in business, you usually get two untrustworthy errors and you're out.

Beware the sesquipedalian

The *sesquipedalian* is a person who uses big words in an attempt to feign superior intellect. These people are particularly prevalent in high-tech areas where the language barrier between the insider and the outsider is enormous. It's easy for a slick shyster to convince you that he is doing all sorts of wonderful things. He must be. He knows so many big words and uses them so freely, he must know what he's doing and he must be good at it. Don't fall into that trap. If you can't get a straight and understandable answer from a high-tech support person, watch out. You're probably being led astray.

If everybody agrees, you're in trouble

I've never been in a meeting of high-tech managers where everyone was in total agreement. Data managers have trouble agreeing on what day it is, so if they all agree on a particular technical question, I begin to worry. It usually means that someone got lazy and didn't ask the right questions, or the managers have been in collusion and are trying to put forth a unified front. Neither of those situations is healthy, and I always send up red flags if too many people agree.

Two or more experts almost always disagree

After the first concerns were raised about the so-called Y2K problem that computers were supposed to experience at midnight on December 31, 1999, I asked our executives and M.I.S. team to draft opinions on what this problem may mean for our company and what we needed to do to prepare ourselves. The responses I got ranged from, "Don't worry, nothing's going to happen," to "Board up your house, store canned goods, load the shotguns, and buy gold."

Obviously, I believed the truth lay somewhere between those two extremes, and our managers set out on the task of preparing our systems for any problems that may arise. I found the stark differences in opinion to be very telling, however. Here were intelligent and reasonable people who were experts in the same field being asked a specific question pertaining to their field of expertise, and the answers couldn't have been more diverse.

This example helped prove something I have believed for a long time: Even if experts don't have the answers, they never hesitate to give you one anyway.

Chapter 9

Making E-Mail and the Internet Your Friends

- -

In This Chapter

▶ Utilizing the Internet to get and stay organized

▶ Avoiding the pitfalls and potholes on the Information Superhighway

▶ Discovering the advantages and disadvantages of electronic mail

▶ Managing your e-mail

▶ Attaching and downloading files in e-mail

▶ Spotting junk mail

- -

*T*he Internet opens a world of possibilities. Companies selling everything from books to teapots have sprung to life because of the Internet, and a whole new term — *e-commerce* (goods and services bought and sold over the Internet) — has entered the common lexicon. Unfortunately, the Internet is so big, growing and changing so rapidly, and filled with so much stuff (both good and bad) that it is difficult to comprehend and keep up with where it is headed.

By far the most common use in network computing (whether on the Internet or through an internal network within a company or institution) is electronic mail or e-mail. It is, as the name implies, correspondence delivered electronically between computers. E-mail has become much more than simple notes, however. Today it is a mechanism by which people in different departments or companies — who may live in different parts of the world — can collaborate on projects, deliver messages, and stay apprised of current events.

The Internet: An Invaluable Tool or a Time Trap?

The Internet is the fastest-growing communications medium in history. Every month, a group of people equal to the population of Great Britain logs onto the Internet for the first time. Because the Internet is a massive, complex, and ever-evolving organism, it is impossible to grasp all the intricacies in this mother of all networks, and every day, some noted sociologist, economist, or think-tank expert comes out with a new theory on how the Internet may change society as we know it.

In some cases these think-tank experts are right. Sitting in my study at 4:30 in the morning, I can shop for my wife's birthday present, check airline rates and flight availability, scan the morning headlines, get a running update on the Asian stock markets, watch a replay of the winning point from the week-end's championship tennis match, and download the scores and highlights from the Australasian PGA Tour for future viewing — before I ever have my second cup of coffee.

Unless you have countless hours on your hands, however, don't try to stay abreast of all the changes. Like e-mail, the Internet can be an invaluable tool for the person looking to improve his organizational skills, but it can also be a time trap filled with wasteful temptations and enticing distractions. With the right attitude, the right approach, and a healthy dose of self-discipline, you can save many hours and lots of money by availing yourself of the wonderful services offered on the Internet. You can also spend hours surfing through lots of pretty sites that seem interesting at the time, but lead you no closer to your organizational goals.

As people conduct more commerce and communication, everyone may eventually need to gain some level of Internet efficiency. You can get ahead of the trend by incorporating the Internet into your organizational plan.

What's the Internet?

The *Internet* (or *Net* as it's sometimes called) has become such a common part of our daily discussions that many people are embarrassed to ask what the Internet is, or how it got its start. In fact, many long-time Internet users don't understand what they are using, or where it originated. They just know to point and click to get to the good stuff.

The Internet is simply a vast network of computers linked together by other computers called *servers*. The best analogy is to compare the Internet to the evolution of the telephone. Originally, every telephone call had to go through an operator. Callers cranked handles on bulky wooden boxes mounted to their walls and friendly operators came on the line and manually connected the callers with the people they were trying to reach. As technology progressed and the number of calls exceeded the number of operators who could handle them, a network was established so each caller could dial a series of numbers and reach his party directly. Later, conference calling came along, and suddenly callers could link up with multiple parties at the same time.

The Internet grew the same way, only faster. As personal computers became popular in academia, many scholars wanted to share information with their colleagues in other institutions. That desire for free information led to the development of a computer network between researchers. Some bright professor named it the Internet, and soon the Net evolved and grew well beyond the campuses and research libraries. Today, the Internet remains a vehicle for information, but it is also an advertising and entertainment medium, a communications tool, and a vehicle for commerce.

The Internet is its own virtual ecosystem. Things grow and flourish, things die, and the entire system expands and evolves through a series of constant changes. The subject you researched yesterday, which produced 1,000 documents, may yield 10,000 documents today and 50,000 documents tomorrow as more information is posted on the Net and more computers join in the process. That sort of growth and change is chaotic, but it also ensures up-to-the-second data on anything in the world.

What's in the World Wide Web?

Many people confuse the Internet, which is a network, with the *World Wide Web,* which is interconnecting data on the Net. The best way to clarify the difference between the Internet and World Wide Web is to use the well-worn analogy of a highway (an *Information Superhighway* for those of you who've been living in a cave and haven't heard that term yet). The Internet is, quite simply, the roadway. It is a series of intersecting highways so vast and complex that traveling on them without guidance would be suicide. The World Wide Web is the traffic on those roads. Each Web site (which is usually predicated by the acronym www) is a vehicle on the Internet highway.

The great thing about this highway, however, is that you can jump (or surf) from car to car. By accessing a World Wide Web site dealing with the Autobahn, the famous highway that runs through Germany, you may run across a reference to Porsche, the German automaker. Although the reference may be passing, the word Porsche could be highlighted or appear on your screen in blue. By clicking on that word, you can jump (or surf) from the article on the Autobahn to the Porsche Web site where you can take a tour of the latest sports cars on the market. From there you may surf your way over to the Maserati Web site in order to compare vehicles. While you're looking through the design features of the latest Italian sports cars, however, you may notice a reference to Venice, Italy. One more click and you're browsing through the Web site of the Venice Tourist Board.

While explaining the features of the World Wide Web, that example also perfectly illustrates how the Internet can degenerate from a useful tool into an addictive time bandit. One interesting subject leads to another fascinating topic, which lures you to yet a third intriguing area, all within your reach by simply clicking a button on your computer.

Commerce

One of the fastest growing Internet companies — and one of the biggest success stories in business history — is the online bookstore, Amazon.com. Without actually opening a physical store, Amazon.com rose to prominence as a convenient alternative to traditional bookstores. Simply by clicking onto the Web site, customers can review books, read excerpts, see what other purchasers have had to say about various titles, and examine a list of other books relating to the same topic as the one being reviewed. With the click of a few keys (and a credit card number), you can order and have books shipped to your home or office within 24 hours.

Amazon.com is a pioneer in the book industry, but the company is only one of millions of virtual stores conducting business online. In fact, the successes of companies like Amazon.com have caused traditional retailers to rethink how they conduct business. Most major chain stores now offer online alternatives to complement their traditional walk-in stores.

The reason e-commerce has grown so rapidly and successfully is because, like the Sears catalog in the early 1900s, the Net brings the store to the customer in a convenient and extraordinarily fast and efficient way. If I am looking to buy a lamp for my study, I can go to the mall, visit a half-dozen stores, and hope to find something among the dozens of models available, or I can shop online and look at hundreds of lamps without ever getting up from my chair. I have increased my options while saving time! It's the best of all worlds.

Of course, I can't actually pick up the lamps to feel how much they weigh, and I am able to gain only a two-dimensional perspective of what the lamp may look like in my study. For some people that isn't shopping at all. For these people, the experience of getting in the car, traveling to the store, touching the merchandise, and chatting with the sales associate is just as important as the purchase itself. I'm not one of those people, and there are millions like me who forego the bright lights and mindless banter of the shopping malls for the convenience and speed of the Internet.

If you are serious about becoming more organized and saving time, purchase a few items online. After you start shopping online, you may find the experience just as rewarding as making that trek to the mall. And you're sure to finish in half the time.

A lot of people don't use the Internet for commerce because of rumors they have heard about the safety and reliability of doing business online. Some of these concerns are valid, but most are unfounded. I want to take a moment to dispel some of the most common myths:

> ✔ **Ordering something over the Internet doesn't automatically put you on someone's mailing list.** You may get plenty of unsolicited e-mail and advertisements galore from your online service provider, but none of those come as a result of a purchase you made over the Internet unless you specify otherwise.

- ✔ **No one can track your name and address over the Internet until you give it to them.** Just because you are browsing through an online store doesn't mean that "Big Brother" is watching you. Until you make a purchase and type in your name, address, credit card number, and telephone number, no one knows who you are or where you live. The Internet isn't like the telephone — you can't be traced.

- ✔ **Reports of credit card hacking are grossly exaggerated (by egocentric hackers).** Credit card theft exists, even on the Internet, but not through the means most people assume. Despite all the Hollywood plot lines to the contrary, hackers have yet to steal one credit card number by breaking into the Internet and intercepting a transaction. The only real online theft has been the good old-fashioned scam, where customers unknowingly give their card numbers to crooks. It isn't as glamorous as swiping a card number out of thin air, but the con artist is the still the most common thief, even in the virtual world.

- ✔ **You take no greater risk online than you do at a conventional store.** In almost all instances, assuming that you're dealing with a reputable merchant, you can return merchandise if you're unsatisfied and you can cancel an order if you change your mind before your purchase has been shipped.

WARNING!

Even with all its advantages, shopping online isn't utopia. There are some legitimate drawbacks.

- ✔ **Too many stores.** Virtual stores are springing up online by the thousands every month, and, unless you're a savvy enough researcher to know who is legitimate and who isn't, the potential for dealing with a scam artist is relatively high. Usually the quality of a Web site can tell you a lot about a company (those multi-page, fully interactive sites are not cheap). Never do business with a company whose reputation is suspect. If you have a question, don't give out your credit card information until you get an answer.

- ✔ **You can't touch the merchandise.** I have a friend who says that he will never order books from Amazon.com or Barnes&Noble.com or any of the other online bookstores, because, in his words, "You have to smell a new book before you buy it." He, like many others, believes that in order to know what you're getting, you have to see, feel, and smell the product ahead of time. Shopping online isn't for him.

- ✔ **You don't get what you buy instantly.** As tough as it is for many people to admit, a fair number of purchases are based on impulse (see Chapter 27 for more information on how to avoid impulse buying). You see a tie that catches your eyes, or a shirt that you like, and the next thing you know you have bought it. With the Internet you have to wait, even if it's just one day, for your purchase to be shipped. If you are leaving tomorrow morning on a business trip and you need two new ties before you pack, Internet shopping won't work. Nor is it very helpful if your vacuum cleaner breaks the day guests are to arrive. In that instance, you had better get in your car and make the drive to your local home appliance store. For the most part, Internet shopping forces you to plan ahead, if only for a couple of days, in order to allow for shipping.

Travel

Whether you go by road, rail, or air, the Internet is an invaluable resource for making effective and efficient travel arrangements. Not only can you shop for the best airfares online, but you can purchase train tickets, rent cars, confirm hotel arrangements, get directions, and plan your extracurricular activities.

Most airlines now offer *e-ticketing*. You can purchase a ticket online and — rather than pick up a physical ticket at the ticket counter — all you have to do is show up at the gate with your driver's license and confirmation number. Eliminating paper tickets saves the airline money, and it saves you time and energy. Another win for the Internet.

Research

The day the Cox Congressional Committee Report on Espionage at U.S. Nuclear Facilities by The People's Republic of China was first declassified, the complete report could be downloaded from the Internet within minutes of committee chairman Christopher Cox's press conference. Supreme Court rulings, complete with affirming and dissenting opinions, are available online the days they are announced, and you can access up-to-the-second stock quotes from the NASDAQ, NYSE, Asian, and OTC markets at any time, or access news from any one of hundreds of news sources.

I write and publish an annual golf book entitled *The World of Professional Golf.* These encyclopedic volumes chronicle the various professional golf tours and provide year-end snapshots of how the game has been played at the professional level. When I first began writing the annual in 1968, there were no other outlets for the information I was providing. If you wanted to know who won the German Open and who finished second on the Japanese Tour money list, you could either call the tour offices in Germany and Japan or read my book. Today, however, that information is a click away. Not only can you receive up-to-date information on all golf tours around the world from various Web sites, you can even download video of key shots or hear audio of the winners' press conferences. My golf annual is still an important tool, however, because much of the information on these Web sites is dumped after a few months. My books are reference tools forever.

One of the downfalls of research on the Net is the volume and reliability of information. Remember that anyone can post anything, so all information should be viewed with a skeptical eye. Network search engines, such as Yahoo and Alta Vista, can help you in your searches, but before you engage in any Internet search, you need to have an idea about where you are headed and you should be very specific about what you want to find.

A superstar travel agent

Even though she has a number of travel agents at her disposal, tennis star Monica Seles makes many of her own travel arrangements over the Internet. Recently Monica told me that she had purchased a ticket online for an entire year of travel. Because she knew which tournaments in which cities she would be playing, Monica prepurchased round-trip air travel between Sarasota, Florida, and Paris, Palm Springs, Miami, Hilton Head, Rome, New York, Chicago, Australia, and many other locations. The entire package cost her approximately $21,000 for the year. Had she purchased each of those tickets individually, even through her travel agent, the cost would have been $35,000.

I immediately asked Monica if she would like to run the IMG travel department after she retired from professional tennis — an offer she politely declined.

Entertainment

Certain video games have an addictive quality that I find unhealthy, but a good game of chess with a friend who lives in Bangkok can be quite enjoyable. The Internet makes games like that possible. It also allows you to store certain video files — news features, sports highlights, or even short movies — for viewing at your convenience. It sure beats a trip to the video store.

What should you sidestep?

Just as there are plenty of time-saving, money-saving, organizational-helping features on the Internet, there are also millions of ways to waste away the hours online. Here are just a few of those time-thieves:

- **Chat rooms:** For the most part, they are as useless as the name suggests. You may occasionally stumble upon a small chat session that interests you, but the vast majority are so inane that they aren't worth browsing. If you're serious about saving time and becoming more organized, stay away from these things.

- **Bulletin boards:** These offer all the disadvantages of a chat room, only slower.

- **Casinos:** These are dangerous sites. Ostensibly located offshore to get around U.S. laws regarding such activity, these casinos take your credit card number, sell you a certain number of credits, and promptly take those credits away at the online craps table, roulette wheel, or blackjack table. The biggest problem with these sites is the lack of regulation. Players have to trust that the games are not rigged or risk losing everything in a scam. It's a risk that all too many are willing to take.

✔ **Get-rich-quick sites:** These are the same slick hustlers who've been around for centuries. The only thing new is the packaging.

✔ **90 percent of the games:** Some of the games are good, offering a chance to interact with friends or acquaintances in distant locations, but most are a waste of time. If you're predisposed to losing track of time while on the Internet, you would be well served by staying away from all games.

The Internet is a great tool for your business and your personal life. It brings the world to you on your time schedule. Use it wisely and you may be better organized as a result.

What Is E-Mail and How Can You Use It Effectively?

Sending and receiving electronic mail isn't much different than the service that the post office provides. In order to receive mail, you have to have an address (a P.O. box or a street address); in order to receive e-mail, you have to have an e-mail address. If you're Internet active (see "The Internet: An Invaluable Tool or a Time Trap?" section, earlier in this chapter), your access software most likely provides an easy-to-use e-mail package. AOL, MindSpring, and others provide step-by-step instructions for accessing and using e-mail effectively. Of course, you can find plenty of other e-mail programs such as Eudora, Outlook Express, and Netscape Messenger, each with its own advantages and nuances, but for standard e-mail service, the program that your Internet provider offers should be fine.

After you sign up for e-mail as a first time user, the Internet service provider (ISP) asks you to choose a *user name,* usually something like your name or initials. Unfortunately, as more and more people become Internet active, user names are becoming harder to choose. All the John Smiths of the world can't have the same e-mail name, so some companies are assigning numeric user IDs like 353589,2601@Mindspring.com. Hopefully, you can still choose an acceptably simple user name of your own because the thought of memorizing such a stream of numbers would turn almost anyone away from e-mail.

The @(name) portion of the address is called the *domain.* It is like the street address, city, and zip code of e-mail. If you're an America Online (AOL) customer, your e-mail address is probably (your user name)@aol.com. The .com is called the *zone* portion of the domain, and it tells you that AOL is a commercial enterprise.

Zone abbreviations include

✔ .com — Commercial enterprise

✔ .org — Nonprofit organizations such as the International Olympic Committee

✔ .mil — United States Military

✔ .gov — U.S. Government

✔ .edu — Educational institutions

✔ .net — Networks

✔ .firm — Service business

✔ .store — A store (both real and virtual)

✔ .web — Organization relating to the World Wide Web

✔ .arts — Cultural and entertainment sites

✔ .rec — A recreational organization

✔ .info — An information service provider

✔ .nom — An individual

My corporation's domain is IMGWorld.com, and all the people in our company have e-mail addresses that read (User Name)@IMGWorld.com. Employees at The New York Times have addresses that read (User Name)@NYTimes.com, and the e-mail address of the president of the United States is President@whitehouse.gov. Your e-mail address includes your user name followed by the @ sign, followed by your domain.

The person to whom you're sending e-mail has a similar address, and in order to send a message you must type an address into the "To" section of the e-mail. If you don't spell the user name correctly or if you inadvertently add a space or other character to the domain, your e-mail returns to you as undeliverable — just like the U.S. mail, only quicker.

Using e-mail is much simpler than it may initially sound. After you get the hang of it, e-mail addresses are easier to master than zip codes, street numbers, and the two letter abbreviations for Maine, Minnesota, Missouri, Mississippi, and Michigan.

Composing e-mail

After establishing an e-mail address, you're ready to write and send your first e-mail. But e-mails aren't formal letters. In fact, they are somewhere between conversations and memos. Most e-mail programs have features that allow you and a friend or associate to send messages back and forth instantly if you're both online at the same time — sort of like carrying on a written conversation complete with all the clunkiness that oxymoron infers.

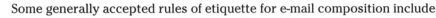

Some e-mail is written informally (often haphazardly) because it isn't considered formal documentation. Although attached text that's e-mailed may be laboriously written, the messages that go with the attachments are often informal, and often grammatically and stylistically incorrect. Messages like "Part three attached. Send comments ASAP. Thanks," can be transmitted as e-mails, even though the attachments themselves were much more formal. These are the same kinds of information I may handwrite on a sticky-back note, but that level of informality is acceptable for most e-mails.

It's not War and Peace, so make it snappy

The reason abbreviated and informal use of language is so acceptable in the e-mail medium is because e-mail is considered a fast and convenient tool with the emphasis on *fast*. Long prose has its place, but e-mail isn't it. You want to get your message across clearly but quickly. The person receiving your e-mail has better things to do than spend all day reading your electronic letters.

Some generally accepted rules of etiquette for e-mail composition include

- ✔ **Sentence fragments are okay as long as the point is made.**

- ✔ **Spelling errors are not okay.** They show disrespect for language that even e-mail users find offensive.

- ✔ **E-mail tone should be conversational, but unless you are adept at the nuances of humor writing, don't try it in an e-mail.** Sarcasm and sardonic wit aren't communicated as easily in writing, and you risk looking foolish or rude if you try it.

- ✔ **Don't use all capital letters.** It reads as though you are shouting.

- ✔ **Rants and long diatribes are unacceptable.**

- ✔ **If you attach a file as part of an e-mail, let the recipient know what the file is before he or she downloads it.**

- ✔ **Use the "regarding" or "re:" line in an e-mail address.** If you don't have a subject to discuss or an issue to write about, don't clutter the Net with another e-mail.

One big difference between e-mail and regular mail is security. In the United States. it is a federal offense to open, withhold, read, or otherwise tamper with mail. If a letter is addressed to you, it may not be opened and read by anyone else — under penalty of law. That is not the case with e-mail. In fact, employers (much to the chagrin of their employees) routinely download and read their staff's e-mails.

Legislation may change that practice in a few years, but until that time you shouldn't write e-mail with an unrealistic expectation of privacy. Unless you would post whatever you have written on a bulletin board, you may want to reconsider sending it as an e-mail.

Attachments

Virtually any file that can be downloaded into a computer can be attached and sent as part of an e-mail, a feature that's particularly helpful in conducting business with people in different cities. If, for example, our accounting office in Cleveland has assembled a spreadsheet containing income and expense projections for the tennis events we plan to manage in the upcoming year, that data can be downloaded and sent to me in an e-mail. No matter where I am in the world, I can retrieve the spreadsheet, download the file into my hard drive, and make corrections or comments electronically.

This technology has been a lifesaver in dealing with staff in our overseas offices. Because of the time differences between our U.S. operations and our offices in Hong Kong and Tokyo, it's been difficult for various staffs in those respective offices to collaborate on projects that require input from several sources. E-mail — in particular the attachment feature — allows different executives in different parts of the world to work together without traveling around the globe and wasting time.

Attaching a file is easy. Click on the Attach icon on your e-mail toolbar and, after the file menu pops up, double-click on the filename you want to attach. It can even be a video or audio file or something you find on the Internet.

E-mailing *Getting Results For Dummies*

This book is a great example of how e-mail can help you become more productive: One IDG Books Worldwide office is in Chicago, but the project editor for this book lives and works in Indianapolis. I split my time between New York, Orlando, Cleveland, and London with a fair amount of travel in between. Getting everyone together to collaborate on this project would have been impossible. If we had waited on the U.S. Postal Service or other shippers to deliver manuscripts back and forth between parties, this book may never have been finished.

E-mail solved those problems. As I completed various parts of this book, I didn't have to worry about printing the pages, making copies, boxing up manuscripts, and entrusting shippers to deliver everything in a timely fashion. I simply downloaded the files and attached them to e-mails. Within seconds, editors in Chicago as well as the project editor in Indianapolis had my work in their mailboxes. When they had ideas and suggestions for additions or corrections to the book, they simply added their comments to the manuscript and e-mailed them back to me. A process that may have taken days — if not weeks — under the conventional system of communication took minutes by using electronic mail.

But be careful. The larger the file, the longer it takes to download. If you're sending a large file in the middle of a busy day, it can tie up your computer for a substantial period of time. The same problem exists if you are receiving an e-mail attachment from someone else. Always check the size of a file before downloading it into your hard drive. The last thing you need is tie your computer up downloading a file while you're attempting to complete another project.

Also make sure that you have the necessary software to run the file that you're receiving. If someone sends you an audio or video e-mail attachment and you don't have audio or video software capabilities, or if you are working on an older, slower computer, the file could be worthless to you.

The files you can attach to e-mails include

- ✔ Photos in image files
- ✔ Videos in video files
- ✔ Audio tracks in audio files
- ✔ Other computer programs in executable files
- ✔ Text or spreadsheet data in text or word-processing files

Never, ever download an attached file from anyone you don't know. E-mails, in and of themselves, are text files and therefore incapable of carrying deadly computer viruses, but attachments come in all kinds of formats — many of which could contain viruses that may cause serious damage to your system. Unless you're comfortable with the integrity of the file you are downloading, don't open or download the file until you can check it out. Antivirus software can check for viruses before they attack your system.

Becoming e-mail savvy

You can easily spot an e-mail neophyte. He's the person who sends out e-mail copies of every article he reads and every advertisement he finds online, whether or not the information is germane to anything. This person is playing with e-mail. It's easy, and, if you're new to the e-mail game, it's fun. Simply click on the article you have found, save it, and attach it to an e-mail for all your friends and acquaintances.

However, this practice is an annoyance in the first degree. Every day my e-mail is loaded with articles, advertisements, news briefs, and bits and pieces of gossip picked up from chat rooms and bulletin boards all over the Web. Almost none of it is useful or insightful, and, in almost every case, the sender is someone who has only recently become Internet active and is spreading his e-mail wings.

Surprise success

A fair number of underground networks have been established by using the Internet, particularly as a result of e-mail. Many of these networks have expanded and redefined the way conventional mediums think about their products.

The television show *South Park*, a poorly-drawn animated series featuring foul-mouthed third graders living in a bizarre Colorado town, first appeared on the Internet after the show's creators produced a 10-minute short feature as a Christmas gift for some friends. One person liked the short so much he e-mailed it to a friend, and that person passed it along to several of his friends, until suddenly the kids of *South Park* were an e-mail cult phenomenon.

Executives at the Comedy Central network soon received e-mail copies of the short feature and they promptly signed the creators of *South Park* to a multiyear contract — all because of a creative Christmas gift that was passed around via e-mail.

Don't fall into the same trap. Whenever you find something on the Web that you think may interest someone else, ask yourself some simple questions:

- ✔ Is this information important enough that the person receiving it should stop whatever he is doing and read it immediately?

- ✔ Am I doing this because the information is useful, or because sending it is easy?

- ✔ If this same information were printed in a magazine, would I take the time to clip it out, make a copy, write and attach a handwritten note, fold it, put it in an envelope, address it, stamp it, and send it through the mail? If not, maybe you shouldn't clutter the e-mail wires with it, either.

Avoiding e-mail pitfalls

For all its attributes, e-mail can be an enormous distraction, especially if you don't establish some strict guidelines for when, how, and what you plan to send and receive via your e-mail.

Just like regular mail, you can do four things with an e-mail message:

- ✔ File it.
- ✔ Forward it.
- ✔ Read and act on it.
- ✔ Trash it.

The biggest difference between e-mail and regular mail, however, is that you don't have to choose one option over another. You can do all of these options to each piece of e-mail you receive. If, for example, you get an e-mail note from a friend, you can read and answer it, forward it to another friend who may be equally interested in the note, file it in another area, and then trash it from your e-mail.

This is the disorganized person's worst nightmare. I have seen computers so overloaded with stored e-mail files that it would take hours to read, act, or delete the volumes of information some people store for future reference.

If you're a virtual pack rat, here are some steps you can take to become more organized:

- **Establish time limits on reading and acting on e-mails.** If you don't read and act on a particular e-mail within a certain number of days, trash it and forget it. That may seem harsh, but if you have been able to ignore an e-mail message for several days it obviously isn't earth shatteringly important, so trash it.

- **You don't have to answer everyone.** You don't even have to answer a majority of your e-mails. Unless a particular e-mail requires a response from you, it is better to say nothing.

- **Touch e-mail as few times as possible.** Just as you do with your regular mail, pick a time to read your e-mail when you have some time to act on what you receive, whether it is to forward the message to someone else, respond to it, or trash it. The fewer times you deal with the same piece of e-mail, the more efficient and fun the process becomes.

Spotting junk

Junk mail isn't always easy to spot when it comes to your home, but *spam,* the e-mail version of junk mail, is almost impossible to catch until it invades your hard drive with pornographic or fraudulent advertising. The reason spam is so prevalent is because it's cheap and unregulated. Paper junk mail has some cost (however marginal), and the government monitors material that passes through the mail system. A fraudulent scam artist soliciting funds through the postal service is in violation of U.S. federal law and is subject to prosecution for mail fraud. No such restrictions exist on the Internet, so crooks and sleaze merchants are free to peddle their wares to everyone who has an e-mail address.

The best thing to do with spam (which got its name from a 20-year-old *Monty Python* skit) is to ignore it. If you respond to it, even by clicking on an icon that says "No thanks" or "Remove," you're acknowledging to the sender that you exist and have actually read a portion of what has been sent. This response only fuels more spam. As furious and frustrated as you may become by some of the junk you receive in your e-mail, your best course of action is to trash it and move on.

Avoiding gossip

Because e-mail is quick, cheap, and immediate, the quality of discourse often degenerates to a level where calling it sophomoric would be an insult to sophomores. Unless you have an endless amount of time to kill and nothing else to do with your day but chat with people you don't know and may never meet, then entering any of the thousands of discussion mailing lists is a waste of your time and energy.

E-mail mailing lists are little more than glorified revolving bulletin boards. By signing up for a mailing list, you place yourself at the mercy of every other bored computer owner who has signed onto the same list. The list has its own e-mail address, and after you send a message to that address, it's instantly posted. The result is a running conversation between a large group of people — in other words, noise.

You also have to be suspect of any information that comes to you through mass e-mailing, chat sessions, or e-mail lists. Remember that e-mail is cheap and unregulated. Anyone can say anything about anyone with virtual impunity. Because of that, the quality and reliability of the information you receive via e-mail can range from okay to worthless. I recommend that you err on the side of worthless.

Moving on: Don't turn into a pumpkin

E-mail is a wonderful tool that can lead to many time-saving opportunities, but in order for it to be effective, you have to know when to turn the computer off and move on to other things. It is tempting to stay online indefinitely, and there are always plenty of other people online who would welcome your company. But just like Cinderella lost track of time when things seemed to be going well, you can also get so engrossed in your e-mail that you may never get out and accomplish anything else.

If you look at e-mail as a time-saving tool and if you limit the amount of time you allow yourself to be online, you may find that the benefits of this amenity far outweigh the blemishes. Ultimately, however, whether e-mail is your friend or your foe depends entirely on your discipline and on your ability to cut the cord and turn the computer off.

Chapter 10

Creating Storage Solutions

● ●

In This Chapter

▶ What to store

▶ When to store

▶ Where to store

▶ How to store

● ●

A friend of mine keeps everything. To call him a pack rat would insult even the largest and most voracious rodent. His home and office are filled with boxes, files, stacks, and mountainous piles of papers, books, clothes, pictures, and knickknacks — all strewn about in such a way that even he admits that both places look like the targets of recent bombings.

After spending years watching my friend stash away every letter, photograph, and tattered sweater he has ever owned, I asked him why he insisted on keeping everything, even though he had long-since run out of storage space.

"I used to tell myself that I might need some of this stuff someday," he said. "Then, after I realized I would most likely never touch any of it again, I convinced myself that my children and grandchildren might want to have it to remind them of me after I'm gone. Of course, even I can't imagine what anybody would do with my old fishing shirts. Now, I just keep everything out of habit. I know storing everything doesn't make sense, but after all these years I can't bring myself to throw away any of my belongings."

As I studied the problem of storage and the propensity of people to hold onto things longer than they should, I came to realize that my candid friend is typical of most pack rats. He can't even convince himself that he needs the things he stores, but the habits of disorganization are so ingrained he can't break them. If you have a storage problem, chances are good that you suffer from some degree of the same affliction.

Accumulating Stuff

One of the funniest comedic skits of the past 20 years has to be George Carlin's all-too-real account of the accumulation of "stuff." According to Carlin, you have your own stuff, which gets lumped with someone else's stuff when you get married so that you now have "our" stuff and "her" stuff, but none of "your" stuff. When you get too much stuff, you buy a bigger house, which you immediately fill with more stuff. The comedian's delivery of this diatribe is hilarious, but what makes the piece so extraordinary is the fact that, like most good comedy, the message rings true. As absurd as the action seems, many people do, in fact, buy larger dwellings and rent massive storage units at great personal expense simply to store things they haven't touched in years.

The accumulation of stuff hasn't always been a problem. In fact, the phenomenon only took hold in the last 50 years (just look at the size of closets in homes built prior to 1940). Hoarding goods is, in some ways, tied to economic prosperity, but the biggest reason for the recent glut of stuff is a decreased sense of organization and simplification.

Discarding an item requires a permanent decision: If you throw something away, it's gone forever. Sometimes this permanency is too much for our mortal minds to handle. Even if we haven't touched an item in years (or have forgotten that it exists), the item might spark fond memories of an old friend or a good time. The emotional attachment at the moment we rediscover an item makes throwing it away almost impossible — as if getting rid of the item somehow means throwing away your past.

Emotional connections to inanimate objects are fine to a point, but when you refuse to pitch the mood ring you got from a disco date in 1972, because of all the memories you would be throwing away, you've taken the attachment a little too far.

Pitching Half Your Stored Items

If you are like most people, you could literally throw away half of the items you currently have stored in your home and office and never miss any of them. If you don't believe me, go through your office and home and arbitrarily stack all stored items into two piles. Then flip a coin. Heads means that you throw the right-hand stack away and tails indicates that you pitch the left-hand stack. Even though you might have some things in each stack that you will miss, chances are better than average that you would get along fine without the items you arbitrarily threw away.

Now, imagine how much happier you could be if you got to choose what you throw away. The good news is, you do.

Throwing away half the items you currently have tucked away in storage takes courage, self-discipline, and at least two (if not more) tries. Whether the area you want to tidy up includes a closet you haven't cleaned out in months, an attic, a basement, a file drawer, a desk, a cabinet, or a garage, you should make your goal to throw away half the items you have in storage within the next 30 days.

The rules of pitching

To determine whether an item should be kept in storage or pitched, whether at home or in your office, ask yourself a series of questions:

- **Have I touched this item in the last year?** A "yes" doesn't automatically mean that the item is worth keeping, but if you haven't touched it in a year, the item should probably go.

- **If I haven't touched it in a year, does it have sentimental value?** Be strong in your definition of sentimental. If the item is a family heirloom, why isn't it on display, or why haven't you touched it in a year? Is it only sentimental the moment you find it? Would it be something you would pass down in your will to your heirs? If you can't provide unqualified answers to all of these questions, throw the item out.

- **If it doesn't have sentimental value, should I still keep it just in case I need it someday?** Absolutely not! Even if your first impulse is to put the item back in storage because "You just never know when something like that might come in handy," throw it away and get it out of your sight immediately. Disposing of the item is the only way to break your cluttering habits.

The closet: A primer for storing efficiency

If you're looking for a perfect example of both good and bad storage practices, open your closet to find a consolidated microcosm of every storage area in your home, office, car, and other personal space. The closet is a frequently used storage area, a place to store items you need every day. But the closet is also a hideaway for things such as the Halloween costume from three years ago or the shoes that you meant to get repaired last December. The closet has shelves, space for hanging items, and room on the floor — all of which have become jumbled masses of shoes, dry cleaning bags, empty luggage, hats, sweaters, ties, and items you couldn't put anywhere else. The closet is a combination desk drawer and dungeon, a convenient spot for your most needed items and a final resting place for things you will probably never touch again.

If you want to find out how to organize all your storage areas, start with your closet, and take copious notes.

1. **Pull everything out.**

   The only way to properly organize storage is to start from scratch. Pull out every item so that you are forced to touch it at least twice, once when pulling it out and once when putting it back or disposing of it.

2. **Make four distinct piles.**

   • Things you touch everyday

   • Things you touch at least once a week

   • Things you have touched in the last month

   • Things that you haven't touched in more than a month

3. **Start with the things you haven't touched in more than a month and make sub-piles.**

   • Seasonal items you will need next spring, summer, fall, or winter

   • Items with no seasonal distinction that have been put in the closet and forgotten

4. **Place the "Items with no seasonal distinction that have been put in the closet and forgotten" into two large containers (plastic bags or large plastic containers work well).**

   Label one container "Give away" and the other "Throw away." If you think that an item in the pile has value and you just can't bring yourself to throw it away, do the next best thing and give it to charity. Goodwill is one organization I frequently support, but there are certainly other local and national charities that help the homeless and disenfranchised. Find one of these organizations and donate the items you haven't touched in months. If you're embarrassed to give an item away, throw it out — obviously, the time is well past for the item to go.

5. **Examine the remaining "Seasonal items" sub-pile and determine whether the closet is the best place to store your sweaters, swimsuits, ski caps, sandals, or other items you aren't likely to touch for several more months.**

   If you have a large closet with plenty of room for these items, the closet may well be the proper storage area. If you're strapped for closet space, however, box those items up and put them in the attic, garage, basement, or other out-of-the-way place until they are needed.

6. **Go through the "Items you have touched in the last month" pile and put a portion of those items in the "Give away" and "Throw away" bins.**

   This step is tough. If you've touched an item in the last month, you might have a legitimate use for it, but the likelihood of needing every item you have touched in the last month is extremely small. Some things you currently handle need to be removed from your life. How many sweaters, for example, do you really need? Is having a jar of snacks in every room really a necessity (or for that matter healthy)? Take this opportunity to throw them out or give them away.

7. **Place the remaining items from the "Items you have touched in the last month," pile back into the closet first.**

   Stack or hang these items in the back of the closet or in the areas that are most difficult to reach and work your way toward the door. Never pile or throw an item into the closet. If you need to retrieve it every month, you need to be able to reach it, so be conscious of accessibility to each item.

8. **Fill in the closet with the remaining items you touch every week, constantly remaining mindful of the "Give away" and "Throw away" bins.**

   No matter how often you touch that 10-year-old paint-stained running suit, the time has come to give it up.

9. **Put the items you touch every day in the closet last, and keep them front and center.**

   The items you need the most should always be within easy reach.

10. **Repeat this process every six months.**

    After reorganizing your storage area, the number of items you thought you couldn't live without but that you haven't touched in six months will shock you. In reality, you didn't need them as desperately as you thought. You also need to make room for the new items you have acquired since you last went through this exercise. Your stuff may change, but if you are diligent about what you keep and how you keep it, your storage areas should always remain orderly and manageable.

A closet was used to illustrate this ten-step program, but the fundamentals are the same whether you are cleaning out a barn or a billion-dollar factory. Keeping these principles at the forefront of your organizational agenda helps you get the results you need from the areas where you store your belongings.

Pitching items in the office

All those notes you took at the corporate retreat last year (the ones you were sure would change your career the second you got back to the office) are, for the most part, worthless and should be thrown out. If you acted on those notes, they are now a part of your organizational system, and you have incorporated them into your things-to-do lists and your long-term goals. If you haven't acted on them, the time to do so is now. Wad up the notes, throw them into the recycling bin, and forget about them. If they weren't important enough to cause you to act quickly, keeping them now only prolongs your disorganization.

Investing via "the storage room" method

A friend of mine makes capital investments in small, start-up companies that show great growth potential. So far, he's done exceptionally well, investing on the ground floor of several Internet companies, and reaping big returns. Oddly enough, this man knows very little about the Internet, and, until recently, didn't own a personal computer. He has also invested in such diverse companies as a luxury yacht manufacturer and a sod farm, even though he doesn't sail and knows little to nothing about grass. Still, he is able to identify a successful start-up venture, see the potential, and invest wisely.

When I asked him what he looked for in a start-up company, he ran through the usual financial parameters, as well as the strength of the management team and the market potential for the product or service. When he got around to his physical examination of the business, however, something he said struck me.

"I always go to the storage room first," he said. "Anybody can keep an office neat and clean, especially when a potential investor is coming by to visit, but the storage room is where the rubber hits the road. If it's neat, organized, and not over-stocked, I know that somebody takes care of the little things. If the storage room's a mess, I look around to see what else might be done halfway. This method may sound crazy, but I have had investment decisions turn on how neatly someone keeps his storage room."

If you look at my friend's success, his advice doesn't sound crazy at all.

The same rule holds true for ancient computer files. Even though computer files don't take up space in the same way as the mountain of junk piled inside a cluttered closet, the old information stored in your hard drive takes up valuable memory space and should be purged from your system on a regular basis. The best rule for deciding when to delete a file from your computer is the hard-copy rule: If the file or document only existed in hard copy (a physical paper file of whatever length) would you still keep it? If so, where and why? If you can't legitimately answer the question, or if your answer is, "Well, you never know when it might come in handy," point, click, drag the file into the garbage icon, and delete it forever.

Here are some more tips on organizing office storage and throwing away unnecessary stuff:

✔ **If a file has outlived the project it dealt with, strongly consider throwing it out.** Unless the file contains compelling procedures or notes that are applicable in the here and now, keeping it around "just in case" doesn't make a lot of sense. Historical relevance is the biggest excuse used for keeping old files, but unless the information in those files is being accessed, they serve very little purpose. A permanent record of a memo for an event that no longer exists isn't as significant as you might think.

✔ **If a file has outlasted the tenure of its primary author, examine why you are keeping it.** Sometimes good, solid reasons exist, many of which deal with legal protection for employees and employers against potential future claims. You do not, however, have to keep everything ever written by a former employee. If a file has outlived its usefulness in your office and no long-term legal reasons exist for keeping it, throw the file out. If there are legal reasons for keeping the file, transfer it to a safe place (perhaps the legal department or an independent attorney's office), but don't keep it stashed away in a closet or file drawer in your office.

✔ **Store your reference materials nearby.** If you frequently use a dictionary, thesaurus, or phone book, keep those items on a shelf or in a drawer within easy reach. They should be stored, but in a spot where you don't have to search for them when you need them. The same principle holds true for other materials you use regularly. Keeping them on your desk or piled on top of a filing cabinet only adds to the clutter, but storing regularly-used reference materials in a place where you can easily reach them is a critical part of effective storage.

✔ **Delegate or eliminate.** If you don't touch a certain item in your office on a daily or weekly basis, either hand it off to someone else or throw it away. A file, document, letter, or memo that has been sitting around your office in the "Oh, I've been meaning to get to that" pile needs to move on out. You have already demonstrated that you probably won't get to the item, so delegate it to someone else, or take the plunge and trash it.

Chapter 11

Organizing Your Home

• •

In This Chapter

▶ Organizing in the family dynamic

▶ Structuring the organized home

▶ Managing the family schedule

▶ Expecting the most from your kids

• •

Some of the biggest challenges you face as a newly organized person do not come from bosses, clients, co-workers, friends, colleagues, or acquaintances. Your toughest obstacles come from members of your own family who know you in your disorganized state and have no real desire to see anything change. From their perspective, you are not a manager, a task-driven achiever, or a results-oriented organizer. You are a spouse, a child, or a parent, and none of your other past accomplishments or future goals are as important as your relationship with your family.

Juli Inkster, the talented professional golfer who is one of only two players to win all four Grand Slam women's golf titles in her career, summed up this particular dynamic by describing her home life and her relationship with her two children. Inkster said, "Having kids keeps me grounded. No matter what I accomplish in golf, I know that the kids are going to say, 'That's great mom, now can we go get some ice cream?' It's then that you realize your family sees you differently than the rest of the world."

Even though your family looks at you from a different perspective, you can still do many things to make your home a more organized and productive place — and to perhaps bring your family along for the ride.

Getting Everyone on the Organization Train

If you woke up one morning and suddenly changed everything in your family routine — from the time you devoted to breakfast, to the demands you made of your spouse and children — there's a better than average chance that you would have a mutiny on your hands. Of course, becoming more organized and getting better results out of your time and tasks requires you to change things in your life. Your old habits and routines lead you into your current disorganized state, so you must change these habits if you want to improve your results and reach your goals.

So how do you make changes in order to improve your personal organization without inciting a riot in your family? Some answers include

✔ **Call a family meeting.** Your family deserves an outline of your objectives and a description of the changes you hope to make. Sharing your long-term, intermediate, and short-term goals with your family, as well as the strategies you hope to employ, helps you win them over to your side. Those who love you most are the most supportive of your efforts, but you have to share with them in order to gain their support.

✔ **Ask for advice and listen to the answers.** Nobody knows your idiosyncrasies better than your immediate family. When you share your goals and objectives with them, request feedback and pay close attention to what they say. Their opinions will likely be honest and to the point, and their suggestions will be specific. If you are someone who overschedules, because you consistently believe that you can accomplish more in a day than is humanly possible, your family will keep you in line and offer suggestions on how to improve in that area. You can also rest assured that your family will let you know when you're being unrealistic in your expectations. If you pay attention, you can use their advice to modify and ultimately codify your organizational plans.

✔ **Involve them in the process.** You have to include your family because you can't complete the process of getting organized all on your own. Suppose that your personal goals include training for a 10-kilometer run, starting a home-based Web page design business, and reading a book a week for the next year. In order to achieve any of those goals, you need the help, encouragement, and support of family members. Your spouse might take over some of the housekeeping duties so you can run. Your kids could assume a more active role in preparing dinner. All of your family could encourage you by insisting that you run on days when you don't feel quite up to the exertion, and they can offer suggestions on how to effectively market and grow your business. The important thing is to get them involved. Results require teamwork, and no team is more important than your family.

> ✔ **Encourage family members to set their own organizational goals.**
> Leading by example sets the tone for the rest of your family. Just as
> falling into a disorganized stupor is easy if you are constantly surrounded
> by scatter-brained, unproductive people, if you blaze an organized,
> results-oriented trail in your home, your family will follow.

Organizing Your Surroundings at Home

If you're serious about getting your life more organized and attaining your
lofty personal goals, you need to structure your home environment to
encourage a focused, results-oriented approach to your days. This restruct-
uring requires removing or changing those things that create confusion
and clutter, and fostering those things that encourage organization and
productivity.

If, for example, you own a personal computer and have Internet access, you
have probably struggled over where to locate the computer in your home.
Your kids want it in their room so they can chat with friends, surf the Web, do
homework, and play games, but your spouse would like to read some on-line
newspapers and shop on-line. You have needs as well. Whether keeping the
family books on the PC or accessing your favorite Internet sites, you need
time for yourself on the computer.

Then there's the issue of parental control. As wonderful as it is, the Internet
is also full of smut. Your computer's location is critical to your monitoring
capabilities as a parent. These are all issues that should be addressed in a
family meeting where everyone's opinions can be expressed and everyone's
needs can be outlined. From there, you have a basis on which to budget time
for everyone to use the family asset, and a place that is neutral, comfortable,
and productive for everyone.

Making Every Space Have a Purpose

The office in my home is at the opposite end of the house from my bedroom,
because I want to have some physical distance between the area where I
sleep and the area where I hold meetings, make business calls, and conduct
my work. The simple walk from one end of my house to the other helps prepare me for the work that lays ahead after I enter my office, and the distance
between the office and bedroom helps me put everything behind me before I
put my head on the pillow at night. Each of the spaces has its own purpose —
even the in-between space serves a role.

Every corner of your home also has a purpose. Your job is to identify what task
you hope to accomplish in a particular space and use the area for that task.

I remember an old still cartoon (perhaps an advertisement, although I don't remember the product) that showed a woman in a one-room apartment attempting (unsuccessfully) to manage her day. Most of the floor was taken up by a television set, and an ironing board occupied much of the rest of the room. The woman, still dressed in her nightgown, had an iron in one hand and a baby in the other with the telephone cradled between her shoulder and her ear. The television glowed with the latest daytime drama, and a dog sat in a corner of the room looking up at the woman as if to say, "What a curious life you lead."

I always remember that cartoon when I see someone attempting to do too many things in an area that's too small. For example, I never read while watching television, because I end up doing neither well. Nor do I answer my phone while I'm meeting with someone — I would rather have the caller leave a message than interrupt the person I'm meeting with to take an unexpected phone call. When I read in my bedroom I sit in a chair, because I want to reserve my bed for sleep.

In short, every space in my home has a function, and I try to reserve each area for its intended purpose. Of course, I'm not always successful. Many discussions spill over from my office to the kitchen, or even out to the pool. Some crossover is inevitable and even encouraged. But if you want to become more productive in your home, pick certain spots for certain tasks and try to remain true to those objectives.

Setting the Family Schedule

Just as colleagues in your office have slightly different agendas and schedules that must be coordinated to accomplish common goals, members of your family have different things to do, different times to do them, and different demands on the limited resources shared by the family. The most common example of differing family schedules is the school-age child involved in extracurricular activities who must be shuttled back and forth between games, practices, competitions, rehearsals, and performances. This taxing process is always a strain on the shuttle driver and other family members who might need the car or have other conflicting activities scheduled. If you have children, you have no doubt experienced this dynamic.

Each family member's priorities differ with various intersections along the way. Getting around the inherent conflicts that arise from varying family demands is impossible, but you can incorporate some strategies to minimize the chaos:

> ✔ **Post a family calendar.** A dry-erase board usually works well. Each family member is responsible for posting his or her activities, time frames, and resource requirements. When a conflict arises (for example, who is going to get the car on Friday night), one member of the family

(the mother or father) acts as arbiter, and resolves the conflict. Not everybody will always be happy with this system, but it beats having no system at all.

✔ **Make certain activities non-negotiable.** Church, dinner at home two nights a week, or other family activities you see as high-priority items are placed on everyone's schedule and deemed mandatory. In addition to setting a good standard, this mandate teaches everyone in the family to work their schedules around certain predetermined, non-negotiable events, a lesson that will serve them well in their careers and life.

✔ **Negotiate time and resources.** When schedules conflict, enter negotiations with members of your family over the resources in question. If the car is in dispute, discuss alternative means of transportation. If your time is requested, negotiate your schedule to accommodate as many family members as possible without jeopardizing your own goals and objectives.

Careers change, goals change, and priorities and objectives change, but your family is always your family. Bringing them into your organizational goals benefits them and you, and increases the results attained by all of you.

Setting High Goals for Your Children

If organization is a learned craft, then disorganization is a well-established habit. Like most habits (good and bad), the earlier you teach results-based organization to your children the more likely they are to retain those habits after they are adults.

A number of ways exist to get your kids started in the right organizational direction:

✔ **Assign tasks.** In the old days we called them chores, and you weren't allowed to sit at the dinner table until you completed them. Call them whatever you want, but set a list of assignments for your children and insist that they accomplish their tasks. Even a two-year-old can pick up her toys, so the time is never too early to start giving your kids a list of things to do.

✔ **If your child can read and write, he can make and follow a list.** Teach list writing as soon as children can form letters and grasp the meaning of what they write. "Put away crayons," and "Play with friends," are about as complicated as you need to get, but these lists condition children to organize their thinking and function from a list of tasks.

✔ **Give time limits.** Just as adults operate under deadlines, children must learn to focus their attention on the tasks at hand. If cleaning a room is on a child's things-to-do list, you and the child must set time limits on when that activity is to take place. Otherwise children, just like adults, become distracted and drag the task out much longer than needed.

✔ **Reward tasks completed well and punish tasks done poorly.** Whatever punishment you find appropriate, you must strictly enforce the time and task limits you place on your child. No excuses. If the room isn't cleaned in the allotted 30 minutes, the television and computer are off-limits for the night, no matter what creative reasons the child conjures up for being late. Rewards are equally important. A job done well and ahead of schedule should be rewarded by allowing children to engage in a favorite activity during the time they saved by doing their jobs right and finishing ahead of schedule.

✔ **Teach creative self-sufficiency early on.** When a child wants something (such as a new video game or computer program), encourage the child to earn the money to buy the item by using whatever creative means he can reasonably think of. Given some freedom, children can be amazingly resourceful.

✔ **Have children write and post their goals as early as they can grasp the concept.** If a child wants to play a sport, ask the child to list the goals she hopes to ultimately achieve in that sport and post the list on a bedroom door or other prominent place. Then help the child break those goals into manageable short-term bites. Monitor the progress with the child so she becomes accustomed to methodically working toward a regimented series of goals. Goal setting is a skill she will thank you for when she reaches adulthood.

This advice may sound like Parenting 101, but the number of children who enter upper levels of education having never written a things-to-do list, and having never set any long- or short-term goals for themselves, consistently amazes me. Even then, the time is not too late, but these children are certainly at a disadvantage in terms of their life skills. Getting organized is like learning a second language — if children learn the skill at an early age, they not only pick up on the skills quicker than their adult counterparts, but they retain and apply those skills more effectively throughout the rest of their lives.

Chapter 12

Dollars and Sense: Organizing Money

*N*othing frightens disorganized people more than an open and honest discussion about money and finances. Even successful people — people who make lots of money and are considered financially astute — grow increasingly uncomfortable when discussing money, how it is spent, how it is saved, and how it grows. The discomfort stems from the fact that the financial world is constantly changing. You have a job, a family, and many other things to think about in a day other than how your mutual fund performed in the Asian market overnight.

Many people simply ignore their personal finances. They pay their bills but put off everything else until some nebulous time in the future that never seems to come. When tax time rolls around, they tally their total earnings for the year and say things like, "Wow, look how much I made this year," but quickly follow up with, "Where did it all go?"

Until you know where all your money is going, you can't consider yourself financially organized. (And until you get financially organized you will never reach your long-term personal goals.) This chapter gets you started on the path to financial organization.

Understanding the Money Mental Block

Disorganized people have no idea where their money goes. It slips through their fingers, and they constantly see others in their same income strata taking more lavish vacations, buying more expensive cars, and generally living a more posh lifestyle than they do. "What do they have that I don't have?" the disorganized person asks. "I am paid reasonably well for what I do. Why can't I seem to get ahead while neighbor X next door, who makes the same salary I do, is flying to Paris on the Concorde and taking her family to Aruba for a week?"

The answer is simple: Neighbor X has made consumption choices that don't match those of her disorganized neighbor. She might be flying to Paris or taking the family to Aruba because she chose to forego luxury edition cars, three-nights-per-week restaurant bills, and a credit card spree at Christmas.

Unfortunately, the concept of consumption choices escapes a lot of people, primarily because they can't discipline themselves to think within the boundaries of their income. For example, the disorganized person in the previous example can't understand why his neighbor can afford luxury vacations. Look at the following hypothetical income and expense projections, and you can see how the disorganized neighbor's money escapes him.

If both neighbors have after-tax household incomes of $10,000 per month, their average monthly expenses might look like Tables 25-1 and 25-2.

Table 25-1 Disorganized Neighbor's Monthly Expenses	
Expense	*Actual Cost*
Mortgage	$3,000
Car lease payments (two luxury vehicles and one midsize for a teenage child)	$1,500
Insurance (life, home, auto, and dependent health coverage)	$600
Accumulated credit card debt	$1,000
Entertainment (health club, golf, sports tickets, and so on)	$1,000
Restaurant bills	$850
Other food	$600
Clothes	$500
Yard mowing and maid services (Once a week for each)	$450
Utilities	$300
Other monthly household expenses (gasoline, napkins, toothpaste, and so on)	$400
Total	$10,200

You are watching a man march headlong into bankruptcy while bringing home $120,000 a year in after-tax income. But he can't understand why he is bailing water on a sinking ship while his neighbor takes extravagant trips abroad.

Table 25-2	Organized Neighbor's Monthly Expenses
Expense	**Actual Cost**
Mortgage	$2,000
Savings and Investments	$1,500
Charitable contributions	$1,000
Insurance	$800
Entertainment	$600
Household expenses	$600
Food	$600
Home repair and maintenance	$400
Credit card debt	$400
Restaurant bills	$300
Clothes	$300
Children's allowances and school expenses	$300
Utilities	$300
Auto repair and maintenance	$300
Vacation savings account	$300
Other monthly household expenses (gasoline, napkins, toothpaste, and so on)	$300
Total	$10,000

Frugal living, mowing her own lawn, and putting money into savings enable the organized neighbor to take a couple of lavish annual vacations. These money-saving measures also allow her to save for retirement, make substantial charitable contributions, lower her mortgage payment (by making a more substantial down payment on her house), eliminate auto lease payments (by purchasing less expensive cars with cash), and live comfortably within the parameters of her income.

The choices made by both of these neighbors reflect their priorities and goals. The organized neighbor has definitive long-term financial objectives and a plan for achieving those goals. The disorganized neighbor would rather look good today driving his new Lexus as the yard workers and housekeeper are working than plan his financial future. He digs a deeper hole every month, and will eventually be forced to revamp his lifestyle or forfeit on many of his obligations.

Being in the sports management business, I continually witness examples of financial buffoonery far worse than the disorganized neighbor's mistakes. Young athletes coming out of college without enough money to buy a hamburger at a fast food restaurant suddenly find themselves showered with riches beyond their wildest expectations. Most do not have the maturity or wherewithal to handle their newfound wealth, and all are too busy competing in their sports to monitor every dollar invested on their behalf.

The results are usually disastrous. After buying expensive cars, clothes, homes, and many of the trappings that they assume go along with being young and wealthy, these athletes squander their remaining money on friends and family who are more than eager to share in the new lifestyle. Before they know what's happening, these million-dollar athletes exceed their limits by spending more than they earn. The situation is compounded when an athlete's tenure in her sport runs its course and, suddenly, this perfectly healthy 36-year-old is forced to retire from competition with little to show for her efforts.

The average working tenure for most athletes is under a decade, meaning that they are forced into retirement at an age when most people are just entering their peak earning years. Unless the money an athlete has earned while playing is properly managed, invested, and set up to work for him in the future, he could be faced with serious burdens he cannot meet, and career decisions he isn't prepared or equipped to make.

Most average citizens can't fathom the kind of money professional athletes make, and only a small percentage can relate to the previous example of the neighbors making $120,000 a year, but the concepts are the same for everyone. I've chosen to use these high-dollar illustrations to show you that making more money isn't necessarily the answer to monetary woes. Someone who organizes his money and lives within his means can live on a much smaller salary than these fictional neighbors and on a fraction of the salary paid to professional athletes. Allowing money to slip through your fingers and finding yourself in dire financial straits is not a function of how much you make (as the previous examples clearly show); it's a function of how organized you are.

Money manager's financial woes

Even people who are in the business of monitoring markets at the highest levels sometimes have trouble keeping up with their personal finances. David Stockton, a cabinet member during the Reagan Administration who headed the Office of Management and Budget (the people responsible for drafting the trillion-dollar budget of the U.S. government), consistently bounced personal checks and received past due notices from his power, water, and cable television companies.

Stockton could tell you how much money the U.S. government spent on sugar subsidies, highway projects, and missile defenses, but he had no idea how much money he had in his personal checking account or when his rent was due. I'm sure that a lot of people in much lower-profile positions are exactly like David Stockton. They can tell you, to the penny, how much money their company earned from their efforts last quarter, but they couldn't come close to telling you how much money they have in their personal savings accounts, nor could they tell you the cash value of their retirement and investment portfolios.

Exploring Your Cash Flow

The two most important financial words aren't "income and expense," or "profit and loss." Whether you're talking about a multibillion-dollar business or your household budget, the most important words in the English language arc "cash flow."

Cash flow is a measure of the money you have coming in, and the obligations and expenditures you have going out. Balancing cash flow sounds simple enough, but if you ever had a mountain of bills come due three weeks before your next check was scheduled to arrive, you understand the kind of problems that can arise if you don't pay close attention to your personal cash flow. The same rule holds true in business. If your company commits $20 million in expenditures for a plant expansion based on revenue projections that don't pan out, you are in the throes of what is known as a *cash flow crisis.* These crises aren't pretty, nor can you dismiss them as temporary anomalies. Some cash flow crises result in layoffs, cutbacks, and bankruptcy.

At home, a severe cash flow crisis means that you can't pay your power bill before the cut-off date because you spent all your earnings (plus a few extra dollars) on a vacation earlier in the month and didn't set aside enough in savings to handle such inconvenient emergencies. Or a severe cash flow crisis could be that the second home you've always dreamed of owning has just come on the market, but because of your current cash commitments and other obligations, you don't have the cash to cover the mortgage.

These sorts of crises are easily avoidable with a little prior planning. Here are some key points to remember about cash flow and its importance in your overall financial organization.

- ✔ **Yearly budgets don't put food on the table this week.** Accurately projecting your annual income is wonderful, but has very little to do with the bills you have to pay this week or this month. The people who take on additional fixed monthly expenses (such as mortgages, car payments, and club memberships) based on a skewed income projection amaze me. If someone made $75,000 last year and expects to make the same amount this year, you might easily assume that he could handle fixed expenses based on a monthly pretax income of $6,250. However, if $10,000 of that $75,000 came in the form of a year-end bonus, budgeting expenses based on $6,250 a month in income leads to an immediate cash flow crisis.

- ✔ **Cash flow must be constantly monitored.** Cash flow isn't an annual financial check-up you look at once and forget about for a year. I request no fewer than three personal cash flow projections a year from my financial advisors, and I want explanations for any major cash flow changes that occur in between. The reason I am so diligent in monitoring cash flow is because I don't want to make the mistake illustrated in the preceding example. If I know that I have a certain amount of money coming in at a specified time, I make my investment decisions based on that cash flow. If most of my income is being deferred to a later time, I wait to invest until I am more comfortable with my cash flow.

- ✔ **Betting that money will come in is a gamble you will eventually lose.** An employee at our company once came into the office fuming over having bounced a personal check. Of course, no one held a gun to his head and made him write the bad check, nor was he accusing the bank of any mistakes. His complaint centered on a promise. "I was told I would have the money in my hand by Thursday afternoon, so on Thursday morning I wrote a check assuming that the amount would be covered in plenty of time," he explained. "Well, the money I was promised didn't arrive until 4:00 p.m. on Monday, and by then the check I had written had bounced."

  "The check is in the mail" is one of the oldest lies known to man and one that will certainly burn you at some point if you let it. Betting on money you don't have in hand is a bet you are going to lose more times than you win. That game is not worth playing.

- ✔ **Slow to pay, fast to spend.** If you provide a service for someone, insist on being paid at the time the service is rendered. Otherwise, you have little recourse. If you sold someone a car and the check bounces, you can always repossess the car. If you provide consulting services for someone, you have nothing to repossess. The client possesses your advice and you have no way of getting it back.

We are faced with such issues quite often with our clients — especially the athletes who make personal appearances at outings, banquets, or golf tournaments. In all cases, we insist that our clients receive the agreed-upon compensation on or before the day of the event. Even though some of the appearance fees are quite hefty, this policy is non-negotiable for most of our clients. To agree otherwise would be a serious error on our part.

✔ **Invoices do not age gracefully.** Putting an invoice in a drawer in the hopes it will go away is the most serious form of denial imaginable and can lead to serious financial problems. Not only does the invoice become larger and uglier as time goes on, you earn a reputation as someone who is slow to pay. That reputation is hard to overcome, no matter what your cash flow situation is in the future.

Organizing Your Finances

No matter what your monthly income is, the following financial strategies can help you manage your money more efficiently, and instill habits that help you reach your long-term financial goals.

Paying yourself first

Before you pay the light bill, the mortgage, the insurance company, or the pizza guy, you should always pay the most important bill first: the one to yourself. Whenever your paycheck, commission check, or bonus check arrives, the first order of business is to take a portion of that money (preferably as much as 15 percent) and put it into a savings or investment account.

Unfortunately, many people take the opposite approach. They pay all their other bills first, and if anything is left over (which is rare), they stash a few of those dollars aside. That approach always leaves you wondering where your money has gone when the rainy day you should have been saving for finally arrives.

Most people do save for retirement and the education of their children. Other items such as vacations and a second home seem to be managed throughout the normal course of their business careers. The areas of primary concern are how and how well they will live when they retire, and what kinds of schools they can afford for their children.

Retirement and college costs are worthy long-term objectives, but other things you need to consider when saving and investing for the future include

- **Keeping nine months salary where you can reach it if you need it.** Today's business environment is more volatile than any in recent history, and just because your company is doing well today does not mean that success will continue forever. What would you do if you were laid off? Would you be in a financial panic? Would you take a job you might not want and enter a career path that might not suit you just to keep the paychecks coming? Unfortunately, too many people are in that boat. To avoid the stress and shock that comes with losing a job, keep at least nine months' salary in liquid savings. This money might be in a mutual fund, savings account, money market certificate, or stock, but you must be able to access it without incurring substantial penalties. When you don't have to worry about paying the power bill, looking for a new job is much easier.

- **Saving for the short term as well as the long.** Opportunities arise when you least expect them and with no warning. A public offering of stock in a company you know and you trust will be successful, for example, is an event when having short-term savings available is important. So is purchasing a new washing machine when yours breaks down. You certainly don't want to dip into your retirement account for such expenses, but if you have earmarked certain dollars for the short-term, you at least have options available when unexpected opportunities or needs arise.

- **Looking to your company for the best savings plans.** Most corporate benefits packages contain programs that encourage savings among employees. 401(k)s, for example, allow you to put money aside in an account and earn a substantial tax benefit. Also, most companies match the employee's contributions up to a certain amount — just one of many benefits your employer may offer. If you aren't involved in your company's savings plans already, check out the available programs and get involved.

Cutting spending

No magic potion exists for saving money. If your expenses are such that you can't afford to put even the smallest amount in savings, then cut your expenses. At first you will no doubt say that you can't. You're tapped to the max, and there's no way you could possibly cut one dollar out of your monthly budget. If that's the case (and it probably is), take the amount you intend to save (say, 10 percent of your net earnings) and pretend that cash doesn't exist. If your paycheck suddenly dropped 10 percent, what expenses would you cut in order to survive? Start from this assumption and continue working until you come up with a formula that allows you to save.

Establishing a family controller

Every company has a *controller,* a person responsible for the accounting practices, who ensures that all income is monitored and all expenses are paid. Your family also needs a controller — one person who controls the monthly bills and monitors the income. The family controller writes the checks, balances the checkbook, files the invoices, and monitors the cash flow.

However, just like a corporate controller cannot and should not make unilateral spending decisions, the person in the home responsible for the checkbook should not make spending decisions without discussing them with other family members. If you approach your family's checkbook in this fashion, you will have far fewer surprises in the family budget.

Hiring a professional

Financial markets change so rapidly and new products and services become available at such an amazing pace that assuming you can make intelligent investments without the help of a qualified professional is pure folly. Whether you're interested in a mutual fund, an index fund, estate planning, an IRA, or a life insurance policy, trained financial planners and money managers know the markets, know the products, and specialize in developing strategies that match individual needs. Unless you have nothing to do with your days but study monetary funds and investment trends, you can't possibly know as much as the professionals in those areas.

Of course, there are good money managers and not-so-good money managers, and you can't tell the difference by the color of their suits.

When searching for a good financial planner, consider the following:

✔ **Who recommended this person?** Word of mouth is still the best way to find a financial professional, but pay attention to who is recommending a money manager and why.

If your cousin is recommending his daughter because she's just starting out in the insurance and financial planning business and needs some clients, the recommendation might not be the most worthwhile tip you receive. If, however, your richest friend gives you the name of his personal financial planner, that recommendation might carry a little more credence. As long as you know the motivations of all sides, you can make an informed decision.

✔ **What is your financial planner's track record?** Check him out. Find out what kind of successes he has had in recent years, and talk to references. You want to maintain the relationship with your financial planner for the long-term, so taking your time and gaining a comfort level with the person you choose is important.

✔ **Find out how your planner is paid.** Some money managers and financial planners work on a flat fee and others are incentive- or commission-based. Each of these structures has good and bad points, but you should understand the agreement you are signing. Neither of these arrangements is better or worse than the other — as long as you understand them both and enter an arrangement with your eyes open.

Part III
Time Is on Your Side

The 5th Wave   By Rich Tennant

"I SENSE YOU'RE IN A HURRY, SO I'LL BE BRIEF."

In this part . . .

Time has always been an elusive concept for most people. People know how it's measured, and know that they never seem to have enough of it, but other than a few physicists like Einstein who devoted years to the subject, most people have no idea what time really is and how it relates to the other elements in the universe.

The good news is you don't need to understand the physics of time to get better results. In fact, all you really need to do is change the way you think about the clock and the calendar. That's what this part is all about.

Chapter 13

Time: The Unrecoverable Asset

- -

- -

*E*ver had a day in which people were late, traffic was awful, calls were not returned, the computer was down, and it was raining? Nothing goes your way, and you accomplish very few of the things you set out to do.

The good news is that you're not alone. Everyone, from the most organized CEO in the world to the most scatter-brained time-waster, experiences these same ups and downs. How they manage them, however, separates the organized from the disorganized, the productive from the unproductive, and the content from the frustrated.

In this chapter, I offer three time-efficiency questionnaires to help you pin-point your time-wasters. I also introduce six basic time-efficiency skills that you can quickly master.

Three Time-Efficiency Questionnaires

People are somewhat self-delusional when evaluating their own time management skills. Everyone wants to believe that they can accomplish more in shorter periods of time than they can. When completing these questionnaires, honesty is (as always) the best policy. You may look at these questionnaires and assume that you can complete this test in ten minutes or so and move on. On the contrary, some of these questions are agonizingly long, especially if you do the kind of soul searching necessary to answer each part truthfully and openly.

How to complete these questionnaires

Give yourself no less than 15 minutes and no more than 30 minutes for each questionnaire. I hope you devote enough time to each test to ensure that you give a fair and accurate description of your current time management skills.

Grading codes appear at the top of each quiz. Total your scores after each questionnaire, and check yourself against the corresponding grading key. You will certainly score better in certain areas than in others, but this disparity is taken into account when you total the scores at the end of the chapter.

Work-life questionnaire #1

Scoring Key: Grade yourself with the following numbers. On the line beside each statement, record the number next to the word that most closely matches your current time management skills:

- ✔ **0:** Rarely
- ✔ **1:** Sometimes
- ✔ **2:** Often
- ✔ **3:** Almost always

_0_ You plan every day from start to finish, meticulously outlining every minute, hour, and detail of your day, before the day begins.

_2_ You know exactly what time you will wake up tomorrow morning and what you will do first.

_0_ Your day contains no *dead times* (gaps in your day when you have nothing scheduled).

____ Very few frenetic times in your day rear up when two or more demands are made on you at once.

____ You write down all your daily tasks for today, tomorrow, and the day after tomorrow where you can easily access them at any time.

____ You know exactly how long getting dressed, making a business call, driving to your office, writing a memo, and attending meetings take, and you rarely overschedule or underschedule the time required for those events.

____ You are rarely late for anything, and on the few occasions when you are late, never more than a few minutes.

____ Whenever you schedule a meeting with someone else or request someone else's time, you let her know in advance how much time you need and what you want to discuss.

____ If you are granted an hour of someone else's time, you never take an hour and a half.

____ If you grant an hour of your own time to someone, you always stick to your schedule. If the person is 40 minutes late, the meeting becomes a 20-minute affair. You don't adjust your schedule to accommodate the tardiness of others.

____ Your schedule in your personal life is just as organized and time-specific as your schedule at the office. Each task has a distinct time to be handled and very few occasions interfere with that schedule.

____ Total score

If you scored:

✔ **0 to 8:** Time slips through your fingers like water from a fountain. You must wonder where your days go, and the overwhelming mountain of tasks backlogging your schedule no doubt frustrates you.

✔ **9 to 15:** You don't easily understand the asset of time, and managing this asset isn't a comfortable process. Spend time working on your time-management practices. Start slowly by writing everything down, but don't become frustrated when you slip up. With time, you can gain a firmer grasp on your life — if you employ a few of the simple principles I outline in this part.

✔ **16 to 25:** The principles are in place, but you are a diamond in the rough. You need to hone your skills in time management through practice, and you must make awareness of time into a habit, not a chore. Continue to work with your schedule and practice. You should see dramatic results in a reasonable period of time.

✔ **26 to 30:** You've got it! You slip up a few times along the way, but no one, not even the most time-conscious chief executive in the world, can control every second. Perfection is unobtainable (although you can have some perfect days), but it is certainly a goal worth striving for. Continue to hone your skills and you will become a master of your time and space.

✔ **31 to 33:** I think that you're fibbing. Perhaps you believe that you're a perfect time manager, when, in fact, you probably need to work on a number of aspects of your schedule. Go back and complete this questionnaire again, but this time, be specific. Count the number of individual instances when you have been perfect or near perfect in a category. If you can't think of any specific instances, perhaps you aren't being truthful in your answers.

Home-life questionnaire #2

Scoring Key: Grade yourself with the appropriate number:

- ✔ **0:** Always true
- ✔ **1:** True
- ✔ **2:** Sometimes true
- ✔ **3:** Never true

_____ You regularly miss meetings because of overwhelming circumstances.

_____ People interrupt you at least twice a day for emergencies that take you out of your schedule and disrupt other plans you have for the rest of the day.

_____ You want to be home for dinner with the family, but rarely leave the office in time because of your overwhelming workload.

_____ You apologized to a date, your spouse, a friend, or one of your children at least once in the past week because you missed a significant event or meeting with that person.

_____ Conducting meetings in your office is difficult because you are constantly interrupted by phone calls and intruding guests.

_____ No matter what is on the agenda, you always arrive at the office at the same time.

_____ You rarely know what tomorrow brings. Each day is a new adventure.

_____ When you have a few moments alone or to spend with your family, the spare time is a pleasant surprise — never an opportunity that you have planned.

_____ You and your spouse haven't been out on a real date since you got home from your honeymoon.

_____ You try your best to be scheduled, but your kids and other family members make it impossible. Your schedule is subject to the whim of others.

_____ Your family and friends understand that work comes first, and they know you can be called away at any moment.

_____ Total score

If you scored:

✔ **0 to 15:** Major problems in your life (both personally and professionally) are most likely the direct result of your ineffectiveness in managing your time and setting meaningful priorities. A healthy look at what's really important to you could go a long way toward improving your interpersonal skills as well as making you a happier person.

✔ **16 to 25:** You are at a crossroads in your interpersonal relationships with family and friends, as well as with colleagues and acquaintances in the workplace. So far, you have adequately managed your time and retained control of your people skills, but one more responsibility or major project could be a turning point. By practicing the good time-management skills you are implementing today and remaining disciplined in your approach to dealing with others, you will free yourself of the friction between your relationships and your responsibilities.

✔ **26 to 33:** Some people may consider you curt — and you might even be criticized for being impersonal at times — but if the relationships that matter most to you are intact and you are progressing nicely in your professional career and personal life, who cares what others think? Life is not a popularity contest. If your friends can count on you and your colleagues know your dependability, you should do whatever you can to continue in the same vein.

Scheduling questionnaire #3

Scoring Key: You know the drill.

✔ **0:** Rarely happens that way

✔ **1:** Sometimes, but not often

✔ **2:** That sounds about right

✔ **3:** Of course, all the time

_____ You write specific six-month, one-year, two-year, and five-year goals in your planner, and read those goals at least once a day.

_____ Before you leave the office every afternoon, you know the exact time you will arrive at work the next day, even though that time varies from day to day, and week to week.

_____ You coordinate your work schedule so you don't miss a family-oriented event like a little league baseball game or a piano recital. Sometimes, accommodating these events means coming in earlier and working weekends, but you have gladly made that choice.

____ You have scheduled at least one meeting for a specific date three months or more from now.

____ You never make out-of-town trips where you attend only one meeting or accomplish only one task.

____ You have already scheduled some specific times and tasks for a week from today. Your standard procedure is to schedule specific items three or four days in advance.

____ You know how much time you devote to interruptions and unpredictable events every day, and regularly build those times into your schedule.

____ You make at least twice as many calls as you take — and the majority of your unexpected incoming calls are returned at a predetermined time later in the day.

____ You not only know your main priorities, both personally and professionally, but can recite them from memory and you have them written down within easy reach.

____ You are adept at negotiating your time so that you can accomplish the things you want and still accommodate as many requests as you feel are justifiable.

____ You are constantly re-evaluating your long-term projects and priorities to make sure that they are still appropriate, given how times have changed.

____ Before you leave the office every day, you always initiate one more phone call.

____ Total score

If you scored:

✔ **0 to 12:** A long-term project for you rarely extends past tonight's dinner options. It doesn't have to be this way. You don't have to go through life with little direction or nonspecific goals. You need to improve your skills in managing the clock and managing the calendar. All you have to do is start by committing your priorities and objectives to paper, and then map out the path you will take to accomplish those objectives using both your calendar and your clock.

✔ **13 to 25:** You have potential, but you need to fast-forward your thinking. Effective time management extends beyond the minute, hour, or even the day. Extend the same time-efficient strategies you now employ in your daily planner to next week, next month, and next year. Planning ahead isn't that difficult once you get the hang of it.

✔ **26 to 30:** I would love to see your long-term goals, because, even though they might be aggressive and almost outrageous if taken out of context, I'm confident you will come close to achieving your objectives if you continue on your current path.

✔ **31 to 33:** Are you sure that you're telling the truth? Try completing this questionnaire again.

The grand total

Total your totals and come up with your grand total.

_____   Grand total score for the time management test

If your grand total was:

✔ **Under 50:** Time is not your friend. The habits and attitudes ingrained in your psyche over the years make managing your time with any sort of efficiency almost impossible. Not to say that you are a lost cause, but, to reorganize, you must make fundamental changes in the way you approach every aspect of your life. Start small; manage an hour, then two hours, and then a morning or an afternoon. Write down everything that you want to do, then chronicle everything you actually get done, and take note of the disparity between those two lists. The most important advice, however, is *do something!* You've got a long way to go, but you too can eat your elephant one bite at a time (see Chapter 2).

✔ **50 to 69:** Not good. Perhaps you know what needs to be done, but you haven't taken the necessary steps to get there. As you read through Part IV, write down some specifics that apply to your current situation, and create a things-to-do-list. After you complete the list, prioritize the items on the list, set time frames for each, and start the process of getting organized. Now is not too late, but you need to get started immediately.

✔ **70 to 79:** You have the basic outline, but you need to practice, practice, and practice some more. Obviously, the skills of time management do not come naturally to you, so, for a while, setting and managing your schedule is going to be tougher work than the actual tasks you have to accomplish in a day. Even so, working on these skills and turning them into habits is important. Only when the process of managing your time is like second nature will you see a dramatic change in your accomplishments.

✔ **80 to 89:** You're close. You've probably mastered certain aspects of time management as well as anyone, but could use a little work in other areas.

> ✔ **90 to 100:** You have a firm understanding of the principles and practices of time management. These skills will serve you well as you continue to pursue your personal and professional goals.

The most critical hour

The most important hour you spend developing your time management skills is the next one. Take the time to sit down, close the door, and study the results of the test you just completed. If you scored poorly in certain areas, make lists of ways to improve your performance. If you shone in other areas, write down the reasons you performed well, and come up with ways to transfer those principles to all areas of your life. The 60 minutes you spend on this one-hour process could change the way you spend all the remaining hours of your professional career, so don't be distracted. Take your time and put some serious thought into the how and why of time management. Careful consideration is critical to your long-term success as an organized achiever.

Seven Simple Ways to Use Time More Efficiently

The following sections contain powerful efficiency tips to move you closer to your organizational goals.

Thinking outside the box

One of the latest buzz phrases (most of which I dismiss as blather) making the rounds in the business world is "thinking outside the box," which means changing your approach to problem solving by including possibilities outside your normal scope of thinking. In other words, being more creative.

In time management, however, the phrase "thinking outside the box" has some legitimate meaning. We all think of time in terms of blocks. The workday falls between 8:00 a.m. and 6:00 p.m. Lunch begins and ends somewhere between 11:00 and 2:00. Dinner is between 5:30 and 9:00 p.m., and bedtime is between 9:30 p.m. and midnight. There are some variations, but, for the most part, these are the "boxes" we use when we think of time.

Improving your mastery of time requires a change in that "boxed-in" thinking. I am a very early riser, getting up most mornings between 4:00 and 5:00 a.m. depending on what I have on my agenda. By 5:15 (sometimes earlier), I am making calls to Europe. At 5:00 a.m. on the east coast of the United States, the time is already 10:00 a.m. in London, and I can reasonably expect to reach the person I need. If I wait until 9:00 a.m. or later to call, the time is mid-afternoon in London and the chances of reaching my party have greatly diminished. I also take naps. They are scheduled into my day just like business meetings, and I am just as prompt with my nap taking as I am with any other task on my agenda. I don't feel the least bit guilty about my naps, even when I schedule them in the middle of what most people consider the business day, because I have retooled my thinking around getting the most use out of my day without the encumbrances of a 9:00 to 5:00 time block.

Freeing yourself from the blocks of time is a difficult discipline to master. If most people began their workdays at 4:30 a.m. and ended them at 9:30 p.m. as I often do, they would burn out in a matter of weeks. Most people would overload on work because they wouldn't adjust their thinking to incorporate relaxation time, and time to accomplish other, nonwork-related activities during their days. If they started work at 4:30 with phone calls and ended it at 9:30 p.m. with a business dinner, the workday would be 17 hours long. Scheduling a nap, some playtime, or some casual reading somewhere in the middle of that day would never occur to these people, because traditional thinking tells us that business hours are from 9:00 to 5:00, and that we should be working during those times. If you want to master the clock, you must begin thinking outside those boxes.

Knowing that time and space are relative

Einstein proved the concept of relativity, but his theories have nothing to do with the relativity of your time and space management. As part of your new thinking about time, you must also rework your approach to space. If you only conduct business in the office, never taking work home or never accepting a personal call while in the office, you severely limit yourself in terms of your time productivity.

Chairing several internal company meetings in my home, some before I shower and dress for the day, is a common occurrence for me. The attendees expect me to be dressed in a warm-up suit at 5:30 a.m., so my attire doesn't distract from the overall productivity of these meetings, nor does my appearance indicate that I have become a reclusive bohemian who doesn't shave or clip his fingernails. I have simply managed the clock and adapted the space around me in a way that accommodates my needs.

Adapting the space around you requires a great deal of discipline. Because a lot of my business surrounds sports and sporting events, I spend a great deal of time entertaining and conducting business meetings at sporting venues such as golf and tennis tournaments. Envisioning a day at the U.S. Open as work is difficult for some people, but in my business my time at the event is not only productive work time, it presents an opportunity to bring many disparate individuals together in a venue they all find appealing. Many of the deals our company is famous for were direct results of the environment in which we pitched the ideas.

A lot of people, including managers in our company, can't convert a sporting event or any other out-of-office activity into a business venue. They believe too much business in a social environment is disruptive or distracting, when, in fact, the conversations about business are usually more informal in those settings and the amount of information gained is greater than in traditional boardrooms. These managers come ever-so-close to closing a deal or pitching an idea, but pull back at the last minute, making statements like, "It wasn't the right place for that discussion," or "I thought it was better to revisit this issue when (the customer) was back in his office." That lack of closure stems from their concepts of space and time. The office, between office hours, is the proper place to close deals in their minds, and anything outside that environment is uncomfortable and distracting.

REMEMBER

Organized people can break out of that "work only in the workplace" mindset and use the space around them to maximize their available time. They understand the value of a relaxed atmosphere and the opportunities that present themselves in these settings, and they capitalize on those opportunities. If you truly want to master the clock and become more efficient and productive, you need to expand your thinking to take advantage of the space you are given.

McCORMACK MEMORIES

Talking shop outside the shop

Our business is full of deals that were closed because the ideas were formulated on a golf course or at center court during a championship tennis match — outside of the usual time and space of the business world.

One example of this kind of deal is a golf outing I hosted in South Carolina for a group of executives. Jack Frazee, Jr., now the chairman of PageNet and the former chairman of Centel, was in my group. As we enjoyed our day together on the links, we began discussing the seemingly dead years professional golfers experience between their peak performance on the PGA Tour and their ascension to the Senior PGA Tour. Jack and I both agreed that most golfers peak at around age 35, and then coast through their 40s until they are eligible for the senior tour.

This discussion continued through dinner and into the next day. Finally, I suggested that Jack consider sponsoring a 40-something golf tournament for those players who had great name recognition, but were having difficulty competing with their 20- and 30-year-old colleagues on the PGA Tour. He thought it was a wonderful idea, and the tournament soon became a reality with Centel and Amoco as the sponsors.

If that idea had been pitched around a conference table in a high-rise office building, I'm not sure that it would have ever seen the light of day. But because it came from a casual conversation between two golf partners, the tournament went from concept to reality faster than it would have under any other circumstances.

The worthless airline seat

Robert Allen, the former chairman of Delta Airlines, first introduced me to the term "unrecoverable asset," when he used it to describe an empty airline seat. "No matter what price we are charging for a seat on a flight," Allen said. "If the plane takes off and the seat is empty, the value of that seat drops to zero and it becomes an unrecoverable asset. Once that aircraft leaves the gate, the empty seat is gone forever, and we have no chance of getting a penny for it."

I have never forgotten this point. Allen recognized the obvious and summed it up in terms everyone could understand. The value of an airline seat is directly related to the likelihood of having someone sit in it. Whether the price is $1,000 or $1, the seat only has value if it is occupied. After takeoff, the chance for payment is gone forever.

Organized people view time in the same way that Allen viewed his seats. Every second has a value. If that second is wasted, the value placed on that second is unrecoverable. Once gone, a second is lost forever.

Remembering that a minute passed is gone forever

World-renowned physicist and author Stephen Hawking theorizes that time will reverse when the universe ceases to expand. According to his theory, the lamp you broke last year will reassemble itself when space stops growing. This, of course, will immediately precede the universe imploding in a massive meltdown that will make the Big Bang look like a cheap firecracker — so don't expect to make up for lost time when that day finally rolls around.

Dr. Hawking's theories aside, lost or wasted time today can't be recovered. Time is an unrecoverable asset, gone forever the moment it passes. Once a second is behind you, it cannot be replicated, recaptured, or returned.

Spending the majority of your time doing things only you can do

Successful people understand that time is precious and, therefore, do not spend it idly. They also maximize their time by following one simple rule: Spend the majority of your time doing things only you can do.

For example, any of our senior-level executives can handle the travel problems of one of our clients. If Joe Montana is scheduled to appear at a function in New York but is having trouble getting a flight out of San Francisco, I don't need to get involved. In fact, my involvement would only slow the process down and would be a monumental waste of my time. However, because of the relationships I have established over the years and the importance of the business, I personally meet with the Wimbledon Committee a number of times a year to discuss our ongoing marketing and representational arrangements. Only I can meet with this committee, which makes the meeting a valid and productive use of my time.

Only Picasso could paint a Picasso, and only you can do certain things in your life. After you identify those things, spend most of your time focusing on them, and you will be amazed at how productive and organized you become.

Living by the two-minute drill

One of the best ways to put time into its proper perspective is to take on every task as if you have a short deadline. The analogy I like to use is the two-minute drill in American football, during which the offensive team is on the opposite end of the field and needs to drive the ball eighty or more yards with less than two minutes remaining in the game. The skilled quarterback then throws a series of quick passes, and the receivers quickly step out of bounds to stop the clock. Linemen run to their positions, and nobody waits for a huddle.

As improbable as the odds of driving the length of a football field in under two minutes may seem, good football teams accomplish the feat with such regularity that the two-minute drill has become a common part of the game. Approaching many of your daily tasks with that same two-minute-drill mindset, and expecting nothing short of a touchdown does wonders for your time sensitivity and organizational skills.

Here are some ideas on how to start your personal two-minute drill:

- **Make yourself the quarterback.** Call your own plays and control how you spend your time. Whenever someone asks for your help, or simply calls to chat, ask how long the activity will take. If it is longer than the time you want to devote, negotiate a better time for the conversation, meeting, or task.

- **Go for the short pass, not the long bomb.** As any good quarterback will tell you, short, high-percentage passes, executed quickly and efficiently, win more games in the final two minutes than twice as many long bombs down the field. If you approach your tasks with that same short, quick mindset, you will be amazed at how much you can accomplish in a relatively short period of time.

- **It doesn't have to be pretty.** A touchdown is a touchdown no matter how ugly the process is. The processes you implement don't have to be pretty. All they need to do is work.

⌐ **Everybody must know the drill.** The two-minute drill only works in football when everyone on the offensive team understands the approach, knows the objective, and works in concert to reach the goal line in under two minutes. In your world, very few people know your rules, your goals, or your strategies for scoring your personal touchdown. If you are to successfully reach your goal line, you must communicate your objectives to others around you and rally them to your side.

Conserving your (and everyone else's) time

Now that you understand the importance of every second, adjust your behavior so you don't waste your own time or disrespect others by wasting theirs. Nothing is more irritating than having a friend or acquaintance interrupt you when the person knows that you are busy and do not want to be disturbed. In addition to being rude, the interruption is profoundly disrespectful. The person knows that you only have 1,440 minutes in a day, and yet still barges in, disrupting your concentration and stealing precious minutes from you. The action is no different than picking your pocket or robbing your cash drawer. In fact, it's worse. Your wallet could be recovered. Stolen time is gone forever.

McCORMACK MEMORIES

Ted and the two-minute drill

One master of the two-minute drill mindset is Ted Turner, founder of Turner Communications and now vice-chairman of Time/Warner, Inc. Turner began his career in the billboard business, but soon acquired a fledgling Atlanta television station and began the process of building a communications empire including CNN, TNT, TBS, and Castle Rock Productions.

Turner's enthusiasm and leadership practices soon became legendary. When he acquired a new broadcast outlet, the two-minute drill started. In the first months of operation, he worked 18 to 20 hours a day, rallying his sales teams around the projects. In the case of CNN, Turner created the world's first 24-hour news network on a tenth of the budget the networks were spending to produce one half-hour newscast a day. Turner was able to accomplish these amazing business feats because of his aggressive, time-sensitive approach to every project. He spent 20 years running an endless stream of two-minute drills.

He also burned out more than his share of executives in the process, and was resoundingly criticized for what many perceived as unorthodox, even wacky business practices. Arguing with his success, however, is difficult. His successes weren't always pretty, and didn't always win him the admiration of his peers, but Turner scored his personal touchdowns nonetheless.

Some behavioral adjustments you can make to improve your own time management as well as the respect you show for others include

- **Start every conversation by asking, "Is this a good time?"** Doing so shows you care about the other person's commitments and schedule. No matter how important your topic, this gentle courtesy goes a long way toward earning you greater respect from those you meet.

- **Volunteer a time limit.** Our company has over 2,000 employees in 70 offices around the world so there is no way I can meet every man and woman in our organization. However, I am a lot more inclined to schedule a meeting with someone who says, "Mr. McCormack, I need ten minutes of your time at your convenience to discuss one of our upcoming projects," than I am an employee who says, "I would like to chat with you about some ideas I have for the company." The first is time- and task-specific, and I almost always make time for that kind of thoughtful request. The second request scares me because it is open-ended in both subject and time.

- **Don't hesitate to ask for an agenda.** When someone calls or wants to schedule a meeting with me, the first two questions I ask are, "How long do you need?" and "What is the subject of our meeting?" These questions might seem rude, especially if the person only wants to get together to reminisce about old times, but I earn a great deal of respect (even from family members!) if I make this a preamble to all my discussions.

- **Stick to the committed time.** If someone grants you ten minutes, stick to the time limit. If you give someone ten minutes, end the discussion on time. People respect you for honoring their time, and will grant you the same courtesy.

Preparing yourself for meetings

Arriving unprepared for a business meeting is worse than missing the meeting all together. Not appearing leaves everyone wondering if you are inept; showing up unprepared removes all doubt. In fact, a direct correlation exists between your effectiveness in a meeting and the amount of advance work you do in preparation for the meeting. If you are prepared before you walk into a meeting, you know the salient points before anyone speaks and have enough background information to keep up without asking any unnecessary questions.

This prepartion keeps the meeting moving and keeps everyone focused on the subjects at hand. Too often, an unprepared meeting participant can drag a meeting into a time-consuming rap session simply because she showed up unprepared. Avoid those meetings if possible, and never be the guilty time-bandit (see Chapter 14) who steals everyone's precious minutes because you didn't do your homework.

Recognizing that the difference is in the details

I can always spot someone who has done her homework, even in a one-sided meeting such as a sales presentation or a speech. The prepared person listens attentively, but confidently, jotting down notes at important points throughout the meeting. When the time arrives for questions, she isn't too eager, but asks detailed and specific questions (usually some of the toughest to answer) with a quiet confidence that shows her genuine interest in the answer.

Sometimes the differences in being prepared and unprepared can be so subtle and obscure that most people miss the nuances altogether. A friend of mine, who has been in the resort and hotel development business for many years, is fanatical about his preparation before venturing into a meeting. His preparation has paid off many times over the years, but none more so than at a recent meeting with the Phoenix, Arizona, City Council to discuss zoning and permits for a new resort he hoped to build in the area.

Because of Phoenix's accelerated growth — particularly in resorts — over the past two decades, many in city government were leery of allowing new developers into their midst. My friend knew of the council's reticence (because he had done his homework), and also knew which council members were pro-development and which were going to be hard sells. During his first trip to Phoenix, he focused on the hard sells, inviting the councilmen to show him around town.

"There's nothing a politician loves more than to show off his district," my friend said. "So I rode along as a passenger with these councilmen as they pointed out other developments they claimed had destroyed the landscape or encroached on natural areas. Of course, I knew what was coming, because I had researched their voting records on all previous developments. When we got to a development that I knew had received unanimous approval and praise from every council member, I piped up and said, 'Wow, now there's the kind of development I'd like to build on my site.' Nothing else had to be said. We were unanimously approved that evening."

Indeed, nothing else need be said.

Too many people attend meetings just to be seen or to discuss subjects on which they have no business commenting. The result is a waste of precious time and a diminished reputation for the unprepared attendee.

Letting the other party know that you're prepared

There are always subtle cues to let someone know how much research you have done before a meeting. In the old days — when I practiced law and negotiated contracts on behalf of clients — I would get the name of the attorney on the other side of the table a few days before our first meeting so I could research her background in *The Martindale-Hubbell Law Directory* (a legal publication that gives the backgrounds of all licensed attorneys).

The background information gave me a bit of a tactical upper hand. If, for example, I saw in *Martindale-Hubbell* that counsel for the other side went to undergraduate school at the University of North Carolina, I might make an off-handed comment about the city of Chapel Hill, or the school's recent basketball record. Or, if I read that the attorney grew up in St. Louis, I might mention the Cardinals recent winning streak. All these comments sent a subtle, yet unmistakable, message to the other attorneys: Don't try to slip anything past me; I've done my homework.

My training as an attorney also helped me solidify the importance of letting others know just how prepared I am. One of the first things I learned in law school was never to ask a question in court if I didn't already know the answer. Contrary to countless television courtroom dramas, surprises are the bane of a lawyer's existence. Knowing the answers before the questions are asked is crucial for an attorney, but equally important is letting everyone else know that you know the answers. You control the tempo and direction of the discussion. Allowing others to know that you are an insider also keeps everything above board, it keeps everyone honest, and, above all, it ensures that you remain in control.

Asking the next question

No more important question exists than the follow-up question. Asking one additional question on a topic — even if you only ask yourself — opens more doors and gleans more information than simply resting after obtaining your first answer.

How one last question saved the day

One of our salespeople learned a valuable lesson, quite by accident, when he called on a potential sponsor for a golf event we were proposing. After going through his presentation and making every possible pitch he could think of to win this sponsor's business, the executive simply said, "No thanks. That was a great presentation, but I don't think that kind of event is right for us."

The salesman was dutifully packing up his briefcase when another question dawned on him, one that couldn't possibly hurt. "Just out of curiosity, do you play golf?" he asked the executive.

"No, I don't," he said. "Actually, I race yachts, so if the weather's pretty enough to be out on the golf course, I'm always sailing."

In the course of the next 20 seconds, our salesman retooled his presentation and sold the customer a sponsorship in one of the many regattas we own and manage. The relationship has continued for years, and the sponsor couldn't be happier.

Like him or hate him, Sam Donaldson of ABC News is a master at the follow-up. In fact, when Donaldson covered the White House his standard follow-up always began, "With all due respect, Mr. President . . .," which was his polite way of saying, "The answer you just gave was lame, so here comes a doozie of a follow-up." The tactic didn't win Donaldson many friends, but earned him great respect as a journalist.

You would be well-served to employ Sam Donaldson's tactics (with a little softer bedside manner) in your business and personal life. Never resting on a single answer, and always being prepared with a follow up, leads you down paths you would have otherwise never considered.

Scheduling in advance to show respect and a level of importance

I never make a trip without scheduling more than one meeting. Even if the trip is for one day and scheduled on short notice, I do my best to maximize my time by meeting with more than one person. Recently, I flew from New York to Atlanta on short notice for a round of golf with Arnold Palmer and Atlanta developer Tom Cousins at the East Lake Golf Club. The trip was quick and set up on short notice, but I still met an associate for breakfast at the airport before venturing to the course. After the round, I attended another quick meeting in the car as I was riding from the golf course back to the airport. One day and a quick trip, but I conducted two very productive meetings around the golf.

The longer I give myself to plan, the more likely I am to schedule several important meetings. If, for example, I know I will be in London five months from now, I might try today to schedule an important meeting for that time. I know very few executives who have completely booked schedules five months out, so the likelihood of getting an audience with the person I want to see is pretty good.

Scheduling a meeting four or five months in advance is also impressive to the person you are contacting. The meeting takes on a new level of importance when someone knows you have gone to that kind of effort. Even if you are making a trip to her city anyway, having something on the books months in advance carries much more weight than an, "Oh by the way, I'm coming to town next week, do you want to meet?"

Of course, anytime you book that far in advance, you run the risk of circumstances changing between the time you schedule and the time you actually meet. Still, if you are making the trip anyway, you have lost very little by setting up a meeting far in advance. You will be surprised how many of these advance relationships work out for the best.

Chapter 14

Beware the Time Bandits

. . . .

In This Chapter

▶ Identify the people who steal your precious time

▶ Be aware of their methods to rob you

▶ Attack them or avoid them, but do whatever you must to stop them

. . . .

Time bandits are those thieves who rob you of your time by making you wait for meetings or phone calls, or who make you work three times as hard in order to get in touch with them. They are everywhere — in your office, home, and neighborhood — stealing your minutes, hours, and even days, and corrupting your schedule to suit their whims. You know them. They could include a client, a boss, an invaluable and talented employee, a neighbor, a friend, a spouse, or even a child, and they don't, necessarily, resemble the diminutive thieves from Terry Gilliam's film of the same name. Regardless of who comprises your group of time bandits, however, you must deal with them if you are to regain control of your schedule.

Recognizing Subversive Time Bandits

Time bandits can't be identified on sight. They don't have distinguishing markings, and they refuse to wear distinctive colors or tattoos so we can recognize and avoid them. Even if they did stand out, however, ignoring or disassociating yourself from those individuals bent on robbing you of your time is often impossible. Clients are still clients, even after you realize that some of them are also time bandits. The same goes for co-workers (especially if they rank higher in the organizational structure than you), family members, and even some employees.

Seeing Through the Lies of Time Bandits

In addition to robbing you, time bandits also lie to you, even if they don't realize that they are being untruthful. Some of the most egregious tall tales of time bandits include

- **"Sorry I'm late."** No, she's not sorry. If she were truly sorry she wouldn't have been late in the first place, and she certainly would not make arriving late a habit, which all time bandits do.

- **"I don't know what happened. I'm never late."** This statement means that he is always late. In his mind, this occasion might be an isolated event, but in reality the time bandit is consistently late for every meeting, call, and activity on his schedule.

- **"I've been meaning to get back with you."** But she hasn't done so, which either means that you fall somewhere below the dry cleaner and the dog groomer on her priority list, or she had no intention of ever getting back with you. This lie is exceptional, because both the liar and the liee know that the statement is an untruth. Sometimes the time bandit chuckles when she says it, as if laughing about the lie makes it more palatable.

- **"I'll call you right back."** This quote is more of a tic than a lie. If calling you back immediately is in the time bandit's best interest, he will no doubt do so. If not, don't expect to hear from him anytime soon.

- **"I hope I'm not too late."** This comment is usually reserved for social functions where the time bandit is so late that not even she can ignore the faux pas she has created.

- **"Can I have a minute? This won't take long."** Oh yes it will. If you agree, you're in for a much longer engagement than you expect.

- **"I've been giving it a lot of thought."** This statement is code for "I completely forgot about whatever it is you asked me to do until this very moment, and now I'm scrambling for a good answer."

- **"I've been terribly busy."** Maybe, but "being busy" is still no excuse for not calling someone back or providing a timely update on whatever projects remain outstanding.

- **"You can count on me."** If he has to say this out loud, watch out. Uttering this phrase is a little like saying "trust me." Trust should be implied. If not, something is wrong.

- **"I won't be long."** There is an air of doom around those words. Whether a spouse makes this comment while adjourning into a favorite store, or a child informs you of this while discussing his evening plans, this lie has an implied insincerity. Expect the time bandit to be a very long time indeed.

McCORMACK MEMORIES

The bandit mother

One of the most notorious time bandits we deal with on a regular basis is the mother of one of our more famous clients. Invariably, she calls one or more of our senior people and says "I just need to speak to you for a moment about an upcoming event." Her request seems innocent enough, so the executive in question usually takes the call.

The conversation always jumps from the innocent subject the mother put forth as a pretext to another (and in her mind, more pressing) topic entirely. I have warned our people about this strategy, but my warnings have had little effect. She still calls, still puts forth the same innocuous pretenses, and then launches into a diatribe on whatever subject is really on her mind.

The situation is a delicate one because of the relationship we have with our client, but hopefully our executives are no longer surprised by this little subterfuge.

Uncovering the Traps of Time Bandits

If you understand time bandits' proclivities, you can avoid many of their traps.

- **No project assigned to the time bandit will be completed on time, no matter what she says.** If a project is on time, it will be half completed — a terrible scenario for you, because you have to make up the difference. A time bandit of this magnitude can be a real career-killer, because she expects you to do the work of two people.

- **The time bandit doesn't discriminate about whom he keeps waiting.** Sometimes a meeting can go ahead as planned with or without the time bandit, but other times require his presence. If the person who is waiting for the time bandit with you is important to your business or your career, you could be in just as much trouble as the time bandit. Avoiding situations where a meeting with an important client hinges on someone who is notoriously late is always a good idea.

- **Time bandits take optimistic scheduling to new heights.** Just look at their schedules. Even under perfect conditions, time bandits never budget enough time for the projects on their agendas (see Chapter 19). The greatest logistics experts in history couldn't do many of the things the time bandits regularly assume that they can complete in a day. These schedules aren't necessarily based on lies; time bandits may be simply delusional when deciding what they can accomplish.

- **Admonitions don't work.** You can threaten, cajole, even beg the time bandit, and she will still disappoint you. As long as you know what you're dealing with upfront, you can enter the relationship forewarned and forearmed.

Dealing Effectively with Time Bandits

The best way to deal with time bandits is to stay far, far away. Unfortunately, that course of action is sometimes impossible. If you're married to a time bandit, you must work around the idiosyncrasies and develop a strategy for getting along. If you work for a time bandit, you could be in for a rough career stretch, but you can find ways to make life more palatable even when your time is being robbed. The same holds true for a time bandit neighbor, friend, or invaluable employee.

You can't change the fact that these people are time bandits, but you can do some things to minimize the damage they inflict upon you.

✔ **Understand the motivation.** Sometimes, being on time is simply not in someone's nature. Other times, people use consistent tardiness as a passive-aggressive power play. If you are stuck waiting, the other person is in control, even for the few fleeting minutes before he arrives. If you deal with someone motivated by a need for power and control, knowing that motivation upfront is good. If you deal with someone who is simply too scatterbrained to arrive on time, you need to know that as well.

✔ **Don't succumb to their schedules.** If you have a one-hour meeting with a time bandit beginning at 10:00 a.m. and she arrives 40 minutes late, do you stick to your original schedule and cut the meeting short, or do you succumb to her schedule and push other items on your agenda back to accommodate her tardiness? If you are guilty of the latter, you are a victim of your own making.

✔ **Don't expect the unreasonable.** If you expect the time bandit to be late 100 percent of the time, you are never disappointed. Sometimes, expecting the worst means relying on others rather than putting your trust solely in the bandit. Doing so is preferable to being left out in the cold because you believed that the time bandit might come through once in his life.

✔ **Close the doors.** An airliner takes off whether the time bandit is on board or not. When a play or concert begins, the ushers close the doors of the theater. Scheduling yourself in a similar manner can serve you well. If a time bandit is late for a group meeting, shut the door and forbid her from entering. If she is late for a trip, leave her. If she is incapable of responding to your requests, go elsewhere for the information. Usually, the best way to get the time bandit's attention is to shut her out. Locking her out might not change her conduct, but it will at least heighten her awareness of the behaviors you consider acceptable.

✔ **Ask for an explanation.** Put the time bandit on the hot seat by demanding a detailed explanation for his tardiness. When forced to give his reasons out loud (especially in front a group), even he might see how silly and irresponsible being late is.

Time bandits will always be among us. But, if you learn to identify them and adjust your expectations, you can coexist with this group without letting them disrupt your own organizational goals.

Chapter 15

Mastering the Fine Art of Saying "No"

. . . .

In This Chapter

▶ Taking the pain out of saying "no"

▶ Deciding when turning someone down is appropriate

▶ Knowing how and how often to say "no"

▶ Understanding why you should probably say "no" more often

. . . .

*U*nfortunately, a lot of people break into hives at the thought of having to actually say "no" to someone. In some ways this reaction is understandable. People want to be accommodating and liked, and, because they know how being disappointed feels, they want to spare everyone else those same feelings.

Although wanting to protect others from negative feelings is admirable, it is also impossible. No one can say "yes" to every request (or even to half the requests) and adequately follow through with every single commitment. Too many people are bidding for your time. If you try to accommodate everyone, you end up pleasing no one and you lose control of your time, space, and personal agenda.

In this chapter, I help you understand why you have to say "no," and then give you step-by-step methods for saying "no" — even when you feel pressured to say "yes."

Why You Have to Say "No"

Why do you have to say "no"? The simplest answer is because saying "yes" all the time is impossible. But even more important than your own sanity, not giving someone a firm answer — even if that answer is "no" — is unfair and deceitful. Even though you may have the person's feelings in mind when you say something like, "Gee, I don't know. Maybe some other time," what you really do is set the person up for future rejection and simply prolonging the process, wasting both her and your time.

The best example of this type of slow letdown is a woman who is asked out on a date by a man she is not interested in. Rather than turn him down outright, she says something like, "I can't tonight. Maybe some other time." When the man asks a second time, another excuse is proffered, and so on. When the lady finally tells the man she isn't interested in dating him, the blow is much harder than if she had simply said "no" the first time he asked so both of them could get on with their lives.

Of course, at some point, everyone has said "yes" when "no" was the more appropriate response. The results in those situations are always the same: You kick yourself for having committed to a task you really didn't want to do; you dread it from the moment you say "yes" until you finally get it done; you try to come up with any conceivable reason to back out; and, even when you follow through with your commitment, your heart isn't in it. In short, you wish you had stopped the entire process by simply saying "no" when you had the chance.

No one is beyond making a stupid commitment in a weak moment. In our business, we see this fear of refusing others all the time. Most of our clients are good-hearted people who have spent their lives trying to please others, so saying "no" is hard for most of them to do. They hire us to say "no" for them. Hall of Fame golfer Nancy Lopez makes no bones about this reason. She has openly said that she hired IMG when she first turned professional because she needed someone to say "no" to literally thousands of requests. Being a wonderfully accommodating person, Nancy did not want to be known as someone who turned people down, so she hired our company to do it for her. That motive has been the case with a number of our clients. After they are with us for a while, they appreciate all the other things we do for them, but when they originally sign on, they usually do so because we say "no" for them without ruffling too many feathers.

"No" is one of the easiest words in the English language to utter, and one of the first words we learn as children (just ask the parents of any two-year-old). Only when we become adults do we learn to fear the word "no." If you want to become more organized and improve your results in business and at home, you need to overcome your fear and reacquaint yourself with the word "no."

Different Kinds of "No"

Not all "no's" are heartbreaking turndowns. There are varying degrees of this negative adverb, and different uses — some easy and others not so easy.

Before you can become adept at saying "no" without going into apoplectic seizures, you need to understand how to apply these varying definitions.

- **"No" to a question of fact is easy.** If someone asks you whether it's raining, you look out the window, say "no," and the exchange is finished. The answer involves no anxiety, pressure, or hesitation. Because you are answering a question of fact, you're being helpful by saying "no." The person who asked the question now has an answer, and everyone can move along in a more enlightened state. That kind of "no" is always easy because it doesn't commit you to anything, either positively or negatively. You simply answered a question.

- **Sometimes "no" is expected before the question is asked.** "Mom, may I drive the Mercedes to the beach with my friends?" The question is so outrageous that a positive response would likely send the questioner into a state of shock. Sometimes questions are asked just for the one-in-a-trillion chance that the person being asked will go temporarily insane and grant the request. Sometimes a positive response does happen. When our client David Duval began a winning streak unlike any seen in professional golf since Jack Nicklaus, we were deluged with requests for David to be interviewed for magazines, newspapers, and television. Of course, we had to turn down most of the requests. Had David granted a fraction of the interviews he was asked to do, he would never have had time to hit another golf ball. Still, we presented most of the requests to our client (which is our duty as his agent) along with our recommendations. When *Surfer* magazine requested some time with him, David's agent almost laughed. Imagine his shock when David turned down numerous international publications, but said "yes" to the *Surfer* magazine request. That magazine's request was a one-in-a-million shot, but in that instance it paid off. Most of the time, however, saying "no" to those kinds of requests is easy, because it is expected.

- **Turning down an earnest request is the toughest "no" of all.** This is the "no" that causes the most pain and anxiety. Our clients are approached all the time by their friends or people with whom they have good relationships, all of whom want a little of the clients' time. Saying "no" is hard for them. The people making the requests are usually well-meaning, good-hearted people who often have worthy causes they want our clients to support by making appearances. As compelling as some of these requests are, our clients cannot be everywhere. Tiger Woods, for example, is one of the most sought-after athletes on the planet, because he is such a great golfer and charismatic figure. But because golf makes him a celebrity, he must spend the majority of his time working on his game. Not that he won't appear at a charity ball or a photo shoot, but he certainly won't appear at every worthy event where his presence has been requested. He can't. Unfortunately, some people take this sort of rejection personally — as if Arnold Palmer turning down a request to attend a golf benefit for disabled veterans somehow means that Arnold doesn't care about the plight of the disabled. Thankfully, that sort of thinking is rare, but it still creates problems, especially with people who have a predisposition to say "yes" when they don't really mean it.

When to Say "No"

The best answer to the question of when you should say "no" is "often." Of course, you can't turn down every request, nor should you. If someone calls you and says, "I have two front-row 50-yard-line tickets to the Super Bowl, would you like to go?" the answer is probably a resounding "yes." But if the question is, "Would you be interested in attending a $100-a-plate dinner to raise funds for Barbershop Quartets of America?", unless you are a big fan of barbershop quartets, you don't need to hedge with a "maybe," or a "let me think about it." The answer is an unequivocal "no."

If you have anxiety about saying "no," ask yourself a few basic questions when presented with a request:

- ✔ **Am I capable and qualified to do what's being asked of me?** If you're asked to join a group in climbing Mt. McKinley and you have trouble climbing the stairs in your home, the answer is "no." You aren't qualified or capable to do what is being asked, and to assume otherwise could be dangerous. That example is an easy one, though. What if you are asked to speak in front a group of 300 professional people on a subject about which you only have a vague knowledge? You may want to say "no," but if the person making the request is persuasive enough, you might acquiesce. Although no one's life is in danger, agreeing to this request is just as foolish as the Mt. McKinley example. Unless you are a professional speaker or you have such a firm grasp of your subject matter that you can speak to an auditorium full of people without any egregious gaffs, you are neither capable nor qualified to make such a presentation. Unless you want to embarrass yourself, the proper answer to that request is "no."

- ✔ **Do I have time for this task or activitiy ?** No matter how attractive or flattering a request is or how noble a cause you are asked to support, most requests require that you devote your time. Even if the request is nothing more than for you to think about something in the future, a time commitment is still involved on your part. If your gut tells you to say "no" because of time constraints, you should probably listen to your instincts. People in our company face these circumstances all the time. In one week I might be asked to be the guest of honor at a dinner being held at the U.S. Open golf championship, attend the NBA Finals, play golf at Pine Valley Golf Club, and take in a Yankees home game with the mayor of New York. Unfortunately, I would have to turn all those requests down if the week in question falls during the opening matches at Wimbledon where my presence is required. My priority is the long-term relationship I have with Wimbledon. You have no doubt been faced with similar choices. How you responded could be an indicator of how successful you will be at saying "no" in the future.

✔ **Do I want to do this activity?** Selfish personal desire is not always a bad thing, especially when someone else requests your time. If you are asked to do something you do not particularly want to do, you have to gauge the other benefits you will receive. If a dentist says, "You need to stay a little longer, we have some cavities we need to fill," your first inclination is to say, "no thanks." Of course you don't want to get your teeth filled — nobody does — but the alternative is to put off a relatively simple procedure for what could become a longer, more painful, and more costly one. In that instance, you should say "yes," even though you want to say "no." Other situations aren't that easy. If I am asked, "Do you want to go the mall and shop?" I can't say "no" fast enough. Even if I have nothing else to do and the request is reasonable, I would rather stick myself with thumbtacks than stroll aimlessly through a mall. I don't want to do it, and unless a compelling reason changes my mind, I almost always turn down that request.

✔ **What are the ramifications of saying "no?"** If you turn down a friend's request to accompany him to a baseball game, will he cease to be your friend? Obviously not, but people's assumptions are sometimes that outrageous when imagining the ramifications they might suffer when they say "no." I am constantly confronted with clients or employees who have committed to things they desperately want to get out of. When I ask these people why they committed in the first place, the response is always the same: "I didn't want to hurt person X's feelings." Instead, they would rather commit first and cancel later, thus putting person X in an even greater bind. Turning down a request does not mean that you are personally rejecting someone and, therefore, banishing him from your life. Just as you have been turned down on many occasions without any ill will, the person making the request has certainly done his share of saying "no" as well.

After you answer all of these questions, you may find saying "no" a lot easier than you thought it would be.

How to Say "No"

Try this exercise: Place two fingers of each hand on the corners of your mouth and push your lips into a slight pucker. From that position you can say "no" very easily, but you can't say "yes." Try it. You sound foolish when you say "yes," and look even worse.

Of course, if saying "no" were always that easy, we would all be walking around with our hands on our faces. The word "no" has become so reviled in our language that people have now come up with a seemingly endless array of kinder, gentler replacements for the monosyllabic negative.

Some of the more common ways that you can say "no" — without actually saying "no" — include

- ✔ **"I'm sorry, I simply can't right now."** This replacement is a good one. Opening with an apology is a wonderfully disarming tactic that takes away confrontation and softens the turndown by letting the person hear you say that you're sorry (no matter how disingenuous your sorrow might be). The statement is also framed to imply that your inability to comply is based on far-reaching circumstances well beyond your control. "I simply can't right now," is an almost helpless plea akin to saying, "I would love nothing more than to accommodate you, but the world is aligned against me and I can't break away." How could anyone not accept that?

- ✔ **"I'm going to have to pass on that one."** This turndown is a little more forceful, but still softer than simply saying "no." Taking a pass is also something most people understand, because we all pass up opportunities, both good and bad. The phrase also connotes deferral. By passing, you are deferring the option to someone else, or until another time. This is a simple word play, but can help temper the act of rejecting someone, even if the person you are rejecting plays the same game and understands exactly what you are doing.

- ✔ **"Thanks for asking, but I'll be unable to help you."** Arguing with that response is difficult. In addition to being reasonably forceful in your turndown, you've also thanked the person for thinking of you while reminding her that she was the one requesting your help. Although this response is unambiguous, it still leaves the rejected person with a good feeling.

- ✔ **"Someone else could help you more than I can."** You have to be careful with this answer. It invites the person requesting your time to heap glowing praise on you, telling you how no one could possibly be as wonderful at whatever he is asking than you are. Unless the person you are dealing with understands that this response constitutes a turndown, you might be in for a more engaging exchange than you bargained for.

- ✔ **"Maybe later."** Again, saying this can cause problems. By inviting someone to make a similar request sometime in the future, you have to be prepared for her to take you up on it. Unless the person you are speaking with recognizes that this answer as a turndown, you might be setting yourself up for future headaches. Saying "no" and getting the rejection out of the way is a better course of action.

Persistence Pains

I always preach to my staff that persistence pays when meeting with someone or selling a product or service. If nothing else, you eventually wear the person down to a point where they agree to meet you just so you won't call any more. This philosophy is wonderful if you are on the selling end, but can be a pain if you are on the receiving end of a persistent caller.

At a certain time, you simply have to say "no" to these people. You can try the other answers, but the most persistent people continue calling until you put your answer in terms they cannot misconstrue. A firm "no" is about as unambiguous as you can get. Learn to say this word, and you will be a lot happier.

Chapter 16
Scheduling Your Time

- -

- -

Schedules are a bit like budget projections: In the end, they are educated guesses. A schedule is a road map — a well-intentioned, practical prediction of future events. Like all predictions, a schedule isn't perfect, nor should anyone expect it to be. Schedules are best-guess scenarios. You can, however, hone certain skills to improve your accuracy and to make your guesses the best they can be.

Taking a Scheduling Test

In order to effectively manage your schedule, you have to know how quickly you can complete certain tasks and how effectively you control the time you have at your disposal. This test can help you gain a better awareness of scheduling.

1. **Do you know exactly how long showering and dressing takes you?**

2. **Do you know what time you have to wake up next Friday?**

3. **Have you added start and finish times to all the items on your things-to-do list for tomorrow?**

4. **Have you given yourself a buffer zone of time in your schedule today in case things don't work out as planned?**

5. **Will you arrive at work before anyone else in your office any day this week?**

6. **Have you combined any tasks on your schedule this week?**

7. Have you added any items to your schedule that won't require action for several weeks or even months?

8. Do you take open-ended phone calls at any time throughout the day?

9. Have you ever left your schedule in your office without missing it?

10. Would your family members be surprised if you committed your evening dinner plans to writing?

For questions 1-7, give yourself a point for every "yes" and for questions 8-10 give yourself a point for every "no. If you scored

- ✔ **8 to 10:** You have a good grasp of scheduling and should continue to hone your skills through practice.

- ✔ **6 to 7:** You're trying to be organized, but you need to focus on the specifics of scheduling and break your old habits.

- ✔ **Under 6:** You're unscheduled and disorganized. Make a change immediately if you want to improve your life.

Changing the way you schedule your days can dramatically impact your overall organization and your peace of mind. Come back and take this test a few more times as you continue to work on your scheduling skills. A few weeks of training can make all the difference.

Making a Schedule versus Making a To-Do List

A *schedule* is a list with an established time frame for each item. As simple as that definition sounds, the meaning escapes a lot of people. For example, many people look at their things-to-do list and assume that heir days are scheduled, which is far from the truth. For example, the to-do list might say:

- ✔ Take the kids to school
- ✔ Buy dog food
- ✔ Meet with office staff on Project X
- ✔ Meet Jack at club for lunch
- ✔ Call Jim to reschedule Thursday's meeting
- ✔ Finish proposal for Linda
- ✔ Pack for trip
- ✔ Go to Jenny's soccer game

Many people look at this list and assume that the items comprise a schedule, even though the list has no structure and no specific times for accomplishing each task. Still, the disorganized person rests comfortably in the assumption that such a list is all he needs to order his day. As a result, he wakes up late, rushes the kids to school, buys dog food at a convenience store for twice the price he would have paid at his regular grocer, and arrives late for his lunch meeting with Jack. The office staff can't be assembled for a meeting on Project X, and Jim's secretary said that he would be out of the office all afternoon. By the time this person gets around to Linda's proposal, he is already late for Jenny's soccer game. Now he must choose between either putting Linda off (and perhaps alienating a colleague) or arriving late for Jenny's soccer game (and breaking his daughter's heart). By the time he gets around to packing, the time is after midnight and his day is in shambles.

A schedule, on the other hand, looks like this:

6:00–6:45	Wake up, shower, and dress.
6:45–7:15	Read paper and eat breakfast.
7:15–7:45	Drive kids to school.
7:45–8:30	Pick up dog food at grocer. Drive to office. Call Jim from car to reschedule Thursday meeting to next Wednesday between 3:00 and 5:00.
8:30–10:30	Attend meeting with staff on Project X. Get timeline and task delineation achieved at this meeting.
10:30–12:00	Handle mail, and dictate letters to Joe, Brenda, and Ian.
12:00–1:30	Attend lunch meeting with Jack at club to discuss Widget contract.
1:30–4:30	Finish proposal for Linda.
4:30–5:30	Return calls.
5:30–6:00	Drive to Jenny's soccer game.
6:00–7:00	Watch soccer game.
7:00–8:30	Have dinner with family.
8:30–9:00	Pack for trip. Include:

> 4 pair black wool socks
>
> Black, gray, brown, and tan slacks
>
> White dress shirts
>
> Undergarments
>
> Three sweaters (blue, red, and white)
>
> Two casual shirts
>
> Warm up suit

Work-out clothes

Dress and casual shoes

Toiletries

Book (on nightstand)

Travel clock

The differences between a to-do list and a schedule are obvious. The preceding example is a schedule, complete with reasonable times to complete each assigned task. Although far superior to the list, even this schedule lacks the level of detail needed to be completely efficient. What are the talking points for the various meetings? What are the subjects that need to be covered in the letters to Joe, Brenda, and Ian? What dinner options present themselves to the family?

Still, this schedule's basic form combines a workable to-do list with the elements of time management. The schedule is realistic, achievable, and leaves little to chance. If your daily planner or organizational system doesn't put you on a time-sensitive schedule, upgrade to one that does.

Understanding the Three Types of Schedules

There are only three kinds of schedules, and I cover each in the three following sections. All schedules fall into one of the three categories, although, there are varying degrees of each schedule type. Whenever you look at a schedule, however, ask yourself which type of schedule it is, and then modify it accordingly.

Optimistic schedules

At some point, everyone overbooks an itinerary, assuming perfect or semi-perfect travel conditions, meetings that flow on time, prompt service, and good weather — none of which is controllable. As a result, the over-planner falls behind on her schedule, becomes frustrated, and allows her organization to fall into the hands of the hungry Huns waiting outside her door.

I am less likely to develop an optimistic schedule simply because I have learned how long accomplishing certain tasks requires and, so, I always schedule more time than needed. For example, my schedule may say, "Pack for trip to London between 6:30 and 7:00." I know that packing won't take 30 minutes because I have done it so many times I have the procedure down pat. Still, I want to leave myself enough time to accommodate the unexpected. If I am suddenly interrupted or if I can't find a certain item I need, I have built enough time into the schedule to handle these distractions without disrupting any future event. I'm not being a pessimist, but I'm not being unrealistically optimistic either.

McCORMACK MEMORIES

The 30-minute photo shoot and other fallacies

In February of 1999, as part of a speaking series, I visited India for the first time. While there, my staff wanted to leverage my time so I could engage in as many meetings and activities as possible in order to reinforce our company's presence and expertise in India. The first itinerary I received looked like this:

Day 1:

12:20 p.m.	Arrive in New Delhi.
3:15 p.m.	Photo shoot on the hotel rooftop.
3:45 p.m.	Leave for airport.
5:20 p.m.	Fly to Calcutta.
8:00 p.m.	Meet with ICC chairman at his residence.

Day 2:

7:00–9:05	Fly to Delhi.
10:00 a.m.	Meet with director of marketing for Coca-Cola.
11:00 a.m.	Meet with directors of LML.
Noon–3:00	Meet with managing director of Mahindra and Mahindra.
3:00 p.m.	Travel to Gurgaon.
4:00 p.m.	Meet with director of Seagram.

5:00 p.m.	Meet with marketing team of Pepsi-Cola.
6:30 p.m.	Meet with director of DLF.
8:30 p.m.	Attend Dinner meeting with director of Stracon.

The itinerary continued in this manner for six days. At one point, I had four interviews and meetings with the U.S. Ambassador and a group of business leaders scheduled before 10:30 in the morning. Not that I am opposed to hard work or to making the most out of an overseas trip, but this schedule was laughably unrealistic. Logistics alone made the schedule impossible. I simply could not travel to all the places I needed to travel, meet all the people I was scheduled to meet, and make any sort of impression on the business leaders in India. If I had tried to stick to this schedule, people would have been left waiting, and all the effort we were expending to send a positive message about our company would have been wasted.

In the end, I toned down the schedule, committing to about 75 percent of the items on the original itinerary. Everyone was happy, and the trip was a rousing success.

Pessimistic schedules

Equally as destructive as the optimistic schedule is the pessimistic schedule — the one that over-budgets time while under-budgeting performance. In an earlier example I scheduled 30 minutes to pack for a trip to London, even though I knew I could pack in under half an hour. I budgeted the extra time just to be on the safe side. The pessimistic scheduler, however, budgets an hour or more for the task, leaving herself a large chunk of unfilled time between packing for a trip and her next meeting or activity.

Pessimistic scheduling disrupts any rhythm the scheduler might develop throughout the day. Focusing and becoming energized by your productivity is difficult with large gaps of dead time scheduled into your day.

Imagine scheduling a trip to another city for two meetings, one in the morning and the other in the evening. With no other activities scheduled, you could sit in your hotel room and channel surf or wander the streets, but the likelihood of being sharp for both meetings is slim. Unless you have some other activities to keep you occupied, the dead time between the two meetings dulls your senses and makes you less productive than you would be if you had slated a full schedule of activities.

Realistic schedules

The real world of scheduling lies somewhere between the optimistic and pessimistic scenarios. Unfortunately, no standard exists for measuring what is realistic. Instead, become comfortable with the realism of your schedule through trial and error (mostly error).

The following tips can help you schedule realistically:

- **Log time for mundane activities.** Just because an activity isn't difficult does not mean that it isn't time-consuming. Packing, for example, can take anywhere from five minutes to half an hour depending on how organized you are and how much stuff you are taking with you. The only way to accurately schedule these types of activities is to time them and come up with an average you can use to comfortably predict the future.

- **Visualize the details.** Most scheduling problems occur because some element of detail has been overlooked in the planning stage. A trip to the store and the bank seems innocuous enough. But, without considering the travel time, the traffic, the items you need at the store, and the amount of banking you need to do, this simple errand can throw the rest of your day off if you don't schedule enough time. The best way to avoid that trap is to visualize the entire trip in advance — assume the worst in terms of the variables you can't control.

- ✔ **Combine activities.** Although considered rude if you are in the company of others, you can read the paper and eat breakfast at the same time. If you have a cell phone, you can call the office while traveling, or you can read important documents while sitting on an airplane. Many activities can be combined in a realistic schedule. When you're outlining your things to do, allow yourself the possibility that several items can be accomplished at the same time.

- ✔ **Put odd time restrictions on yourself.** Just like telling a colleague you will call him up at 10:58 puts an added burden on the person to be ready at precisely that time, giving yourself exactly 16 minutes to read and sort your mail forces you to concentrate on the task at hand and to be more attuned to the clock. This drill conditions you to think about every minute of your schedule.

- ✔ **Schedule everything.** Schedule every activity in your life, from getting up in the morning and showering to watching the evening news. Only when you include every activity in your schedule will you truly free yourself from the burdens of disorganization.

Improving Your Scheduling Abilities

By incorporating the following rules into your daily life, your schedule will immediately become more manageable, and you'll become more efficient and productive in no time.

Finding the most important hour

Everyday you have one critical hour: the one you spend planning your schedule for tomorrow and for the days ahead. That hour is the most important time you spend because it not only sets your agenda, it also gets you focused on the time each task will take and the long-term benefits of each activity you are likely to undertake in the next 24 hours. If you aren't taking that one hour to plan the next 23, you are likely wasting more time on things that have no relevance to your goals than the hour used to focus your agenda.

If you can't find an hour a day to focus on your upcoming schedule, save an hour in other areas:

- ✔ **Cut out one activity.** Consider omitting a meal or an hour of television. Henry Luce, the founder of Time, Inc. and a legend in the publishing world, was ahead of his time in this area. Luce hated eating out, and considered dining a perfunctory necessity. To him, food was simply fuel to keep the body going. Urban legend says that during one business luncheon (at one of New York's finer dining establishments), Luce became so engrossed in the conversation and the work he was accomplishing that he completely forgot he had eaten. After the dessert dishes and coffee cups were taken away, he turned to his lunch guest and said, "The service here is awfully slow. We've been here over an hour and haven't gotten the menus yet." The meal made absolutely no impression on Luce.

Many people forgo breakfast, lunch, or dinner in order to streamline their days and accomplish more during peak hours than if they stopped three times a day to eat. Skipping a meal may or may not be an option for you (depending on your metabolism and what you accomplish during your meals), but doing so certainly saves you an hour.

Time spent watching television can also be cut by an hour. Rarely is the information gleaned from television so valuable that it can't be cut by one hour a day. Your time can be better spent in other areas.

✔ **Steal an early hour.** If you cannot accomplish all your tasks during normal business hours, steal a few early morning hours. By arriving at the office at 7:00 a.m., rather than 8:30 or 9:00, you give yourself 90 minutes or more of pure, uninterrupted time during the most productive period of the day. Imagine how much more you could accomplish if you simply arrived a few hours before the phones start ringing and before chatty colleagues arrive. Now imagine how much better you will feel when you pack up at the end of the day having completed all the items on your schedule.

✔ **Never wrestle with a pig. You get dirty, and the pig enjoys it.** In other words, don't engage in a debate with someone simply for the sake of debating. The person who initiated the argument probably did so because he likes to debate broad philosophical issues — you are just fodder for his ego. The problems of the world will still be around whether or not you engage this person in a debate, so why bother? Pointless arguments waste your time and get you nowhere.

✔ **Ask for bulletins, and only accept briefs.** One of my favorite phrases, especially when I'm inundated with suggestions, requests, and ideas, is "give me one paragraph on that." These single-paragraph briefs give me a little information about a lot of things, and allow me to decide which things I need more information on and which I don't. Most people want bullet information these days — just look at the way news is delivered in short briefs — but those who know how to use bulletin information save lots of time over those who pour over every detail in a 40-page document.

✔ **Don't double-check what doesn't need double-checking.** If you ask a trusted assistant to mail a letter or return a phone call, double-checking those activities is unnecessary. In fact, watching over your assistant's shoulder undermines the bond of trust between you and your assistant. Of course, if you write a proposal or a letter, you should double- and triple-check your work, but plenty of items in your day do not need your second look.

Growing comfortable with time and your personal long- and short-term goals takes practice, but you must do so if you are to pull everything together and maximize your results.

Knowing the pecking order

Scheduling requires an endless series of negotiations. If you want to attend the opera at 8 p.m. on Friday night, but a colleague needs your advice on a project during that time, and one of your children wants to borrow the car for a date, you have to negotiate your time between these interests.

Sometimes scheduling works in your favor, and sometimes it doesn't. If an emergency occurs between 7 p.m. and 9 p.m. on Friday, you probably miss the opera, your child has to make other transportation arrangements, and your colleague must wait. An emergency is higher on the pecking order than your desire to see the opera or your colleague's need for your advice. As for your kid, she only thinks the world is going to end.

If you are the boss, the pecking order becomes much easier to manage. You can call a meeting of your employees during the workday and be reasonably sure that everyone will attend. However, if a client calls and wants to meet with you on an important matter, you can't delegate or otherwise dismiss the request. You are the boss, and you have to go to the meeting.

Every relationship, whether family, business, or social, has a pecking order. If the president of the United States called the chairman of General Motors and asked for a meeting at 10 a.m. next Tuesday in the Oval Office, I imagine the meeting would take place at exactly 10 a.m. If the chairman of General Motors wanted to meet with a dozen of his senior vice presidents, that meeting would also take place whenever and wherever the chairman requested. Pecking orders are a fact of life. Knowing where you fall in that order allows you to schedule your time more efficiently.

Keeping your schedule a full-time commitment

The people who attempt to keep rigid schedules at work but totally dismiss the idea of scheduling their home and personal lives also amaze me. They monitor every minute of the workday, but assume that, once they arrive home, the need for a regimented schedule stops. Scheduling at home is at least as important as scheduling at work.

Organization is a little like being pregnant. You either are or you are not. There is no in-between. To fully achieve the kind of organizational efficiency you are seeking, start your schedule at home and branch outward.

Making the calendar just as important as the clock

My notepad organizational system extends through approximately six weeks, which means that I can plan ahead and make notes throughout a six-week period. Sometimes that six-week window is plenty of time, and sometimes it isn't. Meetings, calls, follow-ups, and major projects can extend for weeks and even months. Whenever a project extends beyond the life of my notepad, I write a follow up on the last page and transfer the item to the appropriate calendar date in the future. I then write "ff" for "fast forward" beside the item to remind myself that it requires action in the future.

My system works well for me because it's easy, fast, efficient, and extends the same scheduling effectiveness to the calendar that I demand from the clock.

Planning Wednesday's schedule before Tuesday

If on Tuesday night you turn to your Wednesday planner and have nothing scheduled, what do you do?

- Say, "Yippee, I don't have anything to do tomorrow. I think I'll go play golf."
- Scramble to add something to your list so you don't waste a day.
- Fill the day with proactive items you have been meaning to get to but haven't had the time.
- Wait to see what materializes when you show up at the office on Wednesday morning.

Unfortunately, kicking yourself was not listed as an option, but should certainly go to the head of the list. Having a blank day shows a complete lack of prior planning and an inability to think beyond the next 24 hours. A blank day is almost akin to no list at all.

Why wait until Tuesday to complete Wednesday's schedule? If you complete Wednesday's schedule on Sunday, Monday, or even earlier, you are far ahead of the game in terms of your time-management skills.

Chapter 17

Scheduling the Unschedulable

In This Chapter

▶ Adapting and modifying your schedule to handle emergency situations

▶ Scheduling time for family, friends, or nothing at all!

Certain situations defy the laws of scheduling. In a perfect world, for example, people would never experience emergencies or interruptions, flights would always leave on time, and traffic would always move at an acceptable pace. Of course, the real world is unpredictable. But the organized person prepares for the unexpected, even when it can't be scheduled. This chapter shows you how.

Scheduling Emergencies

At face value, the idea that you can schedule emergencies seems silly. Emergencies are, by definition, unpredictable events that disrupt our normal routines, so, unless you are psychic, you aren't likely to write, "Attend to emergency," in your daily planner. You can, however, prepare yourself for the inevitable emergencies of everyday life by learning to remain organized both during and after an emergency.

Recognizing that an emergency is in the eye of the beholder

Whether an emergency consists of an irate customer or an overdue library book, a gap always exists between your own and other people's expectations about the use of your time. The easiest way for someone to sway you to her side is to convince you that her needs are emergencies. Emergencies are disruptive events that take you out of your routine and off your schedule, so defining what is and what is not an emergency and communicating that definition to those around you is critical. Otherwise, you will be constantly interrupted with "emergencies" that could consume most of your schedule.

An emergency rests in the eye of the beholder, or the person being most adversely affected by the circumstances. You must determine when those circumstances warrant your time and attention.

- ✔ **Keep in mind that a *problem* is not necessarily a *crisis*.** The best way for someone to get you to react quickly and without deliberation is to call a situation a "crisis." Just look at politicians. Whenever our tax bill is about to be raised or gobs of money are about to be spent in an area, we are told there is a "crisis." The United States has had a health-care crisis, an education crisis, numerous Social Security crises, a military-readiness crisis, a budget crisis, an ozone crisis, a pork-belly crisis, and a crisis over the number of crises in America. Crises have become so commonplace that people have become completely desensitized to the word. All of these social problems are legitimate, just as most of the so-called crises you are presented with have some validity, but they are problems, not emergencies. They deserve to be considered, debated, and strategically acted upon; they do not require a rapid reactionary response.

- ✔ **Don't give in to the shrillest cry.** The old saying, "the squeaky wheel gets the most grease" is often taken to extremes. Many people believe that if they squeal loudly enough they can get almost anyone to jump to their attention. Attending to the person crying the loudest is a trap you should avoid, because the loudest shrieks often represent the least critical problems you need to address. As annoying and frustrating as the squeaky wheel might be, sometimes ignoring it is worthwhile.

- ✔ **Remember the old adage: "Ineptitude on your part does not constitute an emergency on mine."** Legitimate emergencies are usually unforeseen and often unavoidable. Illegitimate pseudo-emergencies normally arise from a lack of preparation and effort on someone's part — usually the person screaming "emergency!" the loudest. The perfect example of this kind of self-imposed "emergency" is the school-age child who puts off a class project until the last minute, and then cries to his parents that he has an emergency need for construction paper and library books. The child's lack of planning has constituted an emergency for the entire family. Helping your child complete his school project is acceptable (after a proper lecture on the evils of procrastination, of course), as is helping a colleague or co-worker when she is in a bind. Don't fall victim to the claims of an emergency, however. You shouldn't be forced to disrupt your schedule just because of someone else's foolish lack of effort.

- ✔ **Set a trend by vigorously controlling interruptions.** The more you allow interruptions for real or perceived emergencies, the more you are interrupted. By setting a high interruption bar for yourself, you make others think twice about the importance of a situation. Is the emergency important enough for you to be interrupted? The answer lies in how tolerant you have been of past interruptions.

One person's emergency is another person's minor annoyance. With the exception of events such as fire, accidents, or life-threatening medical crises, all emergency situations are relative and subject to interpretation by the people who are directly affected.

The emergencies on which everyone can agree

A fire is an emergency. If a fire starts, you stop whatever you are doing and handle the situation in the most expeditious manner possible.

There are also plenty of other emergencies on which everyone can agree:

- ✔ Theft or other crimes require immediate attention and action and are, therefore, emergencies.
- ✔ Physical injuries that require first aid or other immediate medical attention are certainly emergencies.
- ✔ Accidents or natural disasters are events that require immediate attention and therefore constitute emergencies.

Subjective emergencies

A client calling in an outrage about a particular event may or may not be an emergency depending on the circumstances. If the client threatens to terminate the business arrangement with you or your company because of the incident — thereby damaging your business and your reputation — the incident is clearly an emergency, and you should adjust your schedule to handle it. If a client is upset over a relatively minor issue and simply blowing off steam by threatening to sever your relationship, the situation might not be as critical (especially if the client has made similar threats in the past).

Conversely, if you are meeting with a new client or prospect at the time the "emergency" situation arises, a real emergency might ensue, especially if the prospect gets wind of the situation. Unforeseen calamities can certainly jeopardize future business if you don't handle them well. Whether or not current or future clients are sitting in your office, they always watch the way you handle real and perceived emergencies.

Getting stuck as the official problem solver

People gravitate toward the things they like the most. In your job, you tend to spend more time on the areas that you like, while putting off the things that you don't like. At home, you do the things you enjoy first and put off the chores for later.

A career in crisis management

I have a friend who spent over a decade managing and disposing of distressed country club and resort properties for banks and other institutions. An expensive country club real estate development or resort operation would run into financial trouble, a bank or other lender would take over ownership, and my friend would arrive on the scene to manage the property and make it salable. He did this for CitiGroup, Prudential, NationsBank, and even the U.S. Department of Justice, each time taking a nonperforming asset and turning it into a salable property.

Then, all of a sudden, he quit. After carving a wonderful niche for himself in a growing industry, he walked away from his career and went in an entirely different direction. I couldn't help but wonder what had happened, so I asked him why he suddenly quit such a successful and lucrative career.

"I couldn't stand dealing with the same problems at every property I entered," he said. "The names and faces changed each time, but the problems were always the same. I had to be the bad guy, telling vendors that they weren't going to be paid, and explaining to the members that the rules were going to have to be modified. I had to fire most of the staff at these places, which didn't make me very popular and didn't help my state of mind. No matter how good of a job I did in cutting the red ink and making a project viable for a new owner, the members never once said 'thank you.' Finally, I decided life was too short, so I quit. I don't make anywhere close to the same amount of money I did, but I sleep much better now."

I'm happy my friend was able to recognize his career trap and make a change for the better. For him, crisis management was fine for a while, but he didn't want to build his life around it.

If you like handling emergencies — if the thrill and adrenaline rush of managing a crisis gets your blood flowing, and you gain a high sense of accomplishment by being in the thick of an emergency situation — you are bound to be presented with plenty of opportunities. People will seek you out and dump all of their last-minute, critical problems on your desk. You will become the problem solver in your office and in your home. However, do not expect to accomplish much in terms of advancing your own agenda.

Gunslingers are a necessary part of fixing problems, but the men who cleaned up Dodge City are not the same people the citizens wanted running things after the bad guys left town. If you are comfortable being the problem solver, you should prepare yourself to be boxed into that niche for a long time.

Managing emergencies — real or imagined

The following tips can help you respond appropriately to the "emergencies" that you face:

- ✔ **Ask yourself what will happen if you do nothing.** Sometimes things happen that are beyond your control. Usually these events don't require any worry, effort, or follow-up on your part, because whatever has happened cannot be changed. The number of people who rally around a problem — often attending meetings, working overtime, and offering their advice and opinions — when the outcome is already determined stuns me. If there is nothing anyone can do about a situation, then do nothing.

  For example, over the years several IMG clients have decided to terminate their relationships with our company in order to become more independent. Jack Nicklaus left our company in order to form what became Golden Bear Enterprises. These departures have prompted many "emergency" meetings among our executives, who proceed to bring every nuance of the ending relationship into question. Sometimes I attend these meetings, and other times I don't. After three decades I have learned that gaining and losing clients is a natural part of any business. If I am comfortable that we did everything in our power to manage our clients' affairs to the best of our ability, when one or two of them choose to leave our company, I wish them well. Viewing the departures as a crises might make us feel better, but won't change the ultimate outcome.

- ✔ **Determine whether the emergency adversely affects your business, your reputation, or your relationships.** Disagreements are a standard part of life, and certain misunderstandings and unpleasantness are inevitable in every relationship. Not every disagreement, angry exchange, or unforeseen problem constitutes an emergency. Emergencies, by definition, require immediate action. Sometimes disputes are better left alone. If a disagreement or other disruption is likely to have a detrimental effect on your business, your reputation, or relationships that are important to you, consider that disagreement an emergency. If not, leave it alone.

- ✔ **Ascertain how lingering the ramifications will be.** If you are late for a date with your spouse, depending on the importance of the date and your reputation for promptness, you might be in for a chilly night, but chances are pretty good that you won't get divorced over the incident. The ramifications do not constitute an emergency. You shouldn't jeopardize your safety or the lives of others by driving recklessly in an attempt to arrive on time. That same approach should be considered when you are faced with other unpleasant unforeseen situations. Before you take a great risk and put forth a lot of your time and effort, think about the ramifications and how long they might last.

✔ **Determine what sacrifices you will need to make if you handle the "emergency."** If you drop everything to handle a crisis, some of the items on your list are going to be left unfinished. Before you can legitimately classify a problem as an emergency, you have to be confident that it's worth putting other items off until another time.

✔ **Get out fast.** Attack the emergency in much the same way you do your standard things-to-do list.

  • Break the emergency into manageable bites.

  • Focus on each task.

  • Put time limits on yourself.

  • Make sure that each action moves you closer to your ultimate goal.

The biggest difference between managing an emergency and conducting normal activities is speed and accuracy. A task under normal circumstances might take two hours to complete with 90-percent efficiency, but the same task in an emergency might take 15 minutes to be completed at 50-percent efficiency. The drop in efficiency is okay. Just as 50-percent complete would be unacceptable under normal conditions, wasting two hours in a crisis to complete something to 90-percent efficiency could lead to disaster.

✔ **Get back on track as quickly as possible.** After you have done everything you can to get a crisis under control, put it behind you and get back to your regular schedule as quickly and efficiently as possible. Getting back on track often requires a great degree of discipline. Real emergencies tend to make your heart pound faster, your breathing accelerate, and your nerves tingle. Adjusting from that heightened state to focus on the routine tasks from before the emergency erupted is difficult.

Getting back on track is critical to effective time management, however. If the actual emergency took 20 minutes to manage, but the recovery afterward took another 20, the emergency stole 40 minutes of your well-organized day. The sooner you get back onto your schedule the better prepared you are when the next emergency rolls around.

Expecting the unexpected

Because my company manages a number of sporting events around the world, our executives are extremely adept at handling disruptive scenarios ranging from rain to bomb threats. Were we not prepared in advance for the most outrageous circumstances, many of those situations would be disastrous emergencies; but, because we go to great lengths to develop extensive contingency plans, a hail storm in the middle of a tennis match is handled as if it is routine. The more prepared you are, the fewer emergencies you are likely to encounter.

The Hingis "crisis"

Not long ago, an executive in our company spent several hours one morning frantically trying to reach me because he had what he termed "a Martina Hingis crisis." Hingis, one of our clients, and the number-one-ranked woman tennis player in the world at the time, was under contract with the Bolle company. After coming off a grueling playing and traveling schedule, however, she had to cancel an appearance at a Bolle press conference. It just so happened that the press conference had been scheduled to unveil a new product the company wanted Hingis to endorse. Needless to say, Bolle officials were less than pleased with Hingis's decision, and didn't hesitate to share their displeasure with our executive.

After he found me and explained the situation, I gave him some advice, but I also questioned his use of the term "crisis" when characterizing the situation. Bolle officials might have been marginally upset, but they were not going to sever their relationship with Hingis because of the incident, nor were they likely to discontinue dealing with us. Hingis wasn't angry or upset with anyone. She was simply exhausted and needed a little rest. Above all, there was very little we could do in this crisis other than apologize. Although we represent Hingis, no one in our company was going to tie her down and force her to attend a press conference. We could promise to do whatever we could to make amends to Bolle, but they understood that our responsibilities rested with our client. This was certainly a troublesome situation, and one that temporarily ruffled some feathers, but it was never a "crisis." Labeling it as such only cheapens the real emergencies that occasionally creep up in business.

Every meeting, project, or personal encounter is worthy of some form of advance work, even if the planning is nothing more than anticipating all the unexpected scenarios that could come up in a day. Expecting the unexpected can be tricky. Unexpected events are, by definition, unplanned, so anticipating what they will be or how much time they will require is difficult. However, out-of-the-ordinary situations that require your time come up every day. Because unexpected situations occur as regularly as the spring rains, not planning ahead for them is foolhardy.

But how can you advance a schedule, study data, and prepare yourself for an occurrence that is unexpected? Try this drill:

1. **Check out your daily planner for the past week, and calculate the number of minutes each day you spent on "just came up out of the blue" items you couldn't possibly have anticipated.**

   Whether the unscheduled occurrence was a phone call from a client with a problem, an emergency meeting with an employee, or an unplanned trip to Wal-Mart for trash bags and toothpaste, write down everything you did that was, by definition, "unexpected." Honestly calculate the amount of time you spent on these projects.

2. **Categorize the items.**

Phone calls you couldn't ignore should go into one category, and unscheduled interruptions should go into another. Trips you hadn't planned should comprise a third group. Splitting your task into groups gives you some idea of the amount of time you spend attending to unexpected occurrences by category. Knowing which unschedulable events take up the majority of your time may help you head them off before they occur.

3. **Calculate the percent of your workday spent on unexpected events by taking an average of several random days and calculating the total as a percentage of your total work hours.**

I spend between 15 and 20 percent of my workday on unexpected items ranging from client emergencies to traffic jams. Of every ten-hour day, I spend two hours dealing with unexpected interruptions or occurrences. That might sound like a lot of time, but, as vigorously as I control interruptions, I would be surprised if you spend less time on the unexpected than I do. I don't let this time bother me, however, because I do the advance work and plan for the unexpected. If I get an hour a day in unexpected phone interruptions, the lost time is no big deal. These interruptions fit my pattern, and I plan accordingly.

Examining how frequently emergencies erupt

Everyone occasionally faces an emergency situation, but if you're presented with one a week (or even one a month), you should closely examine the situations being classified as emergencies, as well as the person presenting you with these problems. Remember that your definition of an emergency should be strict. If you're having a fire or a medical emergency every month, it's time to do a little investigating. If you're categorizing a client complaint or a child's overdue homework assignment as an emergency, you need to reevaluate your definition.

Taking Time to Smell the Roses

The biggest mistake most people make when attempting to become more organized is assuming that scheduling and time management are business skills, and that the techniques for maximizing time efficiency don't translate to their homes and personal lives. This myth is dangerous. Although becoming organized certainly improves your relationships and your effectiveness in the office, you should put more effort into scheduling activities around family, friends, and leisure time than you spend organizing yourself at work.

An old adage says that no one ever laid on her deathbed and said, "I wish I had spent more time at the office." The point is that family and leisure time is precious and should be jealously protected. Of course, work and career are also important. Your challenge is to balance the demands of work and career against those of family, friends, and personal time. Becoming more organized in your approach to your nonwork time moves you closer to an acceptable parity between career and family, work and leisure. The advice may sound corny, but balance is critical to a healthy life. Scheduling time for your family, your friends, and yourself is an important part of finding that balance. The first step in that process is to incorporate nonwork time into your priorities.

Protecting family activities

Each day, as you list your tasks and assign priorities to those tasks, you make choices. Is calling Frank a higher priority at 9 a.m. than attending the project briefing? Is lunch with Pat more important than lunch with Rita? And how do I maneuver my schedule to handle all the items on my desk and still make it home in time to watch the playoff game? These choices are regular parts of any day whether or not you have an effective organizational system in place.

Unfortunately, too many people consistently place work activities above family and leisure activities, and they allow anything that comes up to encroach on time scheduled for the family. This prioritization is part of a false sense of duty to the office, and a misplaced work ethic.

Don't get me wrong; I have nothing against hard work. In fact, I am one of the biggest proponents for working long, hard, and smart work days if you want to get ahead. But I don't know anyone who places a higher priority on the daily activities at the office over his family. Why, then, do so many of us sacrifice the family in lieu of more work?

Over the years I've heard every excuse in the book for finishing work before family activities. Here are a few:

- ✔ **"If I leave work to go home and help my wife with the kids, the boss will think I don't care about my job."** Hooey. I know more than a few CEOs, and I can't name one who doesn't want all of her employees to have healthy and happy family lives. Of course, these CEOs want quality job performances as well. If you produce in the workplace, no intelligent boss would view leaving the office to be with your family as a weakness.

- ✔ **"I have to put the hours in if I want to get that promotion."** Having started my career as a practicing attorney where, like in most firms, billable hours were the lifeblood of our business, I understand the "paying dues" and "putting in the time" mindset. I also know that hours do not always translate into work. If you have legitimate items scheduled that force you to work late, that's one thing. If you're putting in hours for the sake of putting in hours, you need to reevaluate your priorities.

✓ **"If I don't do it, it will never get done."** This is a sign of either poor delegation skills or an inflated sense of self-importance. Certainly there are some things that only you can do (see Chapter 13 for tips on focusing on those tasks). If too many of those things are taking you away from time with your family, however, you need to train someone as a surrogate and share some of your workload with him.

✓ **"I meant to go to my daughter's recital, but a client called as I was walking out the door."** This excuse means that your daughter's recital fell below an unscheduled call on your personal priority list. Granted, sometimes emergencies come up that you must handle immediately, but in over 30 years of working with some of the highest profile clients in the world, I have found that those kinds of emergencies are few and far between.

✓ **"Assuming nothing comes up, I'll be there."** Something always comes up if you let it.

✓ **"I don't know when I'll be home, but it will probably be late."** In other words, you don't have a definitive schedule, and anything that comes up takes precedence over your family.

Scheduling yourself around a go-home deadline

Given the hours I work and the amount I accomplish, I would be the last person to advocate a shorter work week. But, I do believe that, at a certain time, you should turn out the light, close the door, and go home to your family.

Even the most organized and successful business people have trouble knowing when to call it a day. The number of executives who can tell you exactly where they will be at 10:22 a.m. tomorrow morning and whom they will call before lunch constantly amazes me. These executives micromanage every minute of the workday and efficiently organize their calendars. About the only thing they can't tell you is when they will go home. Even though everything else in their days has a definitive start time and end time, they have no idea when they will close their briefcases, turn off the lights, and leave.

The reason most people can't schedule a go-home time is because they haven't effectively handled all the crucial items on their agendas, so they stay a little longer, let dinner get cold, and finish all the projects they set out to accomplish. Although admirable, being the last car out of the parking deck doesn't win you any brownie points at home, and in the long run isn't good for your mental or physical health.

Some alternatives, however, allow you to leave work at a reasonable time *and* finish all the items on your agenda:

- ✔ **Write "Go home" next to a reasonable time on your master list and make the item non-negotiable.** Schedule everything else in your day around that go-home deadline. If you must arrive at the office two hours early to get everything done, get out of bed and get to work early, but view the go-home time as a final deadline for all daily work.

- ✔ **Don't spend large chunks of time on minor issues.** Major in the majors, and devote enough time to the puny items to get them out of your way.

- ✔ **Work when you're at work.** I understand that the office is a social environment, and ignoring your colleagues when they ask you to voice an opinion on the latest baseball trade or the newest blockbuster movie is difficult. But the minutes you spend socializing in the office take away from time you could spend socializing with nonwork friends or family. Certainly, you can't become an antisocial office recluse, but you can pay more attention to the work you are completing at work.

- ✔ **Close your door.** A closed door isn't a hostile barrier; it is simply a way to tell everyone that you have things to do, and interruptions are unacceptable.

- ✔ **Find a surrogate.** People believe that no one else can possibly complete their work as well as they do it. Humans have egos, and so they can't help but think that they are somewhat indispensable at work; they have to do everything themselves. Nobody is above such inane logic. If you don't believe me, find the people in your office who are about to go on vacation and see if they aren't scrambling to finish everything they think that they need to accomplish before they leave. Or find the person who just returned from a vacation and see if she isn't swamped with back-logged work. What is wrong with finding someone who can help with some of the work we seem determined to do ourselves? The only thing finding a surrogate can hurt is your pride.

- ✔ **Don't feel guilty about finishing sooner than you used to.** When I first began negotiating endorsement contracts for athletes, I spent countless hours pouring over every nuance, comma, and "heretofore" in the documents our clients were about to sign. Now, I can just as effectively review those same documents in a matter of minutes. The documents haven't gotten any smaller, but after 35 years of practice, I've gotten better at what I do. You have too. Don't feel guilty because a task that used to take three hours now only takes one. Appreciate the fact that you have gained a measure of proficiency at your job.

- ✔ **A finished project might not be everything you want it to be, but it's everything you have.** Every project could be done a little better or could be made to look a little more professional. Every fact could be triple- and quadruple-checked, and every document could be re-read dozens of times with minimal revisions coming out of each read. At some point, however, you have to go with what you have. By putting a go-home deadline on yourself, you might not end the day with exactly the finished product you want, but you need to be comfortable enough with the product that you can put your concerns to rest and go home.

Making a date with your spouse

With more couples working than ever before and the divorce rate at an all-time high, going out of your way to schedule time to be with your spouse is important. The best way to accomplish this goal is to set a definitive night as "date night," and take your spouse out on a legitimate, hand-holding, movie-going, dinner-eating date — just like you did before you were married.

Initially, date night might sound easy and even silly, but it actually requires a tremendous amount of discipline on the part of both spouses. You have to arrange for a sitter (if you have children), set schedules, and, many times, tell people at work "no."

You will find the payoffs of date night to be well worth the effort, though. Just as you need to have a go-home time that is non-negotiable, your date night should be just as important after 20 years of marriage as when you were going out for the first time.

Calling a friend every day

One of the executives in our company has an interesting rule: When he has finished all the items on his daily list and is preparing to turn out the light and go home for the evening, he forces himself to make one more phone call. The call might be to a client, a customer, a prospect, or a friend he hasn't spoken to in a while, but before he puts on his coat and closes his door, he makes one extra call. Making one last call is not a bad strategy in business and is even more productive in your personal life.

Everyone takes certain friendships for granted, and wishes she had spoken to her friends more often. But busy schedules intervene, and all the good intentions get washed away in a sea of paperwork and frantic deadlines. People lose touch, forget to follow up, and before they know what has happened, their friends dwindle away.

Call at least one friend every day, if for no other reason than to let them know that they are on your mind. Making a call a day doesn't take long (and probably shouldn't if your friends are busy people), but scheduling the time and making the effort to call a friend a day pays off in ways you can't begin to imagine.

Friends for life

Just because you attain a position of power and authority doesn't necessarily mean that you amass a great number of friends. In fact, the adage "it's lonely at the top" is somewhat valid. The more powerful you become, the more tainted the motivations of those who try to endear themselves to you. I see this phenomenon in athletes' lives quite a bit. Kids who had dozens of close friends in college suddenly gain hundreds of friends when they sign multiyear, multimillion-dollar contracts. No matter how often and how forcefully we warn our clients, they learn the hard (and costly) way that new friends often follow new money, and they vanish just as quickly.

One of the best historical exceptions to that rule was President Dwight Eisenhower. Throughout his life, even when he was the most recognized and revered man on the planet, Ike maintained numerous close personal friendships that remained steadfast. George Patton was one; Clifford Roberts, the co-founder and chairman

of Augusta National Golf Club was another. These men didn't hang around Ike for their own personal gains, because Eisenhower would have never allowed that. They were true friends who remained close to each other until their deaths.

Ike never flaunted his friendships. He rarely even spoke of the subject. However, just before the 1956 presidential election, Ike made an off-handed remark to his secretary that turned out to be one of his more prophetic statements on the subject of friendships. As Richard Nixon, Ike's vice president, left the White House one afternoon after a meeting, Ike turned to his secretary and said, "I can't imagine how a man could live his life without any friends."

Nixon had millions of acquaintances over the years, but never made friends. That contrast between Nixon and Eisenhower couldn't be more telling.

Reserving time for nothing at all

We all need down time. Whether that time is spent as a break in the middle of the day, a fishing trip at the end of a tough week, or an hour or so of mindless television surfing, everybody needs some time to do absolutely nothing. Unfortunately, most of us refuse to schedule down time into our days. (When was the last time you wrote, "Do nothing" on your daily planner?) The mind and body need breaks, however. If you don't schedule them, your body takes them anyway — usually at an inappropriate or inopportune time. We call these forced breaks burnout, mental block, fatigue, or stress-related lockdown. All these labels are buzzwords for the same affliction: a need for a little do-nothing time.

To the chagrin of traditionalists, many executives, particularly in the computer industry and other progressive companies, encourage their employees to take regular naps during the day. Some even set aside areas in the offices where pillows and tents are available for a quick snooze. A decade ago, promoting naps would have been seen as blasphemy, but today's executive understands the importance of quality downtime and the positive effects it can have on productivity.

If you haven't written "Do nothing" on your things-to-do list in a while, maybe you should take a lesson from some of the more successful executives in the country.

Chapter 18

Planning for the Long Term

● ●

In This Chapter

▶ Scheduling weeks, months, and years down the road

▶ Getting results from your long-term goals

▶ Failing and moving on

▶ Keeping the season in mind

▶ Remembering to collect the residuals

● ●

1 hope that you harbor some specific long-term goals for your life, but I also hope that you temper those goals with a healthy dose of realism. In 1984, when I wrote my first business book, *What They Don't Teach You At Harvard Business School* (Bantam Doubleday Dell Publishing), the world was a very different place. The Cold War (between the U.S. and the now-defunct Soviet Union) continued to rage, the three major television networks retained over 80 percent of the national television audience, my company didn't own a single personal computer, Lexus, Acura, and Saturn automobiles didn't exist, and cyberspace was only a reality in a William Gibson novel.

Nobody could have possibly predicted the changes that have taken place in the last 15 years, but, in the 1980s, that fact certainly didn't stop us from trying. Back when I was penning my version of street-smart business advice — before cell phones, cyberlinks, and video e-mail — business people spent hours compiling long-term strategic business plans that included detailed five- and ten-year budgets. Growth projections extended for decades, and assumptions about costs, competition, and the general state of world affairs were eloquently predicted in remarkable detail (almost all of which turned out to be wrong).

Today, if I were presented with a five-year business plan, I would shred years three, four, and five and send the presumptuous executive who wrote the plan back to school for a refresher course in business at the new millennium. Because of the speed in which our environment changes today, no way exists to accurately predict anything three years down the road. Companies such as Amazon.com have exploded onto the scene in a matter of months, and Lexus and Acura have blown conventional '80s wisdom out of the water by developing luxury automobiles and making them successful in three years — a feat that took decades in the old days.

This is not your father's business world. Rapidly advancing technologies foster chaotic change, breaking down many of yesterday's barriers and making future predictions seem like silly wastes of time.

These changes make long-term planning even more important and an even greater challenge. Goals for the long-term are paramount to personal and professional success, but responding and adapting to change in the world around us is the only way to achieve those goals. An unpredictable future doesn't excuse you from long-term planning. Quite the contrary. You must plan for the long-term because the future is so unpredictable. To do so, you need to rethink the way in which you structure your long-term plans and strategies.

Looking Down the Road

In order to organize your time, your tasks, and your surroundings, you must go through certain mental exercises, and be able to see results in terms of hours, days, weeks, months, and sometimes years. At times, looking at the long-term is easy, and, sometimes, it's the hardest thing you can imagine, but in all instances the ultimate mark of getting results hinges on your ability to organize your thoughts for both the short- and long-term.

Here's how:

- **Specify the results you want to achieve, and back them up with effective plans.** Writing a goal like "retire by age 50," may seem specific enough on its face, but unless you have some accompanying detail, the goal doesn't mean much. Retire from what? Do you plan to work for the same company until you are 50 and then retire? Even the government, which has always been considered the most stable employer in the country, can't guarantee that kind of security any more. If retirement at age 50 is your ultimate goal, you need to specify exactly what you plan to retire from, and how you plan to accomplish that feat given the time you have left.

- **Visualize yourself having achieved your goals.** Arnold Palmer never won a golf tournament he hadn't already envisioned himself winning. No successful athlete ever attained greatness without successfully visualizing results. Visualizing your goals consists of more than dreaming about holding the U.S. Open trophy and waving to a cheering crowd, however. You must set specific parameters. How old will you be when you finally reach your goals? What physical condition will you have to be in to attain the goals you have established for yourself? What will your lifestyle be?

How will you handle the obstacles along the way? Successful visualization means taking all aspects of your plan into account and putting yourself through the mental exercise of seeing each step ahead of time.

✔ **Set long-term time frames to allow for short-term focus.** Unless you are a lottery winner, nothing of consequence occurs overnight. All worthwhile long-term goals take a fair amount of time to achieve. That's why people whose goals include "making my first million by age 30," or "retiring at age 35" fail more often than they succeed. Unless you have a specific plan for accomplishing those goals in a fast-forward fashion, you need to be realistic in your time frames. I am not saying that you won't make a million dollars before your 30th birthday, but unless you have a career map that shows you how, and unless you focus on the individual tasks that get you there, you don't have a chance.

Shorten the "long" in long-term

No matter what you want to achieve these days, whether your goal is advancing your career, becoming more active in your community, or learning a new skill, your objective can now be reached faster than at any time in history. If you want to become an entrepreneur, your business is only a mouse-click away. If your long-term goal is to become president of your company, you might structure that career plan on a five-year curve rather than as a 10- or 15-year plan. Regardless of what you want to achieve, rapid change enables you to reach your objectives faster than ever before.

Because of that cultural and societal shift, you should shorten the window of your long-term planning. No longer is looking at a long-term problem and saying things like, "We need to schedule a series of meetings and staff this thing out" an appropriate course of action. An objective that might have taken months just five years ago should be shortened to weeks today, and a project that might have taken weeks last year, may be accomplished in days. Obviously, some goals still have a definitive long-term window (like setting retirement goals for 20 years down the road) but in most cases, what used to take months now takes weeks; what used to take days, now takes hours or even minutes.

In the old days (less than a decade ago in some cases), when our executives came forward with new concepts or new marketing strategies for events, others in our company would ask questions like, "How much risk is involved?" or "How much is this going to cost?" Although those questions are still asked today, they take a back seat to "How quickly can we get this done?" Speed has become the top consideration, simply because of how quickly today's business environment changes.

Writing It Down and Setting a Time

Even though the time frames have shortened and more and more projects are placed on a fast track, the basics of long-term goal setting haven't changed. First and foremost, you must write your long-term objectives down (just as you do your daily list) in clear, concise language, and in as much detail as possible. Whether your objective is learning another language, increasing your net worth, starting a home-based business, or getting yourself in better physical shape, if you don't write your goals and objectives down they are not real. The act of committing a goal to paper moves your objective out of the dream-state and into reality.

You must also commit to paper your long-term projects or tasks. No matter how wonderful and fast new technology might be, a Pentium processor can't bring disparate interests together without some planning, patience, and methodical persistence. If you have an idea for developing a new product, designing a new marketing plan, or refurbishing your local community theater, that idea requires bringing people together. Getting people together takes time, organization, and planning, none of which can begin until you have written your objectives down and established a methodical time line for reaching your goals.

But where do you write down long-term objectives? If you're like me, your daily planning pad only extends through a six-week period, and predicting events too far into the future can be pure folly.

Here's how to record your long-term goals:

1. **Write your long-term objectives on your calendar and keep your calendar in your sight.**

   Whether it's on your desk, in your pocket, or on your kitchen wall, having the calendar visible provides a daily reminder that long-term items need your attention, too.

2. **Write your long-term objectives in your planner as constant reminders of what you are striving to achieve.**

   I write "ff" for "fast forward" beside the items in my planner that do not require immediate action, but need to be considered for a later time. Whatever annotation works for you, the main objective is to commit your long-term projects to your short-term lists in a way that you won't forget them.

3. **Develop a specific list of incremental tasks that leads you toward your long-term objectives.**

   This is the old "eating the elephant one bite at a time" strategy (see Chapter 2). A project that takes months to achieve certainly requires some work along the way, even if the effort is nothing more than scheduling an hour a week to think about an upcoming event. You can accomplish plenty with advance work, even if a project deadline is months away.

4. **Add those incremental advance-work tasks to your planner and calendar as well.**

   If you're spending time thinking about your long-term project, write "10 a.m. to 11 a.m., Think about long-term project X," in your planner.

5. **Give yourself deadlines for every step in the process so that you are constantly under the gun.**

   If each increment is completed on time, the project is likely completed on time as well.

6. **Be ready to adapt to changes along the way.**

   The world today is not the place you thought it would be last year, and the things you predict for next year will probably be wrong. Be prepared to adapt your plans and strategies at every juncture.

Using the community theater idea as an example, your written goal might read, "Open refurbished community theater with amateur production of Les Miserables on July 4, 2001." This objective is ambitious and specific, but also obtainable as a long-term goal. The production requires strategic planning many months into the future, but you must also develop a list of time-specific short-term tasks to get the project underway.

The $150 million man

I have a good friend who owns a well-known chain of health clubs. He carries written goals with him that range in scope from 30 days to ten years. He keeps these goals written on two sheets of paper in the front of a notebook that he carries with him at all times under the theory that every time he opens the notebook he sees the lists and takes stock of his progress.

The first sheet lists his immediate short-term goals, which he crosses off when completed. He updates that list on a regular basis. The second sheet lists his year-by-year goals, both personally and professionally. The goals are ambitious, incredibly detailed, but also attainable. For example, on the first page he wrote that in the next 30 days he plans to visit 14 health clubs, and in the next three months he wants to go helicopter skiing in Canada. Within six months his goal is to run a full marathon.

On page two (his year-by-year goals), he wrote that he wants to open 25 new health clubs in year one. By the third year he expects to have a net worth of $25 million and to have all his sons in the business with him. At the end of the tenth year, he wrote, "Sell my business for $150 million." As brash as that goal might seem, it is perfectly reasonable given the methodical detail this man has given to each of his objectives.

First, you need to determine the theater's state of disrepair and develop a budget for refurbishing the structure. Once you have a cost estimate, you likely need to raise funds through sponsorships and contributions. Then you need to hire a general contractor and project manager to oversee the work, as well as engage the cooperation of attorneys, insurance executives, and numerous government agencies in your town. After that, you have to sell your concept to the local amateur theatrical company and gain their support and cooperation.

These steps are just the beginning. Many questions still linger. Who will be responsible for the upkeep of the structure? Who will turn the lights on in the morning and sweep the floors at night? How will the operation generate revenue? Who will share in the proceeds, and how will they be divided? How will you cover any operating shortfalls? What about taxes, licensing, liability, zoning, parking, accessibility, and clean up? The lists could go on forever, and probably will.

Failing Quickly

The following anecdote should encourage you to aim high and develop a strategy that incorporates both the calendar and the clock. Don't be afraid to fail along the way. As circumstances change and new opportunities arise, remain confident in your ability to try, fail, correct, and try again as many times as needed to reach your objectives.

At a recent meeting with executives from a major packaged goods company, I noticed that the most senior executive was a man in his mid-30s with no demonstrable business successes to his credit. But, he was in charge of a $20 billion global company. When I asked him about his career, his candor surprised me.

"I was lucky enough to have a very smart boss who told me that taking risks and failing is fine. In fact, he expected me to have at least two failures a year. If I didn't, he said I wasn't taking enough risks. The only thing he wouldn't tolerate was being slow to recognize a failure. He called the quick recognition of failure 'fast fail.' Failing was perfectly acceptable as long as I did so quickly and moved on."

The executive explained how his boss encouraged him to modify his strategies and take risks as his environment changed. "I wasn't selling in a vacuum," he said. "I had competitors who were eager to take away my market share. If they attacked my product line, say with a coupon program or a front-aisle display, I couldn't ignore the attack just because it didn't fit into my marketing plans. I had to respond on the fly. That's how you learn what works and what doesn't."

McCORMACK MEMORIES

Taking long-term scheduling to new heights

In 1990, right after the International Olympic Committee announced that the 1996 Summer Games would be held in Atlanta, a small-time sports marketing agent in Atlanta started calling my office and requesting a meeting. I get numerous calls of this nature every day, but what struck me about this one was the advance work the man was willing to make. He told my secretary, "I will meet with Mr. McCormack wherever he wants, whenever he wants, as long as it's sometime within the next six years. If he wants me to fly to Tokyo and meet him at three in the morning that's fine. I'll do it."

After a few calls to make sure that this person wasn't a nut case, I finally scheduled a time to meet with him (long before his six-year deadline had expired). This story just goes to show what a little persistence and some advance work can accomplish.

Remembering the Season

Too often in business, people focus so exclusively on the timing of their tasks that they forget the calendar has some important, built-in dates. June 21 is always the first day of summer, and December 25 is always Christmas. January 1 is New Year's Day and the first week in November is baseball's World Series. These dates are absolutes, but how often people forget about them is amazing.

Not long ago, an executive came to me with a proposal for a sporting event that he claimed could be completed in exactly 11 weeks. "I've timed the project out, and we can have this thing ready to go 11 weeks from today," he said with great fanfare. Something about the timing struck me, so I immediately whipped out a calendar and counted ahead.

When I realized what had been bothering me, I said to this executive, "Even if you are right and we could get this event off the ground in 11 weeks, who is going to watch it?"

"What do you mean?" he asked.

I turned my calendar around and showed him that 11 weeks from that day were the opening ceremonies of the Olympic Games. Even if we put together his proposed event, the likelihood of getting anyone interested in a non-Olympic sporting event was nonexistent. Our executive was so focused on his own plan that he failed to consider what else was happening in the world on the dates he had chosen.

The dog days of the PGA Championships

One of the most glaring examples of an organization forgetting the season came in the early 1980s when the Professional Golfers Association (PGA) of America moved its headquarters to a new complex called PGA National in Palm Beach Gardens, Florida. In addition to a beautiful suite of offices, the PGA National site included a luxury hotel and a championship golf course owned by the PGA of America.

In addition to representing over 30,000 golf professionals around the country, the PGA of America owns and operates the final major championship of the golf season — the PGA Championship. When the organization moved to its new headquarters at PGA National, the board of directors decided to move the PGA Championship with the headquarters. The PGA could showcase its new home, and the organization could reap the benefits of increased revenues from ticket sales and concessions without having to pay a lease for the golf course.

The idea seemed great on paper. There was only one problem: The PGA Championship is always held in August. Remarkably, few people on the PGA of America board considered the weather conditions in south Florida in August. So the championship was held in sweltering heat at PGA National and players such as Palmer and Nicklaus trudged around the course looking like they had just stepped out of a sauna.

The final straw came when NBC, the network covering the event, showed a bikini-clad woman sitting at one of the PGA Championship scoreboards, dangling her feet in one of the course's many water hazards. Needless to say, that was not the image the PGA of America wanted its championship to project (although the television viewers didn't mind, golf's majors try to be much more dignified). The next year the association decided to forego the financial benefits of hosting the tournament at its home course, and the PGA Championship once again rotated to a generally cooler and more conducive environment.

Recognizing the Residuals

Because the world changes quickly, you aren't always guaranteed success in your long-term plans. In many instances, you fall short, or conditions change so dramatically that your objectives or projects don't make sense any more. These failures aren't necessarily reflections of your skill or intelligence, nor are they indictments against your ability to predict the future. Change is simply a part of life, and recognizing when your long-term plans no longer make sense is a sign of wisdom and maturity.

Missing the lessons learned along the way, or ignoring the residual benefits gained from an abandoned project, however, are inexcusable errors.

The New York Grand Prix, for example, was a wonderful long-term idea that our company eventually abandoned because of logistics and an inability to pull together the disparate interests necessary to make the event a success. The effort put into that project was not a total loss, however. Through that process, we developed positive working relationships with New York City, local sponsors, and many of the citizens groups in Manhattan. Although the Grand Prix never materialized, the relationships we developed along the way paid off in spades. Fortunately, we recognize the residual assets gained from an abandoned project.

The star of Star Wars

One of the most visible and yet overlooked examples of a successful residual benefit from a failed or abandoned project is the U.S. military's Patriot Missile — the ground-launched guided projectile that everyone saw on television during the Persian Gulf War. The Patriot became a nightly news staple, launching from positions in Saudi Arabia and Israel, and destroying Iraqi Scud missiles in spectacular midair explosions.

What many people didn't realize at the time (and some forget to this day) is that the Patriot is a direct residual from the abandoned Strategic Defense Initiative (SDI), or Star Wars program, that President Ronald Reagan proposed in the early 1980s. SDI was supposed to be a shield of missiles that could intercept and destroy incoming Soviet nuclear warheads before they hit their targets. It was, as Reagan said, "An alternative to simply bombing each other back to the Stone Age."

But the program never got off the ground. Before the "Star Wars" program could be fully funded or implemented, the Soviet Union collapsed, the Cold War ended, and the need for a space-based missile defense system fell sharply down on the priority list. But not before the U.S. military became adept at intercepting and destroying incoming missiles. That technology became the Patriot. Although no one at the time was thinking about the old SDI debates, many lives were saved during the Gulf War because of the leftover technology from that abandoned Cold War project.

Part IV
The Finer Points

The 5th Wave   By Rich Tennant

"Einstein over there miscalculated our start-up costs, and we ran out of money before we could afford to open a 24-hour store."

In this part . . .

Getting results isn't an exact science, and there are thousands of subtleties that achievers have picked up along the way. Organizing your surroundings and your time takes you most of the way there, but the ultimate reward for being organized, other than living and working in tidy surroundings and having an efficient schedule, is accomplishing what you set out to do. Organization is about results. If you don't advance your personal agenda, don't reach your goals, or fail to eliminate stress and anxiety from your daily life, being organized has very little value.

This part shows you the finer points of getting results — those little things that mean the difference between getting maximum results for your efforts and throwing up your hands in frustration. While this isn't an exhaustive list, the chapters in this part alert you to the skills to develop in order to get the most from your organizational efforts.

Chapter 19

Results Aren't Everything — They're the Only Thing

In This Chapter

▶ Thinking like a winner

▶ Having more than just good intentions

▶ Establishing deadlines for your goals

*T*he title of this chapter is a play on an old expression attributed to football coaching great Vince Lombardi, who said, "Winning isn't everything — it's the only thing." That is about as succinct a statement as anyone has ever made on the importance of getting results. Although Lombardi was speaking to a football team, the point he was making applies to life outside of sports. Whether you're meeting a deadline, making a sale, or accomplishing every task on your personal to-do list in a specified time, the focus required to win is no different than that of a football team playing for a title.

All winners, whether in sports, business, or politics, share certain unmistakable traits, the most prominent being a singular obsession with winning. Goals of successful winners are clear and concise, and there is no doubt about the results that winners hope to achieve. For a star quarterback, the objective is to win the Super Bowl; a golfer plans to win a major championship; the successful CEO focuses on the next product launch; and the skillful politician centers his resources on winning the next election. Every winner has a specific result in mind that motivates all actions. As a result, winners never lose sight of their objectives, and they never become bogged down by process.

A Good Game Is One You Win!

Winners never consider losing. They focus solely on the objective in front of them, never letting doubt or guilt seep into their minds. Winning is the only option, and the only reason they're in the game.

Never take your eyes off of where you want to go

Focus is the key to all success. In your business or personal life, you're only as successful as your ability to keep your eyes on the ball.

I had the opportunity to talk to one of our most successful literary clients recently, and I asked him if he ever reflected on his success as an author. He completely dismissed the idea, saying, "The world is changing every day. I don't have time to look back, especially at myself."

"But aren't you sometimes amazed by what you've accomplished in literature?" I pressed.

He shook his head, somewhat annoyed by my question. "If I started thinking that way, I might believe my own hype. The minute that happens and I take my focus off my next project, I might as well retire because I will have written my last decent word."

Vinny Giles, my friend and fellow competitor in the sports management business, once gave me an interesting synopsis of his client, professional golfer Justin Leonard. Giles said of Leonard, "Justin is the kind of guy you love to be around, who is friendly and fun-loving. But once he's on the golf course he's going to cut your throat and stomp on you while you're bleeding. That's what makes him a winner."

Justin Leonard isn't a callous, mean-spirited, heartless ogre who doesn't care about others. Exactly the opposite is true. He's a compassionate, funny, giving man who also happens to be a highly driven competitor. Leonard is a winner because he never considers any other option. Like all successful winners, he doesn't go out on the golf course content to play a "good game." Leonard knows a good game is one you win! That's the only reason he plays.

Winning attitudes like those of Justin Leonard and most other professional athletes can be acquired and shared with others, not just in sports but also in business and at home. In order to gain the results you desire, adapt a winning attitude and incorporate it into your organized daily activities.

Good Intentions Don't Feed the Bulldog

The world is full of nonachievers who believe that intentions are more important than results. For these people, effort is the same as accomplishment.

You see people everyday, putting in countless hours on the job, struggling to keep up with their hectic schedules, and speaking in breathless frustration about how unappreciated their efforts seem to be. But if you ask them to name one significant accomplishment they have achieved in the last day, week, or even month, many would be hard-pressed to come up with a single example. They may tell you how hard they work and offer countless examples of their own good intentions, but when measuring results, most of these people have nothing to show for their efforts. Even worse, they don't understand why accomplishments even matter.

Because so much of my business involves sports throughout the world, it isn't uncommon for executives in our company to attend three or more major sporting events in one week. Sometimes, however, being at these events overshadows any real accomplishments that the executives hope to achieve. During a planning meeting not long ago, I noticed one member of our management team had scheduled himself to attend a golf tournament in London, a boxing match in New York, and a baseball game in Cleveland all in the same week. When I asked this executive what he hoped to accomplish from these junkets, he told me how many people he would be meeting and who would be in attendance at the events.

"That's not what I asked," I said. "What do you hope to accomplish?"

After a long and slightly uncomfortable hesitation, he said, "I don't know what you mean."

He was being honest. This executive mistakenly assumed that simply being in attendance at these sporting events equated with accomplishment. His intentions were good. He wanted to help himself and the company by being at events where we needed a corporate presence. But he was unable to take his good intentions to the next level. He failed to see that his travels needed to move him closer to some desired result. To him, process and good intentions were enough.

If you're not keeping score, you're probably getting beat

The late Paul "Bear" Bryant once said, "If how you played the game were all that mattered, there wouldn't be any scoreboards."

His point was that keeping score is important, not only in determining the ultimate winner of a contest, but also as a measuring device by which a person, team, or company can gauge itself against the competition. Too often when I ask the question, "How are we doing relative to our nearest competitor?" I get a lot of blank stares and less-than-specific answers. If you don't know the score — whether in an athletic competition or a business environment — you have a better-than-average chance of being left behind.

How Much Time Is Left on Your Game Clock?

Just as every game has a specified beginning and ending — whether measured by a game clock, the number of innings, or a predetermined number of rounds — every project in your business and personal life has an effective time limit. Your success in those projects is often a function of how efficiently you manage your personal game clock.

A friend of mine who became renowned in the business world as a "turn around" expert shared with me one of the secrets to his amazing ability to rescue floundering companies:

"If an idea or project comes along, the first thing I look at is not how much potential it has, but how long it will take to start yielding results," he said. "It really doesn't matter whether or not an idea will eventually yield billions if you go broke in the time it takes to bring it to fruition."

That simple advice is often overlooked in everyday life. Whether you're launching a multimillion dollar ad campaign or adding a new sun porch onto your house, knowing how much time is on your game clock goes a long way toward ensuring the project's success.

Chapter 20

Redefining Yourself

- -

In This Chapter

▶ Using your assets

▶ Walking away from your old self

▶ Making the new you known to the world

- -

*W*hether your goal is to become a more organized manager, a more efficient parent, or a more successful entrepreneur, your success depends on your ability to redefine yourself as the person you want to be. As you implement many of the results-oriented strategies in this book, you could easily lose sight of what you want to change and why you embarked on this process in the first place. That's why writing your goals and objectives (see Part I) and keeping them in a convenient location is critical to your success. Equally critical is having a clear description — preferably written down — of the person you want to be.

This new definition of yourself must be specific, and it must center on the results you hope to achieve. If your career goal, for example, is to become the food critic for a major newspaper (which involves lots of taste-testing) but also to be 15 pounds lighter than you currently weigh, your two images are at odds with each other. If you're a secretary, however, and your objective is to become an executive, through observation and inquiry you should be able to develop a reasonable description of yourself as an executive in your company.

This chapter gives you a few rules for redefining yourself.

Leading with Your Strong Suit

Redefining yourself doesn't mean that you should throw away all the skills you know and have mastered over the years. Exactly the opposite is true. In order to effectively redefine yourself, you must hang on to the things you do well, and discard or improve the things you don't do well.

Early in my career, I went to Yale Law School, passed the bar exam, and became a practicing attorney in Cleveland. Over 40 years ago, I gave up the day-to-day practice of law to form IMG. However, I still refer to myself as a lawyer. In fact, when I travel abroad, I always write "lawyer" under "occupation" on the declaration forms.

In many respects, I am still a lawyer, even though I don't actively practice law. My legal training still permeates the way I speak, the way I write, the way I read, and the attention I show to details when I conduct business. Had I been a salesman by training, I may deal with clients in broader strokes; had I been an accountant, I may feel the need to communicate in financial terms. But because I'm a lawyer, I know my strength lies in my meticulous attention to detail, and I have parlayed that strength into every aspect of my professional career and personal life.

Many people fail in reinventing themselves because they throw away the strongest aspects of their personality and training, and try to master skills they have no business trying to master. A healthy dose of self-awareness goes a long way in successfully redefining yourself.

Getting Prepared to Walk Away from the Old You

Even though you should hang onto your strengths when redefining yourself, that doesn't mean that you should continue to do the same things you've always done just for the sake of doing them. Part of becoming a new person is giving up on some of the activities you've loved in the past.

For example, I once visited a ski resort while our company was producing one of our first televised ski races. Upon arriving, I immediately looked for the head of our television division who was overseeing the event. To my surprise, I was told he was out on the side of the mountain setting up camera angles with the crew. That would have been a perfectly acceptable place for him to be if he were still a producer. But as a division head and the most senior executive on the premises, I expected him to be at the base of the mountain with the network executives and ski officials. Because he hadn't come to grips with his new position, this executive reverted back to the old, comfortable definition of himself without realizing that his new position required him to sacrifice some of his old ways.

Manage by objective

Management guru Tom Peters first popularized the business buzz-phrase *management by objective* or *MBO* in the early 1980s. The phrase was used to describe a style of management that focused solely on results and not the process by which those results were obtained. It was revolutionary thinking at the time. Twenty years ago, managers still thought in terms of time clocks and paid leave. Peters pointed out that the successful companies of the future would scrap the old assembly line theories if it meant creating better quality products and services. He was right.

In redefining yourself for the future, you must manage your time and resources to maximize your objectives. That goal requires modifying the procedures you employ in your business and personal life, in order to move yourself closer to your ultimate redefinition of yourself.

On paper, my career might look like a hodge-podge of reinventions. I was an attorney who became a sports agent, who became a salesman, who then transformed himself into a manager. In total, however, my career has been a fluid progression. My objective was to be a successful entrepreneur, and I managed my career with that objective in mind. Every move I made along the way made perfect sense because it moved me closer to my ultimate goal.

No matter where you are in your career or personal life, successfully changing yourself means setting a target and managing all aspects of your life around that objective.

Being Loud and Proud

If you don't communicate to the world that you have redefined yourself, nobody else will. Your choices are simple: You can either let everyone you come in contact with assume that you are the same person you were before, or you can announce your transformation to everyone.

I suggest the latter.

When I decided to reinvent myself and shift from being Arnold Palmer's agent into the manager of a growing sports marketing business, I had to redefine my relationship with Arnold in such a way that I got my point across without offending him. Those tests came early and often. Arnold would call and ask me to run an errand for him, and the newly defined Mark would say, "I'll be happy to have my secretary do that for you, Arnold, but I would be doing more for you if I spent my time clearing up this contract with Allstate Insurance."

It took Arnold and my other clients some time to grow comfortable with the new Mark McCormack, but in the long run, the redefinition benefited everyone. If you don't tell the world you have reinvented yourself, years may pass before people reinvent their impression of you.

Never forget where you came from

At 70 years old, Arnold Palmer has now spent almost 50 years of his life as one of the most recognized athletes and celebrities in the world. He has graced the cover of every major sports and business magazine of note, and his celebrity star shines just as brightly now as it did when he was capturing major golf championships. Arnold is a legend — a true icon in American sports.

But when he goes home to Latrobe, Pennsylvania, he is still Arnie Palmer, Deacon Palmer's son. Arnold simply smiles at this. It's what makes him unique. Not only is he comfortable being Deacon Palmer's son from Latrobe, PA, the fact that he has remained rooted in his background is one of his most endearing qualities. Arnold has achieved mass popularity and success not in spite of his background, but because of it. He is genuine and he never forgets his roots. The public sees that, and loves him for it.

On the other end of that spectrum, I know an actor who refuses to speak about his past, and who won't acknowledge any aspect of his life prior to arriving in Hollywood. It is as though he is embarrassed by the fact that he grew up in a modest household with middle-class parents. He wants to be seen as nothing less than a star.

Unfortunately, after a run of moderately successful films, this actor's career became stagnant, his star-power faded, and he became bitter, often drinking too much in public and openly making snappish comments like "Don't you know who I am?" to people who obviously didn't know and didn't care.

Although there are many differences between Arnold Palmer and the actor, the one that has always stuck out in my mind is the difference in the way they accept themselves. Arnold knows who he is, where he's from, and who the most important people in his life are. The actor wants nothing to do with his past, and as a result, he has little to look forward to in the future.

Chapter 21

Making Your Goals Contagious

In This Chapter
▶ Communicating the results you want
▶ Spreading your dreams to others

You may be the most independent and self-reliant person in the world, but results require the help and cooperation of other people — no matter who you are. Sure, you can probably clean up your office on your own, and if you employ the organizational principals outlined in Parts II and III, you can certainly get more out of your hours and days, but the big results — the lofty prizes at the end of your organizational rainbow — can only be achieved with the help of others. In order to recruit other people to your cause, you must be able to communicate, motivate, and spread your vision to those around you.

Start by making a list of the personal and professional results you hope to obtain in the next 12 months. Maybe you want to remodel your house, or perhaps you have dreams of starting your own company. Whatever your goals, devote a full sheet of paper to each objective you hope to obtain, writing the desired result in bold letters at the top of the page.

Beneath the heading make two lists:

✔ Steps I must take myself to reach these results

✔ Others I must recruit to help me

After you spend a little time with each of these lists, you'll probably find that the "others you must recruit" list is at least as — if not more — detailed than the "steps you must take yourself" list. Whether you're delegating current duties to free up time to take on new projects or bringing in experts to help make decisions, reliance on other people is critical to achieving the results you want.

Communicating Results

The biggest obstacle to getting the results you want isn't money or time; it's communication. People are naturally reluctant to ask for help, and even more reluctant to share information about a desired outcome. If you don't believe it, go ask your boss about his goals for next month's profits. Unless you work for an enlightened CEO, the answer is likely to be something between "Why do you ask?" and "None of your business." Human instinct is to keep goals personal. To share your objectives with others is to put your dreams on the line. And to ask others for help is often perceived as a sign of weakness.

That sort of thinking is hogwash. All successful people have asked for and received the help of other people along the road to their success, and all are great communicators. In order to get results, you must join those who have mastered the art of effective communication.

Recognizing that what you say isn't always what others hear

If you have children, you are probably nodding your head after reading the heading to this section. I'm amazed at how interpretive a simple statement like "clean your room," can become when communicating with a child. Each word must be examined and respoken in order to ensure the outcome you desire.

But even though you may smile when you think of all the communication breakdowns between parents and children, many people fail to realize that the same sorts of communication challenges come up regularly between adults in business and social relationships. How many times have you asked a colleague a question about an issue and received an answer totally unrelated to the subject? How often have you requested something specific from a co-worker and received something totally off the wall? On a more basic level, how many times have you made special requests in a restaurant only to have a meal delivered that doesn't resemble what you ordered?

These are just a few examples of how what you say and what others hear can differ, but the examples illustrate a big problem for those trying to communicate a future objective. If ordering a well-done hamburger with extra onion and no tomato from a single waitperson causes problems, how can you possibly communicate a long-range vision to a large group?

Do not disturb — for the most part!

In her first month of employment, the woman I hired as the assistant for my Orlando residence found herself in a Catch-22, which could have been avoided if I had been more diligent in explaining myself. I was in the middle of a tennis match when my daughter called to wish me a happy birthday. Unfortunately, I had left specific instructions with my assistant not to be disturbed during the match, because I was not expecting any calls and wanted to enjoy the camaraderie and competition this match afforded — especially on my birthday.

When my daughter called, my new assistant said, "I'm sorry, he's in the middle of a tennis match right now and can't be disturbed."

This deeply wounded my daughter. Not only did she wrongly perceive that I placed a tennis match over her call, she was calling from a cell phone in France, which made a follow-up call from me virtually impossible.

Technically, my assistant had done exactly what I had instructed her to do. Practically, however, she was in a no-win situation. She had no idea how I would react if she interrupted me (although in this instance I would have preferred to know my daughter was on the line), and she had no idea how my daughter would react to being told she couldn't speak to me on my birthday. This situation could have been avoided if I had taken a little more time to explain some of the exceptions to my "do not disturb" rule.

Knowing how others process information

Several years ago an executive friend of mine accepted a job as the chief operating officer (COO) of a large company. The plan was for my friend to work a few years while being groomed to succeed the notoriously difficult CEO. At the time, I told my friend that I thought the move, although risky, was a good one. In my estimation he had all the qualities of a great COO: a quick mind, great follow-up skills, good judgment, a mind for details, and an ego that allowed him to study and grow in his career.

To my dismay, however, he quit the new job within eight months. He and the chairman never clicked, even though no one ever sensed any overt personality differences between the two men. When I had an opportunity, I asked the chairman about my friend and what happened with their relationship.

"I liked him," the chairman said. "But he was too much of a 'systems guy' for me. He was always bombarding me with memos and reports that I didn't want to read. I needed a partner, someone I could talk to each day and bounce ideas off of. He seemed to be much more comfortable shoving paper at me."

My friends' promising professional career went askew because he didn't understand how his boss processed information. The chairman didn't want paper; he wanted conversation. He was a verbal communicator, while my friend communicated by using written words.

It may seem small, almost petty, but success depends on figuring out how your bosses, clients, and peers process information, and then communicating with them on their level. In the sports management business, I've seen many relationships between clients and agents sour because the agents didn't understand how their clients processed information. Some clients want the agent to call them every day with updates. Others think that sort of communication is an annoyance. Some want written updates; others want a phone call. Neither is right or wrong, but if you want to effectively communicate your ideas, you must understand how those around you get information.

This strategy is actually easier than it sounds because everybody falls into one of two camps: People either *listen* or *read* to receive information, and people either *talk* or *write* to send information. Unfortunately, most people don't take the time to identify which group their audience falls into, and some don't even analyze their own preferences.

Everyone thinks of him- or herself as a good listener. But how often have you found yourself nodding agreement with someone and then realizing that you have no idea what the person just said? Do you remember a point you read in a magazine article last week better than you remember what a co-worker said two days ago? If so, you're probably a reader/writer. If you can recall conversations from days or weeks ago, but can't remember the headline in this morning's paper, you're probably a talker/listener.

I like to think of myself as a good listener, but when I analyze myself, I realize that I'm really a reader. Even though I have numerous business conversations every day, I almost always end each conversation by saying, "Do me a favor. Please send me a one-page memo outlining what we've just discussed." I may remember the conversation, but after it's in writing I know that I can process the information on my own terms.

Don't call me — write me!

I know one CEO who refuses to meet with anyone until the person has submitted a written synopsis of the meeting topic. His reasoning, although blunt, is simple. "I don't have time for rambling conversations," he says. "If someone has enough discipline to organize and condense his thoughts on paper, I'll read it and then talk to him, but sitting around chatting is a waste of my time. Plus, I can read faster than most people can talk, so it saves a lot of time." This guy is definitely a reader/writer.

Try this exercise: Go to the list I discuss at the beginning of this chapter, and look at the names of the people you listed under "Others I must recruit." Can you identify how each person on your list digests information? If not, find out and accommodate your communications to fit their preferences.

Establishing the confirmation key

If you've ever served in the military or if you're a pilot, you understand the cumbersome formalities of radio communications. For every message, an identification and verification process must be followed before the message is completed. Without *confirmation* (correspondence as to the details of a plan), the sender must assume that the message has not been received.

For example, an air traffic controller can't call a plane over the radio and say, "Hey buddy, you need to turn left to miss a jet that's heading your way." The transmission must be to a specific aircraft (designated by call letters) and the pilot must verify it. If the controller needs the pilot to turn left, the message might be, "November-four-six-papa, turn left flight heading two-six-zero vectors for traffic."

The pilot must then respond. "November-four-six-papa, roger, turning left heading two-six-zero." It's wordy and cumbersome, but that sort of confirmation is crucial for air traffic safety. Any miscommunication, and lives could be in jeopardy.

Although communicating your objectives may not be a matter of life or death, you should still require confirmation after communicating a point. It may be as simple as asking, "What did you take from what I just said?" You may be surprised by some of the responses you get. It's amazing how garbled your message gets once it goes through the filter of a listener. By throwing in a few confirmations along the way, you have a better chance of cleaning up your communications.

Communicating why you are communicating

In the movie *Trains, Planes, and Automobiles* starring John Candy and Steve Martin, Martin's character is a weary traveler who finds himself navigating the midwestern United States with Candy's character in an odd-couple relationship that proves hilarious. At one point during their travels, Martin's character has had enough, and during an insulting monologue, he says to Candy, "Oh, by the way, when you're telling a story, have a point. It makes it so much more interesting."

Too many people forget that advice when they're communicating with others. You may know exactly why you are telling your story to a co-worker, but the co-worker may not have the faintest idea why he is listening. If your communications are to be effective, the person you're communicating with needs to understand how he fits into the picture. Otherwise, although he may not say it, the person you need the most is thinking, "What's your point?"

Spreading Your Dreams

Even after identifying those from whom you need help and after you've determined how to communicate with them, you still have one major task ahead: You have to make others want to help you.

Motivation comes in many forms. If you're a parent trying to get a teenager to clean his room, the reasons you give might range from "Because I said so," to "Your grandmother is coming, and she hasn't had her tetanus shots." If you're the boss and you're asking your employees to get on board with a project, you can say, "This is important to the future of the company," or "This is a top priority for everyone." These motivating slogans are nicer than "Because I said so," but the meaning is the same.

When you deal with people who aren't your children or your subordinates, the task becomes a little tougher. In those instances, you have to persuade people that helping you is in their best interests. The following sections show you several ways to accomplish this task.

Finding out what motivates others

When Steve Jobs (the founder and CEO of Apple Computer) was trying to lure John Sculley (who held the top post at PepsiCo) from New York to California, where Sculley would assume the reigns at Apple, Jobs looked Sculley in the eyes and said, "Do you want to continue to sell sugar water to kids, or do you want to help me change the world?" It was an offer Sculley couldn't turn down.

If you expect others to help you achieve the results you desire, you have to make your dreams their dreams. Money is always a great motivator, as is prestige, a good title, and the promise of a few corporate perks. But if you want those around you to become impassioned, you have to tap into their motivations, and the goals they hope to accomplish in life. If, like Steve Jobs, you can convince those around you to give up selling sugar water to help you change the world, you will have plenty of help achieving your results.

Getting your assistant onboard

Whether you have a secretary, an executive assistant, or a high-school student who helps out around your house after school, the same principles apply. If you want to gain maximum efficiency from your assistant and get him or her on your organizational track, you must first meet your responsibilities to your assistant.

✔ **Communicate your objectives on the front end.** Figure-it-out-as-you-go just isn't enough with an assistant. You become frustrated by seemingly trivial breaches in your organizational plan while the assistant becomes equally frustrated by your constant corrections. Mistakes while training are inevitable, but you can eliminate a lot of unnecessary misunderstandings by sharing your goals, objectives, and expectations with your assistant.

✔ **Incorporate your assistant into your system.** Nothing gets your assistant on board faster than making him or her an integral part of your goals. The best way to include your assistant is to sit down with him or her at the end of each day and discuss the next day's activities. Perhaps your assistant can take over some of the items on your list, or give you some ideas for maximizing your efficiency. Either way, getting an assistant in tune with your plans improves your relationship and your efficiency.

✔ **Evaluate regularly.** The annual or semi-annual review isn't enough when evaluating and training your assistant. If you want to establish an effective long-term relationship, provide constant feedback, both positive and negative, and offer suggestions at every turn. You improve as your assistant improves. Although critiquing may be uncomfortable for you and you may believe letting some mistakes slide is best, that attitude only poisons future relations and causes resentment.

✔ **Remain aware of your assistant's needs.** I often rise between 4:00 and 5:00 a.m. in order to read my newspapers and make phone calls to Europe during morning business hours. Sometimes my early morning activities require an assistant (in the case of dictation or filing), and sometimes they don't. If I do need my assistant to be available at what is, for most people, an obscene hour, I make sure that he has plenty of notice as well as ample time off in the afternoon or evening to compensate for my early morning request. Assuming that an assistant can always bend his schedule to meet your needs is unreasonable, although the nature of the job requires a great deal of flexibility on his part. Assistants are human beings with lives and families and needs. Remaining mindful of that fact only strengthens your relationship.

Sharing the credit

Former president Ronald Reagan used to say, "It's amazing what you can get done if you don't care who gets the credit." It's also amazing how motivated your friends, co-workers, and family members become after you generously dole out credit when they have accomplished certain tasks.

Of course, financial rewards such as profit sharing and bonuses for successful projects also generate excitement, but don't think that you're bound by how much you can pay. Worthwhile rewards don't always have dollar signs attached.

Announcing the results

After you reach a goal, announce your achievement to those who helped along the way. It may be something as simple as a note saying, "I couldn't have done it without you," or a phone call to let the person know that you've succeeded. Whatever means you choose, announcing your success in this way isn't bragging. It's a kind way of saying thank you.

Motivating Your Family

Orienting yourself toward a goal means changing your behavior. Although the change is for the better, it's a change nonetheless. Nowhere is change more difficult than at home, where the family dynamic is well-established and ingrained. Your co-workers expect you to behave a certain way, but when you change your behavior as part of a "getting results" resolution, they tend to accept and even embrace the new you. Family members aren't always so understanding.

If you've always been the glorified taxi service to and from your child's school, baseball field, and favorite ice cream store, placing restrictions on when and how often you will make those jaunts may create some tension. Similarly, if your spouse has been a willing accomplice in contributing to the clutter around your home, any effort you put forth to change that behavior may be met with moderate to strong resistance.

Setting goals

Like any organizational change, the first step in bringing your family onboard to your new approach to projects is goal setting. The most important family member to include in the process of setting goals is your spouse or significant other. A great way to break the ice and make getting organized a family activity is to take your spouse on a dinner date — but take your notepad along with you. After you order your entrée, explain to your spouse that you are devoting yourself to getting better results. No one could possibly argue with that!

The next step is to explain how getting results at home is a family effort, requiring mutual goals and realistic expectations. If both spouses work outside the home and the family can't afford a cook or a maid, for either spouse to assume that the house will be pristine and that dinner will be on the table at 6:00 every night is being unreasonable.

Still, cleaning the house and cooking meals are tasks that have to be done. As part of your goal-setting discussion, you and your spouse must come to terms with what can and can't be reasonably expected. The discussion need not be emotionally charged, and won't be if you use your notepad and segment your goals and tasks into manageable bites.

After you agree on some common goals, the two of you should discuss how responsibilities can be divided. Perhaps one spouse is better equipped to get the kids dressed in the morning while the other is more adept at preparing breakfast. Maybe one spouse wants to read the papers before going to work, but this action creates resentment in the rest of the family. One possible answer is for that spouse to rise an hour early in the morning and explain to the family that this is "newspaper time." The other morning tasks can still be completed, and no one harbors resentment.

This give-and-take plan may require more than one dinner date to agree upon, but the creation of a specific scheme is critical if you are going to change your family life and become more organized at home. Just as communicating with your peers and clients is critical at the office, talking with your spouse about your organizational vision is the first step in bringing your family onboard.

Getting your children involved

One of the biggest favors you can do for your children is to show them how to work toward results when they are young. The principles and practices you teach them as kids will serve them well in higher education and in their careers. Conversely, if you set an example of being scatteredbrained, flighty, frustrated, and generally disorganized, your kids will follow in your footsteps and struggle with the same problems you're trying to leave behind.

Make the children part of the organizational process. After you and your spouse agree on your objectives, the two of you can sit down with your children and explain what you hope to achieve, and what is expected from them. A two-year-old can pick up his toys. A six-year-old can organize her closet, make her bed, and be responsible for dusting and cleaning her room. Their responsibilities at home should increase as they grow older. Children can — and should — help in your plan for your home, even when that plan is as major as remodeling, moving to a new city, or getting rid of debt.

The griping may be persistent and the whining will, no doubt, get on your nerves, but you can give your kids no greater gift than showing them how to work toward goals. If they observe you, it will be second nature to them when they enter the real world.

Chapter 22

Pulling Others Along for the Ride

. . . .

In This Chapter

▶ Discovering what you can and can't control in other people's actions

▶ Getting the support you need

▶ Cutting through organizational frustrations

. . . .

*O*ne of the biggest challenges to getting results is your relationship with those reluctant people around you. Despite what you may believe, you can't change other people. You can train them, you can encourage them, you can inspire them, and you can disassociate from them if they don't meet your standards, but the only person that you can change is yourself.

The inability to change other people presents a number of problems when you're working to get results. No one wants to seem rude, and you certainly don't want to offend your friends, co-workers, or family members. You must, however, send the message to all these groups that you are changing your life, and that a lackadaisical approach to meetings, commitments, deadlines, and clutter is no longer tolerated. No man or woman is an island, so communicating your commitment to getting results is imperative. You can get this message across in a number of ways.

Showing Off Your System

Meetings with people who aren't supporting your initiatives can turn into rap sessions or get bogged down by details. To make these meeting run more smoothly, let others see your organizational system, even if that system consists of nothing more than a pen, a pad of paper, and some note cards. If I am chairing a meeting in one of our offices, I mark through the agenda items on my pad as we discuss them. This action demonstrates to others in the meeting that I consider that particular subject closed for the moment. When I mark through an item on my pad, in plain view of everyone in a meeting, all in attendance gain a palpable sense of closure and the discussion moves ahead to other items. Such cues are subtle, but without them I've seen meetings deteriorate into endless rap sessions with no focus, no agenda, and no definitive conclusion.

Marking through completed items also offers a way of transitioning out of one meeting and into another without insulting anyone. When a meeting is over and you want to move on to other things, you can hope the person you're meeting with picks up on your signals and excuses herself or you can say something like, "Well, that was wonderful. Now, if you will excuse me I have some pressing calls to make," and hope that you don't insult the person. Or you can simply mark through the person's name on your notepad. Without saying a word, you've communicated to the person that the meeting is over — no uncomfortable words and no awkward transitions.

Some people see this method as rude, but it is much more pleasant than dismissing someone verbally. Crossing off the names shows the people with whom you meet that you're organized and efficient. In the end, if they're intelligent and professional, they appreciate your efficiency.

Administering the Odd-Time Test

Nothing captures people's attention faster than setting an odd time for a meeting or a phone call. I have become quite well-known for doing this, often telling a colleague or client that I will call at 10:58 next Tuesday morning or some other precise — but relatively odd — time. Usually I get a chortle from the person on the receiving end of this exchange because the time seems so outrageous. More than once, I've heard people say, "Is McCormack nuts? How can he know that he's going to call me at exactly 10:58 next Tuesday? I don't even know what I'm going to be doing an hour from now."

Without fail, however, the people to whom I give the odd times are standing by at 10:58 (or whatever time I requested) simply because I was so precise.

If I said, "I'll meet you at around 11:00," the time of the meeting could be interpreted as any time between 10:55 and 11:25 (usually the latter). By going overboard in my precision, I send a message to those around me that punctuality is important.

Holding Firm

As anyone who has ever played tournament golf can attest, starting times are inflexible and no excuse earns you leniency if you're late. The penalty for not arriving at the first tee on time is disqualification — no exceptions and no adjustments. If Tiger Woods leads a tournament after two rounds, but breaks down on the way to the course and shows up 15 minutes late for his third-round tee time, he's disqualified from the event. That's the rule. Because Tiger and all other competitive golfers understand that rule, they are rarely, if ever, late. Traffic, warm-up times, and all other variables are taken into account when a golfer learns his starting time. Players arrive at the first tee at least five minutes before their prescribed deadline 99.99 percent of the time.

You can pick up a lot from this rule of golf. If you have a meeting scheduled from 11:00 until 12:00, and the person with whom you are meeting doesn't show up until 11:20, do you extend the meeting until 12:20 and inconvenience your schedule, or do you cut the meeting short by 20 minutes and end it promptly at 12:00? Your answer says a lot about how much value you place on your project, and how much control you exert over your daily schedule.

Even though I have gained a worldwide reputation for being one of the most prompt and organized people in the business world, I am not immune to the time bandits — those people who, because of ego or woeful disorganization, can't arrive at a meeting on time (see Chapter 14). I've heard every excuse in the book for lateness. But I have learned from experience that someone else's inability to be on time should never disrupt my schedule. As long as the person understands upfront that I set aside only a specific block of time for him, my conscience is clear when I must cut our meeting short. He was late, not me.

I'm not saying that I am an ogre who doesn't understand unexpected calamities such as cars breaking down, children getting sick, or flights being canceled. I have been a victim of these circumstances just like everyone else. However, just as I don't expect everyone to adjust their schedules to fit my unforeseen problems, most people don't expect me to shift everything in my schedule to accommodate their tardiness. If someone is going to be late for a meeting and I have another meeting immediately following, I reschedule with the tardy person for a later time or another day. I do not, however, inconvenience the person I am meeting next in order to accommodate someone who is running late.

Pulling Free of the Molasses

During my early years as an entrepreneur, I received some sage advice from Ben Bidwell, president of Ford Motor Company. Ben told me that dealing with Ford (and any large company like Ford) was like trying to get through a wall of molasses. You can get into it, but you can't get through it. Once in it, you can't move from side to side, and, after too long, you discover that you can't get out of it, either.

This was a great lesson for me at the time, because as a strong-willed business owner, I thought all executives and all companies operated with the same lean, mean, growth-oriented mindset that I brought to IMG. I quickly learned the truth. The larger the company, the larger the bureaucracy — and the thicker the wall of molasses.

Submitting a proposal to a junior executive at Ford would be less effective than throwing the same proposal in the ocean and hoping that it washed ashore and landed in the hands of the right person. Contacting a junior officer would be a waste of time and a frustrating exercise in futility.

On the other hand, getting the proposal into the hands of the right person (the president or chairman, in the case of a large company such as Ford) can be very productive. Dealing with Bidwell was always a pleasure, because he could cut through the wall of molasses with one phone call. The trick was getting the proposal in Bidwell's — the right person's — hands.

Some projects aren't meant to be

Imagine how tough reaching five CEOs in five different Fortune 500 companies *and* getting all of them to agree with your proposal would be — just to get your proposal off the ground.

An executive in our New York office designed a music proposal that required the cooperation of television networks, record producers, artists, agents, and concert promoters on four different continents. Even though this man was more likely to be hit in the head by an asteroid than pull off this far-flung venture, he continued to pursue it with blind vigor. He never attended a meeting that he didn't offer an update on his

project — a call to a record executive or a meeting with a concert promoter.

After several months of no progress, I finally had to sit down with this executive and explain the futility of his efforts, telling him that he was jeopardizing his reputation inside the company by pursuing this project. Of course, he was wounded by my criticism, but if he had taken the time to calculate the odds of bringing all those disparate parties together, he might have recognized how unlikely his scheme was. As I told him, it was a great idea, but without controlling more of the variables it was a waste of his time.

Part V
The Part of Tens

The 5th Wave — By Rich Tennant

"I've been working over 80 hours a week for the past two years preparing for retirement, and it hasn't bothered me OR my wife, whats-her-name."

In this part . . .

This part assembles the various traits, tips, warnings, and drills of achievers and divides those tidbits into lists of tens. Each of the chapters in this part provides you with ways to get maximum results from your project initiatives — a road map for achieving the results you expect. From ten ways to emulate achievers to ten traits to avoid at all costs, ten drills to improve your results to ten ways to cut down on clutter, the chapters in this part help you move your agenda forward. I've even included a chapter on how to start each day on the right foot!

You may want to transfer some of the items from this part into your personal planner. If a tip makes sense, incorporate it into your everyday activities and keep it written down in a convenient place so you can reference it often. If you don't possess the positive traits you see listed in this part, transfer the items to your list of goals and set realistic time frames for incorporating them into your day.

Chapter 23

Ten Traits of Achievers

In This Chapter

▶ Recognizing the traits of results-oriented individuals

▶ Incorporating these traits into your daily life

*W*hether they are professional executives, world-renowned artists, athletes, students, managers, or homemakers, all highly successful people have certain common characteristics. These are not traits that *make* them successful; they are merely the common attitudes and actions that are shared almost universally among those who have mastered their clocks, their calendars, and the spaces they occupy.

Understanding each of these traits and how you measure up against achievers is important. After studying the characteristics, look at the people you know who get maximum results out of their time and efforts, and see how they excel in each of the areas I list in this chapter. Then make a list of your own, writing down at least three action items that help you improve in each trait.

None of these traits are genetically transferred. All can be learned and applied to your daily routine. You must make each trait a priority, understand its implications, and make it part of your lifestyle.

Setting Clearly Defined Goals

These goals are not vague or nebulous. They are clear, precise, written objectives with definitive time frames for completion. A successful person's goals are always written — although they are usually short enough to be communicated in one or two brief sentences — and they are kept in a place where the person who wrote them can reference them easily, like a notebook or a wallet.

But the results-oriented person doesn't merely write his goals, frame them, and place them in clear view on his desk as he would some inspirational slogan. This person looks at his goals as tasks to be achieved, much like the daily tasks he writes on his to-do list. He doesn't look to his goals for guidance or inspiration; instead, he looks to accomplish them so he can mark them off his list.

For this reason the achiever's goals are not based on attitude, but are results oriented. They are also more detailed than the goals of his disorganized counterparts. For example, a nonachiever may write as a goal, "Create a net worth of $1 million in the next ten years," which on the surface may seem perfectly acceptable. The statement is specific, goal-oriented, and framed by a deadline. Compare it, however, with what the results-oriented person may write: "Grow widget business by 30 percent annually for five years. Pay off all personal debt in six years by selling percentage of widget company stock. Increase personal net worth to $1 million in ten years through growth of stock value to $20 a share."

Who do you think is more likely to reach his goals? The person with the nebulous $1 million net worth goal, or the individual with the detailed plan? The answer is as clear as the goals you need to write for yourself.

Respecting Time

Those who get results respect their own time as well the time of others. You won't find the results-oriented person frittering away the day as if time were an endless commodity. In fact, achievers monitor every minute, paying equally close attention to how they spend their leisure time and their business time. They don't dwell on the superfluous, nor are they exceptionally tolerant of those around them who spend time unproductively.

I am probably as good at monitoring and respecting time as anyone I know. In addition to having my days mapped out from start to finish, I have, for the last 40 years, kept a running log of the number of hours I sleep. It started when my mother once told me she didn't think I was getting enough sleep. I wasn't sure whether she was right or not, so I started keeping track of my rest time and logging that information in order to develop weekly, monthly, and yearly averages. It worked out great. I discovered that although the time I slept varied dramatically from night to night, my yearly averages were about 6½ hours a night, which is plenty of rest for someone with my metabolism.

Keeping track of the hours you sleep may seem like a strange idea to some, but disciplined people understand the value of this type of information. This information helps them make rational decisions about the time they are spending in certain areas, whether it is sleep, work, play, or doing absolutely nothing. By knowing how much time they are spending in each area and respecting that time as precious, organized people stand a much better chance of reaching their objectives than those who continually let the clock slip away.

Writing Down Everything

Even the most trivial and seemingly inane task makes it onto the achiever's list. Whether it's taking out the trash or finishing an important sales proposal, the results-oriented individual keeps running lists of the things she has to finish and the time in which she has to finish them.

Details confuse disorganized people. Results-oriented individuals keep their long-term, intermediate, and short-term goals written down where they can see them on a daily basis, and their lists and daily planners are with them at all times. A disorganized individual believes that the to-do list she leaves on her desk every night constitutes sufficient planning and organization. Yet, when her organized colleagues accomplish more than she does, and reap the rewards that come with getting results, the disorganized list writer can't figure out what she's doing wrong. She believes that she is as organized as her co-workers, even though she sees them taking their notepads and lists home with them every night while *her* one-page list sits on the corner of her desk.

Writing everything — from when you will sleep, to when you will eat, to what you will do first, second, third, and last — is the only way to truly stay organized and get the results you want out of life.

Prioritizing

People who get the best results out of their days, weeks, months, and years, whether it is in their business or personal lives, always approach tasks in descending order of importance, handling the most important things first and the least important thing last. That is not to say that every important task gets done first thing in the morning. What it does mean, though, is that the most important task gets a priority spot in the day's agenda and all other items fill in around it.

As an example, if you are expecting a phone call from your most important clients to discuss a major piece of business, you will likely schedule the other calls and other tasks you have to finish in the day around that call. If a colleague comes into your office five minutes before your call, the results-oriented person explains that she's expecting an important call and schedules a more appropriate time for the colleague to return. The disorganized person will anxiously sit while the colleague drones on, hoping he will finish whatever it is he has to say before the phone rings.

For those who achieve results, prioritization is a natural process. Everything that comes up is assigned a number almost immediately. If other more pressing items are on the day's agenda, the lower-priority item isn't forgotten; it is merely moved to another day and a more convenient time. The achiever then handles first things first, getting maximum results out of the time she has allotted.

Focusing on the Task at Hand

Because everything is written down and prioritized, the results-oriented person doesn't have to clutter his mind with things that are coming up later or things that he has completed in the past. Each task is given his undivided attention. The most important thing on the achiever's mind at the moment a task is undertaken is completing the task so he can move on to the next item on his list.

The only way this works is if the person writing and carrying out the tasks on the list has total confidence that each item represents the highest and best use of his time at the moment he is engaging in the task. This is where disorganized people often get sidetracked. They commit, for example, to a golf game at 3:00, but when they are on the first tee they know they should be in the office working on the monthly sales projections. Guilt sets in, golf is a blur, and at the end of the day nothing of substance has been accomplished.

The disciplined person not only knows when he will complete the monthly sales projections, he knows how long it will take and what he will forego in order to complete that task with the utmost efficiency. Because of that knowledge, the achiever can go to the golf course at a predetermined time and have a wonderful and relaxing round, focusing on the task at hand, which at that moment is golf.

Studying a Subject Before Acting on It

A results-oriented individual looks before she leaps, not only to develop a strategy for approaching a task, but also to judge whether a subject is worthy of her time and attention. If it doesn't move her closer to her short-term or long-term goals, no matter how attractive it may seem, the studious, disciplined person will turn it down. If it does fit her goals, however, the structured person still ponders a subject in order to ensure that she approaches it in the most effective and efficient manner possible. More than anything, the person seeking results understands that the time she spends developing a plan of action will be made up ten times over once the task is underway and the results start pouring in.

Constantly Looking for Ways to Improve

I have used my particular organizational system (my lined legal pad and note cards) for over 30 years with great success. But that doesn't mean that I haven't kept an eye out for something better. I've studied the systems of dozens of busy executives, and, at times, I've incorporated some of the things they do into my system. I have also looked at hundreds of electronic organizational gadgets and expensive planning folders, calendars, and daily organizers, but none of them have met my needs as well as my pad, pen, and note cards.

I'm still looking, though. As is the case with most results-oriented people, I am constantly looking for ways to improve what I do and how I do it. When I see something that seems to work, I analyze it, sometimes modify it, and almost always try it to see how it could work for me. If my results improve with the new system, it stays. If they don't, I either modify it, or I abandon it and continue looking for something better.

Rarely will you hear an achiever say, "I do it this way because I've always done it this way." Many of us are old dogs, but we're constantly looking to learn a new trick.

Delegating

The proper emphasis on delegation cannot be overemphasized if you want to achieve maximum results. You can't do everything, nor should you try. Not only are you not as accomplished at certain things as other people, but if you try to do everything, you won't finish the things you do well with any consistency. You either have to delegate some items to others, trusting that they can complete the tasks you assign to them, or you have to limit your successes to only those tasks you can physically accomplish yourself.

Better than others, disciplined people understand those things that only they can do, and they spend most of their time focusing on those items. The tasks that can be completed by others are delegated, so that the achievement-oriented person accomplishes more in less time with better efficiency than he would have if he tried to get it all done himself.

Of course, at some point we've all said, "If you want something done right, you have to do it yourself." But only the *dis*organized person believes it.

Knowing When to Quit

When those who get results call it a day, they turn out the light, close the door, and move on without any hesitation, guilt, or anxiety. That is not to imply that an achiever always accomplishes everything she sets out to do. Many times, circumstances arise that keep even the most organized and efficient person from getting the results she had hoped for.

Does that mean that she stays in the office two extra hours fretting about it? Not unless those two hours move her closer to her desired results without impeding on other priority items on her list. More than likely the results-oriented person simply chalks it up as a less-than-letter-perfect day and transfers the unfinished items on her list to the next day. This approach allows her to go home or move on to the next item on her list without worry. She will handle the unfinished item at a later time.

She also knows when to abandon a project altogether. Some things just don't work out, and you have to let them go. Those who strive for results are able to do that and move forward.

Managing Space As Well As Time

Not only does the achiever get maximum results from the time he spends on his daily tasks, but he achieves the most from the space around him, and he maintains an orderly environment in which to live and work. You have certainly seen this person: He is the one who never seems to panic when a deadline is approaching, and continues to accomplish more than those around him while keeping his desk spotless and his surroundings tidy and well groomed.

These orderly surroundings allow the results-oriented person to focus on the tasks at hand without worrying about the upcoming file sitting beside him or the previous project that is still laying open on his desk.

That organization doesn't stop at the office, however. One of the best ways to determine whether someone is a serious results-oriented individual is to check out his personal surroundings. Does he live in an orderly home? Are his storage areas efficiently organized? If so, you can bet that the tasks he undertakes are completed with great attention to detail. If not, look for sloppy thinking and less-than-perfect performance.

Remaining Flexible When Necessary

Those who strive for results are realists. They understand as well as, if not better than, most people that time is fluid and schedules constantly change. Unlike the scatterbrained person, however, the achiever derives great pleasure from being able to shuffle things around and still meet her obligations without disrupting her focus. It is a challenge she finds exhilarating. While others throw up their arms in despair, the organized person takes changes in stride, immediately reorganizing things to maximize her accomplishments within the new parameters.

For example, if the important client whose phone call you had scheduled your day around had his secretary call to say that he couldn't talk to you until two hours later, you could reshuffle your lower priority items in order to accomplish everything on your list within these new circumstances. Or you could throw up your hands and assume that the entire day was a waste. How you handle those sorts of situations says a lot about your chances of success.

Chapter 24

Ten Drills to Improve Your Results

Getting results from your efforts is a learned trait that you can practice and perfect over time. All it takes is patience, an understanding of the principles you are applying, and enough practice to make good habits a natural part of your daily routine. Good habits drive out bad habits, especially where organization and efficiency are concerned. Unfortunately, good habits don't come naturally. They have to be drilled. This chapter provides a few drills to get you underway.

Visualize Your List

Visualizing your list is akin to meditation, only more productive. Your list may be optimistic or pessimistic, but the only real way to know is to put yourself into the list, determine how long each item is likely to take, and calculate the odds of success. Only then can you modify your schedule and make it more realistic.

Visualization isn't telepathy or levitation. Visualization simply requires you to close your eyes and put yourself in the activity you have written on your list. If your first item of the day is a trip to Wal-Mart for cotton swabs, toilet paper, and the latest issue of *People* magazine, you need to mentally put yourself in the car and visualize the trip. How long is it likely to take you to get to Wal-Mart given the traffic patterns in the morning? Then visualize the parking lot that time of day. Where are you likely to park, and how long should you expect to look for an empty space? What about your time in the store? Do you know where the cotton swabs, toilet paper, and magazines are located in your local Wal-Mart? If so, how long is it going to take you to walk through the aisles and pick up the items? If not, how long should you plan to look? How long are the checkout lines in the morning, and how slow are the cashiers? How much traffic should you expect on the way back home?

If, after you have gone through the trip in your mind, you determine that the minimum time for a Wal-Mart excursion is 30 minutes, but you've only scheduled 15 minutes on your list, you should modify your list to allow at least 45 minutes for the trip. This approach gives you plenty of time to speak to a friend whom you may run into in the store or search for a parking space if you underestimated the crowd.

The only way to accurately gauge the time needed, however, is to visualize the activity ahead of time. I use a trip to the store as an example, but you should go through this exercise with every item on your daily list. This strategy will help you think in terms of real time, and it will do wonders for your effectiveness after you get into your daily activities.

Close Your Door, Even When You Don't Need To

If you are prone to accepting interruptions or others have become accustomed to intruding on your time and space, try closing your door, even if you're not involved in a top-secret project. The simple act of closing a door sends a message to those around you, especially if it's something you rarely do.

At first, people will wonder what is wrong with you. "There must be a crisis for her to shut herself off from the rest of the world. It's so unlike her," they'll think.

But the shock eventually wears off, and after it does, continue to close your door when you need to focus and leave it open when you don't. But initially, closing it for the sake of closing it will go a long way toward teaching yourself and others to respect your time and space. There's no time like the present.

Set Daily Goals That Go Beyond Your List

You may have established a one-year goal, or a two-year goal, or three-year, four-year, five-year, and ten-year goals, but until you successfully reach a few of those pre-set goals they are going to seem nebulous and ethereal. You not only need to get into the habit of setting goals, but you need to learn how to reach them. You need to know what it feels like to attain a goal and cross it off your list, and you need to experience the satisfaction of accomplishing a worthwhile goal.

A good way to get into the habit of goal setting and experience the thrill of reaching your goals is to establish a daily goal for yourself that is above and beyond your to-do list. For example, your list of tasks could include a meeting, a conference call, a luncheon, 50 pages of reading material to review, and a basketball game to attend. But your goal for the day may read, "Ask one additional question of everyone I meet today."

This goal isn't a task per se, although it requires action through the course of your day. It is a goal that has a very short-term life and can be definitively measured. It also has enormous payoffs. By forcing yourself to ask one additional question of everyone you meet, even if it's nothing more than, "How are you feeling today?" followed by, "And how are the kids?" you will have expanded your mind and enhanced your relationship with those around you.

As time goes on, make the goals loftier. "Contact two old friends today," or "Go an entire day without making a negative comment." Each of these daily goals is outside your normal list of tasks, but accomplishing them will get you in the habit. By the time the one-year, five-year, and ten-year goals roll around, you will be an old pro.

Check Yesterday's List against Today's Reality

History is the cruelest judge of all. No matter how long you spend visualizing your agenda, and no matter how proficient you become at controlling interruptions, situations will arise that you could not predict — situations that interrupt, disrupt, and otherwise screw up your schedule. How you adjust to those circumstances is a great measure of your ability to get results.

A good drill to help you grade your adaptability to the real world is to take yesterday's to-do list and see how realistic it turned out to be. Did you accomplish all the tasks on your list? If not, why not? Did everything you had planned fit into the time frames you planned? What items took longer than expected? And what things did you finish sooner than you thought? Did anybody stand you up for a meeting or a phone call? If so, how did you respond?

Taking a look at all these questions the next morning gives you a fresh perspective on the previous day's events and allows you to correct any mistakes in planning that you may be consistently, and inadvertently, making. Checking yesterday's list is also a great tool to use in judging your adaptability skills. If the day was hectic, you were interrupted at every turn, and you still managed to complete all your tasks on time, you may be ready for the organizational big time.

Calculate Costs and Payoffs of Your Time

You know that time is money, and you understand that your time is valuable in both monetary terms and in opportunity costs (things you could be doing if you weren't at work or if you had an hour off). But have you ever taken the time to calculate the costs and payoffs of your time? If not, now is the time.

You can't control every second of every day, but it's a good exercise to calculate how much your efforts are generating relative to the amount of time you are spending on a particular project or task. Sometimes that calculation can be tough. If you're working on a project that will generate a million dollars for your company, but you are one of 20 people contributing to the project in varying degrees, your contribution may be difficult to calculate, but it's worth a try. Because no one else is likely to see this analysis, your estimates are as good as anyone's. So is your estimation of how much your time is worth in dollars and opportunity costs.

Keep a running tab of the value of your time and compare it to the payoffs being generated. You're likely to be surprised by what you find.

Carry a Stopwatch and Log Times for Your Tasks throughout the Day

Unless you know to the second how long it takes you to sort and read your mail, call a client, get a cup of coffee, write a memo, and drive from your home to the Burger King and back you need to carry a stopwatch and log those times. In addition to maintaining an accurate record for future review, the simple act of keying a stopwatch will cause you to focus more intently on the task at hand. Nothing brings a task into focus more quickly than putting yourself on the clock. Things become clearer, your adrenaline picks up, and before you know it you've accomplished a task in a matter of minutes that normally takes half a day.

Keep your log for future reference. After a few weeks, you should be able to schedule every activity in your day to within a few minutes based on previous records. You may get some strange looks when you pull out your stopwatch, but when you start improving your results, everyone will be asking for your secret.

Work on Your "Buts"

We all have them. They are the qualifiers — the things you don't like to hear when the subject is you. For example, we've all said things like, "John is a great salesman . . . *but* he doesn't always follow up the way he should," or, "Jean has a lot of potential . . . *but* I don't know if she's a team player." Even though you may be guilty of using these qualifiers to describe your co-workers, employees, friends, or even family members, you probably have never taken the time to address your own "buts."

What are your qualifiers? If your colleagues were to describe you, what would follow the "buts" in their descriptions? If you want to improve your results, you need to identify and address your personal "buts." The more you can eliminate, the smoother your life will become.

Ask What You Can Contribute

Two heads may be better than one, but three, four, five, and sometimes a dozen heads are far worse. The more people you have involved in a meeting or a project, the slower the process becomes (just look at Congress). The fact is, unless you have something substantive to contribute to a meeting, a discussion, or a project, your time could be better spent attending to other things.

This strategy takes a great deal of courage on your part. Everyone wants to be involved or be "in the loop," but it isn't always necessary. In fact, I would venture to guess that 20 to 25 percent of the meetings you currently attend are complete wastes of time. You attend, you take up a seat, you may offer an opinion or two, but in terms of being the highest and best use of your time, a quarter of your current meetings probably don't make the cut.

You should be self-policing the meetings you attend by asking one simple question: "How can I contribute?" If you have legitimate and substantive things to offer, you should definitely attend. If you are there to have weight and take up space, your time will be better served attending to other matters.

Write Proactive Items in Red Ink

Too often we make our lists based on requests or assignments other people have given us or as follow-ups. If you aren't careful, however, you will get bogged down in reacting to situations while all your proactive, agenda-driven tasks fall further and further down your priority list. You still have to handle situations that come your way — everybody does — but it shouldn't be at the expense of all the proactive tasks you hope to get accomplished.

One way to keep visual track of your proactive and reactive items is to use two differently colored pens when writing your list. Every item that falls into the proactive category can be written in red, and all your reaction or follow-up items can be in black. This effort will give you instant visual feedback on how you're spending most of your time. It will also prompt you to change the way you approach your days. Nobody wants an all reactive to-do list, so a little red ink can go a long way.

Read Your Personal Goals Aloud

If you think that writing them was tough, try reading them aloud everyday. This is not a chant or a prayer, but it is a way of making your goals tangible and personal. You want goals you can understand and then get excited about. There's no better way to get yourself motivated than to read your goals aloud. Even if you recite them to your reflection in the bathroom mirror, the act of reading them makes your goals real.

Chapter 25

Ten Results-Oriented Questions to Ask Yourself

*H*onest self-evaluation is just as central to your organizational growth as setting goals, writing lists, and paying attention to the clock. You need to take time periodically to ask yourself some serious questions. If you aren't progressing as quickly as you think that you should, evaluate your progress and determine why you've fallen behind your stated objectives. If you are on track, but still missing a few ingredients, ask yourself how you can modify your behavior to fill in the gaps.

In the beginning, ask some rudimentary questions about yourself, your current habits, your objectives, and how you intend to become more organized and efficient. The following sections offer some examples.

Have I Set Real, Attainable Goals?

There is a big difference between writing goals and writing attainable goals that you can effectively achieve. If you are currently 30 pounds overweight and haven't exercised in years, it's admirable of you to want to run in this summer's Boston Marathon, but it is also unattainable. There aren't enough hours left between now and the starting gun for you to become a marathon runner. You could certainly modify your goals to include running in a 10-kilometer race this summer, and work your way into a full marathon within the next three years, but even that will require a great deal of commitment and personal sacrifice. It is attainable, however. The first scenario is not.

This same principle applies to all areas of goal setting. If you are making $50,000 a year with marginal savings and investments, to set a goal of being a millionaire in 12 months is unrealistic. Unless you have a rich uncle who is about to pass away and leave you a fortune, or unless you have invented a miracle product that is scheduled to hit the market in a matter of days, your goal is a little lofty for your current situation. That doesn't mean that you won't become a millionaire. It just means that you need to restructure your timetable and establish some reachable intermediate goals to get you on your way.

Nothing is more frustrating to the achiever than setting goals that aren't attainable. Be optimistic when you set your goals, but be mindful of the world in which you live. You'll have a much better chance of success.

Am I Working Every Day to Reach My Goals?

Daily routines become just that: routine. If you are not constantly monitoring your progress toward meeting your goals, you have no chance of getting the results you want.

The first order of business when you are writing your to-do list for the day is to ask yourself a simple question: "Are these items moving me closer to my short-term and long-term goals?" If the answer is an unqualified "Yes," press ahead. If you aren't sure, reexamine your list and ask yourself what you can do to ensure that you're not wasting a day on non-goal-oriented items.

Who Controls My Time?

Wouldn't it be nice if we could all say that we control every second of our days without interruption? How would it feel to set the agenda and have the world bend to your schedule? I don't know of many people who have such a luxury. The president of the United States may come close at times. If the president wants to meet with various world leaders, captains of industry, civic leaders, and the starting lineup for the San Antonio Spurs, the chief executive can set the schedule and everyone is likely to acquiesce to the requests.

No one else I know has that measure of scheduling control. We all answer to someone, whether it's a client, a family member, an employee, an employer, a friend, an acquaintance, or the person on the other end of a ringing phone. Knowing who controls your time and what portion of it they control will help you manage your remaining time efficiently.

How Often Do I Accept Interruptions?

How often you accept interruptions says a lot about how prepared you are to control your days. If you regularly allow anyone and everyone to stroll into your office or home and take up your time, you may gain a reputation as a warm-hearted listener who has time for everyone, but you probably won't be known for the results you produce or the goals you achieve.

There is a time and a place for interruptions. How often you accept them sets the tone for your future organizational progress.

Who Dumps Work on My Desk and How Do I Respond?

If you have earned a reputation as a fixer, people will expect you to fix their problems as well as your own. Some of this expectation is unavoidable. If your boss comes into your office with a proposal she needs you to review, edit, or otherwise modify, you don't have much choice but to drop whatever you are doing and heed your employer's wishes. But if you are someone who lets a co-worker, a colleague, a family member, or a friend drop work on you without notice, you are destined to have others control your time and your agenda.

Is My Daily Planner with Me at All Times?

Notes almost always need to be written at the most inopportune and obscure times. A friend asks you to call him tomorrow morning or a client phones you at home and asks what your schedule looks like next Tuesday. Hopefully, you are able to accommodate those requests or at least give the questioner an informed response. But the only way that's possible is by having your daily planner within easy reach at all times.

My legal notepad, the organizational tool I have used for over 30 years, is always with me. I put it on my nightstand when I go to bed at night, and I pick it up first thing in the morning. Because it is with me, I rarely miss anything. You would be well served to follow that example.

Do I Write Everything Down?

It doesn't do any good to have your planner by your side if you only use it during business hours. Everything, from the phone calls you have to make to the list of groceries you need to buy at the market on the way home, should be written down in one place for easy reference. There's no other way to manage your day effectively.

By writing everything down, you free your mind from the burdens of having to remember details. After I commit to calling someone at a particular time, I write it on that date on my notepad, and forget about it. When the day comes to make the call, I have it written down along with a reminder note on the subject. Nothing could be easier.

Do I Know What My First Task Will Be Tomorrow?

If you haven't organized tomorrow before you go to bed tonight, you are going to struggle to get results. It isn't enough that you have a list of tasks written down in your planner, if you haven't assigned specific times for each task and placed your tasks in order of priority, you don't have a schedule; you only have a list.

Plan your days well in advance. If possible, specify time periods for each call, each meeting, and each function you have to complete. If you know that you have to make a 6:00 a.m. call to Europe next Monday and that call is likely to take an hour, you definitely don't want to schedule a 7:00 a.m. breakfast meeting. If, however, you haven't specified a time to call Europe and you schedule the breakfast meeting for 7:30, you risk missing the overseas party with whom you wished to speak.

Times as well as tasks are an integral part of an organized plan. Make sure that you employ both when making out tomorrow's schedule.

Do I Know What Time I Will Go Home Tomorrow?

Stop times are just as important as start times. Knowing when you will call it a day, turn out the lights, and return home to your family carries just as much weight as knowing when you will be conducting the client conference call or chairing the board meeting.

What Are the Odds That I'll Accomplish Everything on My List?

I've never been much of a gambler, but I have paid close attention to people who set odds and estimate the likelihood of a project or a schedule succeeding. The majority, I have found, give themselves great odds at succeeding while setting the odds of their co-workers' and colleagues' success in the stratosphere. If I had wagered $10 every time a person gave odds he could accomplish a task within a certain timeframe, I would have a tidy little nest egg established from my winnings.

It's always amazed me how people extend their optimism and confidence by unreasonable odds for their success. None of us is perfect, and there are going to be times when we fail. If you understand that and set the odds of your success at a reasonable level, you won't become disillusioned when some things don't work out as planned.

Chapter 26

Ten Tasks That Don't Need to Be Done Perfectly

*I*f you have written a sales proposal to an important potential customer, you should proofread it as many times as needed in order to get it absolutely perfect. When you think that you have it exactly the way you want it, give it to two other people and have them proofread it. You cannot be too perfect when making that kind of presentation. There are plenty of times, however, when you don't need to be 100 percent perfect. Sometimes 90 percent will do nicely, especially if you are saving time.

In the following sections, I list a few of those items that don't require 100-percent perfection.

Lists

Anyone who picked up my notepad would assume that I write in code. The fact is, I write quickly and sloppily when I am working in my notepad because I am writing to myself. To spend a lot of time on penmanship and spelling would defeat the purpose. I take notes to save time. The less time I spend fidgeting with my lists, the more time I have to accomplish my daily tasks.

You should get in and out of your notepad or daily planner as quickly as possible. If that means making entries less than perfectly, who cares? You aren't entering your to-do list in a writing contest. Write your schedule and move on.

Notes

The same is true with notes you take, whether they are at meetings, during phone calls, or as you are contemplating a subject. My notes are constantly filled with arrows, unintelligible abbreviations, questions scribbled in the margins, and other equally indecipherable notations. But who cares? They are working notes, and nobody is going to read them but me. If I were writing for publication, I would spend hours poring over language, punctuation, and syntax. With my notes, I simply want to be able to read what I have written to jog my memory about a subject.

Treat your notes like your lists. As long as you get it, nobody is counting off for lack of neatness.

Filing System

Your filing system requires a little more detail than your lists or your notes, because other people will have to access some of the files either in your computer or your file cabinet. Therefore, you can't create your own random system. You have to keep your files alphabetized and properly maintained, but you don't have to keep them pristine and perfect. If you and the people inside your office understand the filing system, and it is neat and orderly enough for others to find the information they need, that's enough. Perfection isn't necessary and shouldn't be the goal.

Informal Meetings

I often chair morning meetings in my home before I shower and dress for the day. These are internal meetings with members of my staff. I'm not making any formal presentations, so the fact that I'm wearing a warm-up suit and a day's growth of beard isn't likely to offend or shock anyone. By foregoing formalities in these internal meetings, I am able to get more accomplished in less time than if I put on a coat and tie and hustled everyone off to a hotel conference room.

Itinerary and accomplishments are the most important things in internal meetings. How you dress and what the room looks like comes secondary.

Internal E-Mail

An e-mail is far less formal than a letter or a memo. E-mail is like written conversation, so certain conversational liberties can be taken for the sake of expediency. A sentence fragment here and a missed punctuation mark there would certainly be unacceptable in a sales proposal or even in a letter being sent outside the company, but when using e-mail to converse and collaborate with colleagues, less than 100 percent is perfectly okay. (See Chapter 9 for more tips on using e-mail.)

Advice on the Fly

How many times have you been walking to a meeting or rushing to catch a plane when a co-worker approached you and said, "Hey, I need some quick advice on something." Certainly you could dismiss the person by saying something like, "I don't dispense quick advice," or "I'm late, and I don't have time to consider anything right now," but if you're like most people, you continue walking while listening to your co-worker's question.

Usually you offer exactly what was asked of you: quick advice. Don't worry if it's not perfect. You weren't asked to provide nuggets of wisdom from some temple of philosophy; you were asked for some slash-and-burn advice on the fly. If it's less than 100 percent perfect, so be it.

Emergency Tasks

When speed is of the essence, efficiency sometimes takes a backseat. The most graphic example is a life-threatening emergency such as a fire or an accident. In those situations, no one would care about the neatness with which you stored certain items or the manners you used in directing your staff. Speed and safety are number one, so if you are a little short or your manners slip a bit in those situations, most people will understand.

The same is true in business. If 100-percent efficiency takes one extra day, but you are in an emergency mode and the task has to be completed in a matter of hours, 80 percent will always do.

Storage Areas

Unless you have a need to organize your clothes by color or by the day on which you plan to wear certain outfits, how and where your clothes hang is largely up to you. If you're 80 percent efficient at storing clothes in your closet, that's fine. The extra time it would take to coordinate by color and uniformly space the hangers probably isn't worth it.

The same principle applies to your storage room, attic, garage, and other storage areas you may use. Storage areas should never be cluttered, and the effort to organize them shouldn't drop below about 80 percent. But the additional 20 percent to reach perfection in those areas may not be worth your time.

Draft Itineraries

Schedules constantly change. Flights are late due to weather delays, traffic forces you to rearrange a meeting, phone calls run longer than expected, the service in a restaurant is slow. All these things combine to throw off the most well planned itineraries. As you are developing the drafts of your varying schedules, leave room for the possibility that things will change.

To painstakingly pore over an itinerary in its draft stages is foolhardy. You know that at least one item will change as the event draws closer, so keep it fluid, and don't worry if it isn't your best work early on.

Leisure Activities

The whole purpose of scheduling leisure activities is to unwind and relax. If you are obsessed with perfection when it comes to your leisure time, you will never truly relax, rest, and enjoy yourself. Scheduling activities is fine, but when things don't work out as planned, go with the flow. You're relaxing. You'll have a much more pleasant experience if you lower your expectations during R and R.

Chapter 27

Ten Ways to Keep Clutter from Accumulating

In This Chapter

▶ Avoiding clutter in your office

▶ Getting rid of clutter in your home

*N*o one intentionally allows clutter to accumulate. It's an accidental and incremental process — slow and piecemeal but cumulative in its effects, like a small virus that never gets better. One minute you are at your pristine desk mulling over the morning mail, and the next thing you know you have stacks of paper strewn about your surroundings, open books lying on the floor, files out of place, notes scattered around, and a desk that looks like a trash heap. You certainly didn't mean for your surroundings to become so disorganized, but things just got away from you. Before you knew what hit you, the clutter monster invaded your premises and turned everything upside down.

The battle against clutter is a continuous one, but one you can win through patience and practice. These sections provide some keys to help you dig your way out from under the piles you have gradually allowed to weigh you down.

Handle Clutter First Thing in the Morning

The end of a long day may not be the best time to try to clean up your surroundings, especially if you're late getting home from the office, or you are scheduled to be at a restaurant across town in an hour and you still have to change clothes and make another phone call. In those instances, leave the mess, but come in an hour early the next morning and handle the leftover clutter first.

This strategy is a departure from what most organizational managers tell you. The guideline you will hear most often is, "Leave your desk clean at night, so you can start each day fresh." It's great advice if it's possible, but the real world doesn't always work the way we would like it to. Sometimes you simply run out of time to put files away, clear the magazines off your credenza, and return all the reference books to their proper places on the bookshelf. Unless you have a boss who will come into your office at night and throw everything into the trash, it's okay to postpone cleaning the clutter until morning.

It's not okay to put it off any longer, however. If you've left something out overnight, take care of it before you answer your first phone call, speak to your first co-worker, attend your first meeting, or do anything else on your list.

Looking at clutter with fresh eyes (hopefully after a good night's sleep) will also bring new perspective to some of the things you allowed to accumulate. That magazine article you couldn't throw out yesterday may be less important to you this morning. The notes you wrote may be clearer, or you may realize how useless some of the items on your desk really are. No matter what you end up deciding about the clutter, handling it first thing in the morning gets it out of your way and allows you to move on with the rest of your busy day.

Touch Paper Only Once

You will never reach 100-percent efficiency when it comes to handling paper, but if you approach each scrap of parchment you handle as a one-time, one-touch affair, you will improve your efficiency, remove enormous amounts of clutter, and save time. You can only do so many things with a piece of paper (see Chapter 7). The sooner you make the decision to act on it, delegate it, file it, or throw it away, the quicker you can remove it from your sight and move on to other things.

Sometimes touching a piece of paper twice is unavoidable. If you want to respond to a letter, for example, but you need to defer your response until a later time, you will no doubt have to handle the original letter at least twice. Any more than that and you are wasting time. The third time you touch a piece of paper, it should be to throw it away.

If You Haven't Touched It in a Year, Throw It Out

No matter what "it" is, the one-year-and-out rule is almost universally accepted as the standard for throwing something out. Sometimes it's difficult. You may run across something while you're cleaning out storage that sparks memories of a happy time or a pleasant relationship. Should you keep the item? Absolutely not! As much as it may tug on your heartstrings, recognize that the item is taking up valuable space while serving no useful purpose. Throw it out.

Some items do serve useful purposes, however. Tax receipts need to be stored for at least five years, and I recommend that you keep them a decade or longer. Other files may contain valuable historical information you don't need immediately, but will serve a definitive, useful purpose in the future.

If your sole purpose for hanging onto an item is the "that could come in handy someday" excuse, do not succumb to temptation. Discard the item immediately.

Pick a Charity and Support It Regularly

I can't tell you how many times I have heard people say, "I know I should throw that old item away, but I feel guilty. It was expensive when I originally bought it, and it just seems so wasteful to toss it even though I have no use for it." That sort of puritan response is admirable, but it also leads to mountains of clutter. Things you couldn't possibly use are kept lying around because throwing them away would appear wasteful. There is an alternative.

Give the stuff away to charity. Pick a local charity that will accept used items such as clothing, furniture, cars, books, computers, radios, televisions, and accessories and give those items away. Not only are you getting rid of them, you are actually helping those who need help. Your clutter could be very useful to someone, so your feeling of guilt should be replaced with a good feeling of accomplishment. You have helped someone else by clearing out items you no longer need.

Giving to charity also encourages you to clean out more items than you would if you were throwing the items away. Giving things away is easier than throwing them away, so an item you might put back in storage because you simply can't part with it is easily given up when you know that it's going to charity. You clean out more, the charity gets more, and everybody wins.

Clean Out All Storage Areas Every Six Months

No matter how organized and results-oriented you are, cleaning out storage is drudgery. It is tedious, mind-numbing, sometimes backbreaking work that offers no demonstrable payoff other than the knowledge that your stuff is well-organized and put away. Still, force yourself to go through the exercise every six months, if for no other reason than to throw away more stored items with each cleaning.

Because the task of reorganizing your closet, your garage, your storage bin, or your company's warehouse is so time consuming, you are prone to throw new items away every time you clean an area out. That cardigan sweater you couldn't possibly part with the last time you cleaned out your closet becomes less attractive after you have handled it two or three times in the course of cleaning out and reorganizing your space. The same is true with that stack of old magazines you've stored "just in case," or that crate of moth-balls in storage at the warehouse. After two or three times of moving them in and out of storage, the items you held dear the first time you put them away suddenly become garbage you can't wait to get rid of.

Cleaning out storage is not fun, but it's like going to a dentist. You need to do it every six months to keep clutter from taking over your life.

Consolidate

If you are making a trip to the grocery store to buy milk, bread, coffee, truf-fles, and figs, and your son needs a paperback copy of Hemmingway's *The Old Man and the Sea,* you will likely swing by the bookstore while you are out, thus consolidating two tasks into one trip. That's a natural example of consol-idation, and one that doesn't require much thought. Other applications, how-ever, aren't so obvious.

Because of the nature of our business, I receive a lot of reports and updates on various projects, events, and client relationships. Sometimes, I get three reports from three different executives on the same subject. That sort of duplication can be bothersome, especially when you have a limited amount of time to read all the items that cross your desk.

I handle those situations by insisting that the reports begin with a one para-graph summary. If I have already read the same information in another previ-ous report, I may skim the summary and move on. If an executive has a different take on a situation, I can quickly discern the differences in opinion by reading the summaries and scanning a few of the salient points in the reports. Regardless of the outcome, however, I am able to quickly peruse the information I need because I have required our people to consolidate data and compress their analysis.

Undoubtedly, some things in your day can be consolidated. If you and a colleague are working on different parts of the same project, spend a fair amount of time together to ensure that you are not duplicating efforts, and that your coordinated and consolidated efforts will result in a project you both will be proud of.

Throw Boxes Away

One of the most common clutter fallacies is the notion that you should keep all your boxes just in case you need more storage, or in the event that you move in the next couple of years. That logic has created more clutter than any other element in the home or office.

Look in your closet. Do you still have shoe boxes from shoes you have been wearing for months? Is the carton of toilet paper you purchased still sitting in your bathroom closet even though you're down to two rolls of paper? How about the boxes of letterhead and envelopes in your office? Are they still sitting half empty on your storage room shelves?

Throw those boxes away. You'll be stunned by the space you will save and the clutter you will eliminate. And believe it or not, you won't miss those boxes at all. If you move in a couple of years, you will have plenty of opportunities to pick up some new ones.

Make Trash Cans Convenient

Often, clutter accumulates because putting an item on the corner of your desk, or throwing it on your bed, or leaving it on the floor is easier than filing the item or throwing it away. Although putting filing cabinets in every room of your house isn't practical, you can make throwing items away easy. Simply place trash cans in convenient locations throughout your home and office.

When you come in contact with a piece of junk mail or a memo that doesn't require any action on your part, rather than place that item aside so you have to touch it again, throw it away in one of the strategically placed trash cans you have conveniently located throughout your home and office. You will be amazed how much clutter you will eliminate by doubling the number of trash bins you keep nearby.

For Every Purchase You Make, Give an Item Away

Clutter is simply the accumulation of things over time. One of the reasons people let clutter sneak up on them is because they are constantly buying new things but never eliminating old things. Look at the shoe closet of Imelda Marcos. Each of the thousands of pairs of shoes she keeps in her closet seemed important at the time she purchased them. But after a while, the cumulative effect of her shoe fetish became comical. No one in her right mind would build a wing onto a house simply to house shoes, but that is what Mrs. Marcos was forced to do when she left Manila with her late husband.

You have an optimum number of shoes that make sense for your space and lifestyle, just like you have an optimum number of shirts, sweaters, jackets, ties, books, files, computer programs, and CDs. Of course, you want to update your wardrobe and your CD collection from time to time, so how do you keep from being caught in the clutter creep?

Simple. When you buy a new item, give an item away. Whether you give to charity, your neighbor, or the garbage collector, the only way to maintain an optimum level of stuff is to think of your belongings in zero-sum terms. Every time you add something you have to give something away. Not only will your purchases become more practical and efficient, you will get rid of a lot of things you should have eliminated long ago.

Avoid Impulse Purchases

I know that you thought you needed that singing bird clock when you saw it displayed so nicely in the store, but was it really an item you couldn't live without? Probably not. In fact, more than a quarter of the items we purchase are on impulse. We see the item displayed in a store window and decide, without so much as a moment's forethought, that it would be nice to own it.

In addition to being a strain on your budget, these impulse purchases contribute to clutter in your home and office. The best thing to do to avoid this problem is suppress your urges. Leave that impulse item on the shelf. If you really need it, you can always go back after considering all your other options.

Chapter 28

Ten Excuses of Disorganized People

In This Chapter

▶ Recognizing excuses of the disorganized

▶ Avoiding using these excuses in your own life

*A*t the root of all disorganization lies an element of self-delusion, a propensity for the lost and disorganized soul to seek solace in irrational untruths. The lies are usually small, and in many instances they are believable, but they are lies nonetheless. Unfortunately, the liar — the disorganized person who is perpetuating the falsehood — would never admit to conscious deceit. Most fervently believe what they say. That doesn't make it true, however. If anything, the delusion only exacerbates the problem for the person who is stuck in a disorganized web of lies.

In the following sections, I provide a few examples of the lies told by disorganized people. (If you've heard yourself use any of these excuses, jump to the chapters in Part II for everything you ever needed to know about getting organized.)

Sorry I'm Late

This apology has become so insincere that it is almost a cliché. If the person who was late were truly sorry, he would have called in advance and explained that he was stuck in traffic or that his car had broken down. He wouldn't have left his party waiting only to offer the lame but expected lie when he finally arrived.

I Know Where Everything Is

This is usually a lie of justification. If an office or a home is so disorganized that it elicits shock from visitors, the curator of these messes will always explain that it is her own personal organizational system, and that what it lacks in visual appeal it more than makes up for in convenience. She knows where everything is, and because she is the only one who must find everything, she is quite content to live and work in a pigsty.

Of course, this lie usually becomes apparent the moment the liar actually needs to find something amidst the jumbled piles of her domain. At that point, even she can't deny the inefficiency of her system.

I Thrive on Chaos

There is a actually a grain of truth in that lie, although the liar has something of a mistaken interpretation of the word "thrive." Usually the person is confusing a momentary secretion from the adrenal gland (something that is common when an individual is immersed in chaotic circumstances) with thriving accomplishment.

Thriving people get results from their efforts, whether in chaotic or calm environments. Disorganized people experience an occasional adrenaline rush when the chaos they have created begins to get away from them. But that rush should never be confused with thriving. Until you can show the fruits of your efforts, you cannot honestly boast that you have thrived.

I'm Too Creative to Be Organized

This lie is also a tired cliché. The person who utters this one labors under the false impression that all artists are starving bohemians who can only find their artistic brilliance while sitting in a soil-stained apartment with empty pizza boxes strewn throughout.

In fact, the most brilliant and respected artists in history have also been among the most organized people of their time. Leonardo da Vinci was considered one of the most thoughtful and productive scientists of his day in addition to being a prolific artistic genius. Rembrandt was also fastidious in every detail of his life and his work. Dali, although having his share of quirks (including placing cucumbers over his eyes to foster creativity), also insisted that his surroundings be structured to his exacting specifications. The list goes on. All great artists have their idiosyncrasies, but disorganization, for the most part, is not among them.

I'll Get Organized Someday

This kind of statement is more wishful thinking than an outright lie. The person saying it doesn't really believe it, but it is a fleeting dream much like winning the lottery or retiring to Monaco. Without a plan and a time frame, this statement may as well be a lie. It is just as unlikely to happen as any intentional lie.

If I Had More Help, I Would Be More Organized

This kind of statement is usually uttered as an admonition to family members or co-workers whom the liar believes are not pulling their weight. Organizing your time and your surroundings does require the help and cooperation of others, but organizing yourself, your thinking, and your attitude is completely independent of all other people. Having the cooperation of others may be helpful, especially at home, but no one is keeping you from becoming more organized and efficient. You're doing that on your own.

I'll Remember That

The person who refuses to write an important event or message down because he is convinced he will remember it is not only disorganized, she is foolish. Why would you stress your brain trying to remember something when all you need to do is write it down in you daily planner and move on?

Some people believe that it is a sign of great intelligence to be able to remember things. If they don't write anything down, they give the air of having a photographic memory or some other higher intellectual power. What they are really showing is their disorganization and contempt for others around them. No one can remember everything. That's why man invented written language in the first place.

I Don't Have Time to Get Organized

This is the ultimate contradiction. Getting organized gives you more time to accomplish the things you really want to do. Blaming your lack of organization on not having enough time is silly. If you took the time to become more organized, you would have more time to get the results you want out of life.

It's a Busy Schedule, But I'm Sure That I Can Get It Done

This is a lie of the overly optimistic, the person who believes he can, through sheer strength of will, work an unworkable schedule. The man who says this will always over-schedule his days, assuming he can do more than is humanly possible in a 24-hour period, and he will become frustrated when he doesn't finish all the tasks on his list.

Of course, it will *always* be someone else's fault. Traffic was bad, or he didn't get the cooperation from his co-workers he needed. If those other obstacles hadn't gotten in his way, he would have successfully finished his Herculean performance by crossing the last item off his list.

You have to applaud his optimism, but this person is just as delusional as the other fabricators in this chapter.

I Don't Know Where My Day Went

This may not be a complete lie, but unless the person who uttered it spent a portion of the day in a coma or had her memory erased by invading aliens, she knows exactly where her day went. She is just frustrated that it didn't go according to her original plan. Good organization and time-management skills would change her attitude, if she would take the time to change her habits.

Chapter 29

Ten Traits to Avoid at All Costs

In This Chapter

▶ Ensuring that you never develop poor habits

▶ Finding tips for avoiding these traits

*J*ust as organized and results-oriented people share numerous distinguishing traits, some critical flaws distinguish disorganized people — and these flaws ensure that those individuals will remain disorganized and continue to under-perform. These flaws range from the simple to the fundamental, and although you won't find all of them in *all* disorganized people, you can certainly identify the most scatterbrained and least efficient individuals by the organizational flaws they continue to perpetuate.

If you see yourself in any or all of the sections in this chapter, you are on a fatal organizational path. You're not terminal, however. You can change — start by checking out the chapters in Part II for tips and techniques to get organized. After you recognize your own flaws, you can correct them and put yourself on the path to better results. All it takes is effort and lot of honesty on your part.

Disorganized People Rely on Their Memories

The greatest minds in the world cannot remember everything, but the disorganized person takes it as a personal challenge to log things in his mind for future reference without writing them down. The results are always the same: Something slips the person's mind and a task goes untouched or a commitment falls by the wayside.

This is the most critical flaw of the disorganized, and it exemplifies the antithesis of what a results-based individual does naturally. It is second nature for an organized person to write everything down. The disorganized person refuses to write anything down, even if he has a pen and paper in his pocket. "I'll remember that," is the common mantra of the disorganized. The disorganized person probably does remember . . . until someone else says something to him. Then his brain cells will become occupied by the next item he is sure that he'll remember, and the first item slips his mind completely. The cycle continues until the only thing he can be sure of remembering is the last thing he saw or heard. Everything else is distant and fuzzy.

Not only is relying on your memory ineffective, it gives those around you good reason to worry. We've all forgotten things. So when others around you see that you aren't writing things down, they wonder and worry about your ability to remember.

If you don't believe it, go to a restaurant where the waiter takes your order without writing anything down. If you've had some special requests — dressing on the side, no onions, and so on — you're going to be worried. Will the waiter get it all right? How could he possibly remember everything? Your level of anxiety is directly proportional to the complexity of your order and how important it is that your meal be prepared correctly.

Now imagine how your boss, your co-workers, or our family members must feel when they give you important instructions and watch as you nod, but make no move toward a pen and paper. Their anxiety is far greater than what you experience in a restaurant — and rightfully so. Chances are better than average that you will forget what they told you and solidify your position as undependable and disorganized.

Disorganized People Create Piles

When a magazine or a letter comes in the mail, most of us put the item in a pile to be handled later. The disorganized person does this with everything she touches. There are piles of clothes she intends to hang in her closet but never seems to get to, piles of magazines and newspapers she intends to read but never picks up, piles of books she knows she'll need but never seems to touch, and piles of dishes she intends to wash just as soon as she catches a spare minute. These piles seem perfectly normal to the disorganized person because she has created them incrementally. To everyone else, they are a mess.

If you are a pile maker, whether it is books, clothes, CDs, magazines, letters, files, or general clutter, you are destined to remain disorganized until you clean up, pick up, and put things away. Of course, you can always tell yourself you will save time by leaving a pile untouched. You have to get to it sometime, and having it out is a constant reminder.

That lie has a short life. You eventually have to reconcile yourself to the fact that your pile isn't there to remind you of anything. It's there because you haven't touched it. And until you do, you will continue to be disorganized and unproductive.

Disorganized People Accept Interruptions

We all accept *some* interruptions. If I'm in the middle of a meeting and the fire alarm goes off, that's an interruption I am not likely to ignore. If my two-year-old little girl comes into my home office while I'm reading a memo, that's also an interruption I am likely to welcome. However, I won't let an unscheduled appointment interrupt a scheduled phone call, nor will I allow someone to barge into my office with an idea while I am in the middle of reading a file or working on other material. No matter how brilliant the idea may be, disrupting my schedule simply because someone is excited about an idea isn't worth it for me. If it's a good idea, it will still be good when I have time in my schedule to hear it.

If you regularly accept interruptions under the aegis of having an "open door policy," you are turning your schedule over to others. Anyone who has a problem, an idea, or simply a need to chat will come knocking on your open door and will not leave until you shoo him out.

Organized people don't have that problem. They schedule everything, and everyone around them knows it. Interruptions are rare and usually important, so the organized person isn't annoyed by them. He does not, however, tolerate or accept ambiguous interruptions. Nor does he interrupt others. He has the same respect for their time as he expects from others.

Which category best describes you?

Disorganized People Answer Other People's Phones

And when they answer other people's phones, they assume other people's problems. Of course, I'm not suggesting that you simply walk past a ringing phone and refuse to pick it up. If you are an employee, the boss will certainly frown on that; and if you're the boss, you should answer every call as if it is your most valued customer on the line. But if you have a habit of answering other people's phones or being available to meet with the salesman who came to see someone else, you will earn a reputation as someone who assumes other people's problems. And when you get that reputation, an endless stream of ringing phones will be waiting to be answered . . . by you.

Disorganized People Overschedule

If there is one thing the disorganized person doesn't lack, it's a positive belief in her abilities. Just look at her schedule. She honestly believes that she can sleep until 8:00 and still attend three meetings, return six phone calls, and read a 40-page document before her lunchtime racquetball game.

Of course, reality sets in about 10:00 when the first meeting isn't finished and the two others have either been pushed back or canceled. The over-scheduling zealot has only returned one phone call, and will have to excuse herself to call her racquetball partner and cancel the game.

None of this is her fault, however. Just ask her. The meetings ran long because a colleague or a boss got caught up in the sound of his own voice, and the phone calls weren't returned because people were out of their offices. All the other items on her list became jumbled because her morning ran long, and none of the things she had hoped to get done were finished by the time she trudged home, a dogged victim of inexorable fate.

If that sounds like you, check your schedule. Have you planned yourself into a corner? Could something outside your control go wrong and disrupt your entire day? If so, you might want to add a little pessimism to your planning. It could mean the difference between getting results and getting frustrated.

Disorganized People Underdeliver

Underdelivering goes hand-in-hand with overscheduling. When a disorganized person tries to squeeze too many things into too little time, the tasks that get done on time aren't done very well. The disorganized person rushes what shouldn't be rushed, and delivers poor work if he delivers any work at all. His options are to complete something fully and turn it in late, or have it turned in on time and in poor or partially completed condition. He is unprepared for the meetings he attends, because he is constantly running late to meetings. He misses the deadlines he can miss (and a few he can't), and he spends many late nights throwing together work for morning deadlines.

Again, he firmly believes that none of this struggle is his fault. If he had only been given more time or if only the other meetings hadn't taken away so many precious hours, he certainly would have completed his projects on schedule, and he would have given each task more time and attention. He is capable of more thorough work, but he just doesn't have the time to give each item the focus it deserves. His schedule is out of control, and his work suffers as a result.

But it's not his fault. Honest.

Disorganized People Say "Yes" Too Often

Every organization has "yes" people — the people who believe that the only way to the top is by agreeing with the boss on all issues all the time. Rarely are those the most organized and efficient people in an organization, however. In fact, the "yes" people are usually rebuked as "suck-ups" or "brown noses."

Whatever they are, people who say "yes" too often are not setting their own agendas. See Chapter 15 for advice on saying "no."

Disorganized People Can't Tell You Where They Will Be Next Year

Disorganized people don't know where they will be tomorrow or next week. Next year may as well be another decade as far as they are concerned. They are incapable of long-term goal setting because their thinking doesn't extend much past the items on their to-do lists for the current day. If you asked them where they're going to be on this day in a year, they probably will respond by saying, "Probably right where I am now, unless I win the lottery."

Organized people on the other hand have one-year, two-year, five-year, and ten-year plans for themselves that are both personal and professional. They know what they hope to accomplish in their careers, in their home lives, with their health, with their education, and with their finances. They know where they're going and how they're going to get there.

Disorganized people are like rudderless ships. The chances of them running aground are good, but nobody knows exactly where they will land.

Disorganized People Never Seem to Catch Up

Disorganized people are the breathless ones. They run from appointment to appointment, place to place, never fully together when they arrive and never where they should be at the right time. Scatterbrained is a nice word for them. Their apologizes are so practiced and poetic they flow like songs. "I'm so sorry. I can't believe I'm late, but you just wouldn't believe the day I'm having," or, "I am *never* late, but I've just had the most incredibly hectic time today. I'm really sorry."

There's usually a sigh or two thrown in for effect. These people suffer from a combination of afflictions ranging from over-scheduling to simple rudeness. They become caught up in their own worlds to the detriment of everyone around them. Be careful. These disorganized people usually have no idea that they are disorganized. If you deal with them, expect the worst. You won't be disappointed.

Disorganized People Change Course on a Whim

The best indicator of someone's organization is her commitment to her goals, projects, and schedules. If someone is committed and focused on a consistent set of ideals, that commitment shows in her actions and attitudes on a regular basis. She will not be swayed from her mission, even when circumstances change and obstacles are placed in her path. This person is the goal-oriented achiever who maximizes results in every situation and gets the most out of every day.

Then there is the disorganized person who changes directions more often than she changes socks. This person can be persuaded to abandon her goals by something as innocuous as her daily horoscope. In fact, she seeks out astrologers and soothsayers in the hopes that someone will set her goals for her. Her objectives are as unpredictable as the weather, and her accomplishments are few and slim.

If you are this person, throw away your crystal ball and make some decisions on your own.

Chapter 30

Ten Great Ways to Start Your Business Day

In This Chapter

▶ Making good impressions

▶ Leaving yesterday behind

*E*very business days starts differently, but if you are like most of us, you want to get your workday off to a good start. Here are some great ways to jumpstart your business morning and set the tone for the rest of your busy day.

Make a Good Impression with an Early Phone Call

London is five hours ahead of New York, so if you want to catch someone early in his London or Paris office, you have to be on the phone by 4:00 a.m. Unless you have reason to call Europe on a regular basis, I don't recommend making too many 4:00 a.m. phone calls, but if you want to make an impression on someone, call early. The person will remember the lengths you went to just to speak to him.

Schedule a Breakfast Meeting

Your mind is usually fresher in the morning, and because everyone has other things to do, you are likely to accomplish more at a breakfast meeting in less time than if you scheduled the meeting for mid-morning or around lunch. Also, canceling a breakfast meeting at the last minute is more difficult. After someone gets to the office, there's always the chance an emergency will come up and your lunch meeting will go away. That's not likely at breakfast.

Schedule Creative Writing for the Early Morning

Before the phone starts ringing and your day gets out of control — and while your mind is still clear and your creative juices are flowing — pen that proposal you've been intending to write, or spend some time writing letters you've fallen behind on writing. Morning is a great time of day to let your words flow.

Eliminate Yesterday's Clutter

If you had to leave some things on your desk, whether it was paper, files, books, project notes, or other materials, clean those items out of your way before beginning anything else. One day's clutter should never spill over into the next day's activities. Eliminate yesterday's clutter first; then start the rest of your day.

Glance at Yesterday's List

You will have a much better perspective on yesterday's list — what you accomplished, what you didn't finish, what requires more follow-up — after a good night's sleep. Fresh eyes provide fresh perspective. Reviewing yesterday's accomplishments in the bright morning light is always a good idea.

Run a Quick Goal Check

How are you doing in relation to your goals? An early morning check of your status not only gives you a fresh perspective on your goals, but it gears your thinking around your goals for the remainder of the day. Not a bad way to get things underway.

Scan the News

I normally read a minimum of three newspapers a day, and I make the news an early morning priority. If I have a 6:30 breakfast meeting, I rise at 4:30 so I can spend half an hour with my papers before preparing for my day. I always feel that I have a leg up by reading the news early. I am more in tune with the world and the events going on around me, and I am less likely to be caught off guard by changing events in the news. No matter how you get your news, scan it early to prepare yourself for the day.

Write Thank-You Notes

The handwritten thank-you note has almost become an ancient ritual, as dead as Victorian decorum. Don't fall victim to today's brash and often rude rules of engagement. A telephone thank-you is fine, but nothing beats a thoughtful handwritten note. First thing in the morning, as the sun burns the haze off the horizon, is a great time to say thank you.

Send Fan Letters

I make it a regular habit to send fan letters to people whose work I admire. That may sound silly coming from someone who has worked with hundreds of the world's top professional athletes as well as members of the Nobel committee, countless CEOs, broadcasters, authors, artists, musicians, and even the Vatican, but I still know a good job when I see it, and I am still a fan of good talent well used.

Not long ago, I sent a broadcaster, who has no affiliation with our company, a note saying how much I enjoy his work. I had no ulterior motive in sending the note. It was simply a fan letter. Shortly thereafter, I received a nice letter from the broadcaster thanking me for the kind words. He feels good. I feel good. Everybody wins.

Greet Everyone You Meet with a Smile

I know a chef, now the owner one of the finer restaurants in Florida, who has a rule that all of his employees must greet every person with a smile. No matter what time of day or night, this man says that it is a requirement of employment that you smile at everybody. I asked him how he came upon this particular policy. His answer surprised me.

> "I was a student in Guatemala during the revolution, and I saw numerous atrocities there. When I arrived in America, I had 59 cents in my pocket and didn't speak a word of English. Now I own my own restaurant. I realized that you wake up every morning with a choice. You can be happy and proud of what you have, or you can be miserable. I choose to be happy, and I insist that those around me spread that same feeling to others."

That story puts things into perspective. Smiling is a great way to start your day.

Index

Notes

Notes

Notes

Dummies Books™
Bestsellers on Every Topic!

TECHNOLOGY TITLES

INTERNET

America Online® For Dummies®, 5th Edition	John Kaufeld	0-7645-0502-5	$19.99 US/$26.99 CAN
E-Mail For Dummies®, 2nd Edition	John R. Levine, Carol Baroudi, Margaret Levine Young, & Arnold Reinhold	0-7645-0131-3	$24.99 US/$34.99 CAN
Genealogy Online For Dummies®	Matthew L. Helm & April Leah Helm	0-7645-0377-4	$24.99 US/$35.99 CAN
Internet Directory For Dummies®, 2nd Edition	Brad Hill	0-7645-0436-3	$24.99 US/$35.99 CAN
The Internet For Dummies®, 6th Edition	John R. Levine, Carol Baroudi, & Margaret Levine Young	0-7645-0506-8	$19.99 US/$28.99 CAN
Investing Online For Dummies®, 2nd Edition	Kathleen Sindell, Ph.D.	0-7645-0509-2	$24.99 US/$35.99 CAN
World Wide Web Searching For Dummies®, 2nd Edition	Brad Hill	0-7645-0264-6	$24.99 US/$34.99 CAN

OPERATING SYSTEMS

DOS For Dummies®, 3rd Edition	Dan Gookin	0-7645-0361-8	$19.99 US/$28.99 CAN
LINUX® For Dummies®, 2nd Edition	John Hall, Craig Witherspoon, & Coletta Witherspoon	0-7645-0421-5	$24.99 US/$35.99 CAN
Mac® OS 8 For Dummies®	Bob LeVitus	0-7645-0271-9	$19.99 US/$26.99 CAN
Small Business Windows® 98 For Dummies®	Stephen Nelson	0-7645-0425-8	$24.99 US/$35.99 CAN
UNIX® For Dummies®, 4th Edition	John R. Levine & Margaret Levine Young	0-7645-0419-3	$19.99 US/$28.99 CAN
Windows® 95 For Dummies®, 2nd Edition	Andy Rathbone	0-7645-0180-1	$19.99 US/$26.99 CAN
Windows® 98 For Dummies®	Andy Rathbone	0-7645-0261-1	$19.99 US/$28.99 CAN

PC/GENERAL COMPUTING

Buying a Computer For Dummies®	Dan Gookin	0-7645-0313-8	$19.99 US/$28.99 CAN
Illustrated Computer Dictionary For Dummies®, 3rd Edition	Dan Gookin & Sandra Hardin Gookin	0-7645-0143-7	$19.99 US/$26.99 CAN
Modems For Dummies®, 3rd Edition	Tina Rathbone	0-7645-0069-4	$19.99 US/$26.99 CAN
Small Business Computing For Dummies®	Brian Underdahl	0-7645-0287-5	$24.99 US/$35.99 CAN
Upgrading & Fixing PCs For Dummies®, 4th Edition	Andy Rathbone	0-7645-0418-5	$19.99 US/$28.99CAN

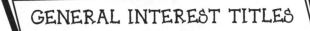

GENERAL INTEREST TITLES

FOOD & BEVERAGE/ENTERTAINING

Entertaining For Dummies®	Suzanne Williamson with Linda Smith	0-7645-5027-6	$19.99 US/$26.99 CAN
Gourmet Cooking For Dummies®	Charlie Trotter	0-7645-5029-2	$19.99 US/$26.99 CAN
Grilling For Dummies®	Marie Rama & John Mariani	0-7645-5076-4	$19.99 US/$26.99 CAN
Italian Cooking For Dummies®	Cesare Casella & Jack Bishop	0-7645-5098-5	$19.99 US/$26.99 CAN
Wine For Dummies®, 2nd Edition	Ed McCarthy & Mary Ewing-Mulligan	0-7645-5114-0	$19.99 US/$26.99 CAN

SPORTS

Baseball For Dummies®	Joe Morgan with Richard Lally	0-7645-5085-3	$19.99 US/$26.99 CAN
Fly Fishing For Dummies®	Peter Kaminsky	0-7645-5073-X	$19.99 US/$26.99 CAN
Football For Dummies®	Howie Long with John Czarnecki	0-7645-5054-3	$19.99 US/$26.99 CAN
Hockey For Dummies®	John Davidson with John Steinbreder	0-7645-5045-4	$19.99 US/$26.99 CAN
Tennis For Dummies®	Patrick McEnroe with Peter Bodo	0-7645-5087-X	$19.99 US/$26.99 CAN

HOME & GARDEN

Decks & Patios For Dummies®	Robert J. Beckstrom & National Gardening Association	0-7645-5075-6	$16.99 US/$24.99 CAN
Flowering Bulbs For Dummies®	Judy Glattstein & National Gardening Association	0-7645-5103-5	$16.99 US/$24.99 CAN
Home Improvement For Dummies®	Gene & Katie Hamilton & the Editors of HouseNet, Inc.	0-7645-5005-5	$19.99 US/$26.99 CAN
Lawn Care For Dummies®	Lance Walheim & National Gardening Association	0-7645-5077-2	$16.99 US/$24.99 CAN

IDG BOOKS WORLDWIDE

For more information, or to order, call (800)762-2974

BESTSELLING BOOK SERIES

Dummies Books™
Bestsellers on Every Topic!

TECHNOLOGY TITLES

SUITES

Title	Author	ISBN	Price
Microsoft® Office 2000 For Windows® For Dummies®	Wallace Wang & Roger C. Parker	0-7645-0452-5	$19.99 US/$28.99 CAN
Microsoft® Office 2000 For Windows® For Dummies®, Quick Reference	Doug Lowe & Bjoern Hartsfvang	0-7645-0453-3	$12.99 US/$19.99 CAN
Microsoft® Office 4 For Windows® For Dummies®	Roger C. Parker	1-56884-183-3	$19.95 US/$26.95 CAN
Microsoft® Office 97 For Windows® For Dummies®	Wallace Wang & Roger C. Parker	0-7645-0050-3	$19.99 US/$26.99 CAN
Microsoft® Office 97 For Windows® For Dummies®, Quick Reference	Doug Lowe	0-7645-0062-7	$12.99 US/$17.99 CAN
Microsoft® Office 98 For Macs® For Dummies®	Tom Negrino	0-7645-0229-8	$19.99 US/$28.99 CAN

WORD PROCESSING

Title	Author	ISBN	Price
Word 2000 For Windows® For Dummies®, Quick Reference	Peter Weverka	0-7645-0449-5	$12.99 US/$19.99 CAN
Corel® WordPerfect® 8 For Windows® For Dummies®	Margaret Levine Young, David Kay, & Jordan Young	0-7645-0186-0	$19.99 US/$26.99 CAN
Word 2000 For Windows® For Dummies®	Dan Gookin	0-7645-0448-7	$19.99 US/$28.99 CAN
Word For Windows® 95 For Dummies®	Dan Gookin	1-56884-932-X	$19.99 US/$26.99 CAN
Word 97 For Windows® For Dummies®	Dan Gookin	0-7645-0052-X	$19.99 US/$26.99 CAN
WordPerfect® 6.1 For Windows® For Dummies®, Quick Reference, 2nd Edition	Margaret Levine Young & David Kay	1-56884-966-4	$9.99 US/$12.99 CAN
WordPerfect® 7 For Windows® 95 For Dummies®	Margaret Levine Young & David Kay	1-56884-949-4	$19.99 US/$26.99 CAN
Word Pro® for Windows® 95 For Dummies®	Jim Meade	1-56884-232-5	$19.99 US/$26.99 CAN

SPREADSHEET/FINANCE/PROJECT MANAGEMENT

Title	Author	ISBN	Price
Excel For Windows® 95 For Dummies®	Greg Harvey	1-56884-930-3	$19.99 US/$26.99 CAN
Excel 2000 For Windows® For Dummies®	Greg Harvey	0-7645-0446-0	$19.99 US/$28.99 CAN
Excel 2000 For Windows® For Dummies® Quick Reference	John Walkenbach	0-7645-0447-9	$12.99 US/$19.99 CAN
Microsoft® Money 98 For Dummies®	Peter Weverka	0-7645-0295-6	$24.99 US/$34.99 CAN
Microsoft® Money 99 For Dummies®	Peter Weverka	0-7645-0433-9	$19.99 US/$28.99 CAN
Microsoft® Project 98 For Dummies®	Martin Doucette	0-7645-0321-9	$24.99 US/$34.99 CAN
MORE Excel 97 For Windows® For Dummies®	Greg Harvey	0-7645-0138-0	$22.99 US/$32.99 CAN
Quicken® 98 For Windows® For Dummies®	Stephen L. Nelson	0-7645-0243-3	$19.99 US/$26.99 CAN

GENERAL INTEREST TITLES

EDUCATION & TEST PREPARATION

Title	Author	ISBN	Price
The ACT For Dummies®	Suzee Vlk	1-56884-387-9	$14.99 US/$21.99 CAN
College Financial Aid For Dummies®	Dr. Herm Davis & Joyce Lain Kennedy	0-7645-5049-7	$19.99 US/$26.99 CAN
College Planning For Dummies®, 2nd Edition	Pat Ordovensky	0-7645-5048-9	$19.99 US/$26.99 CAN
Everyday Math For Dummies®	Charles Seiter, Ph.D.	1-56884-248-1	$14.99 US/$22.99 CAN
The GMAT® For Dummies®, 3rd Edition	Suzee Vlk	0-7645-5082-9	$16.99 US/$24.99 CAN
The GRE® For Dummies®, 3rd Edition	Suzee Vlk	0-7645-5083-7	$16.99 US/$24.99 CAN
Politics For Dummies®	Ann DeLaney	1-56884-381-X	$19.99 US/$26.99 CAN
The SAT I For Dummies®, 3rd Edition	Suzee Vlk	0-7645-5044-6	$14.99 US/$21.99 CAN

CAREERS

Title	Author	ISBN	Price
Cover Letters For Dummies®	Joyce Lain Kennedy	1-56884-395-X	$12.99 US/$17.99 CAN
Cool Careers For Dummies®	Marty Nemko, Paul Edwards, & Sarah Edwards	0-7645-5095-0	$16.99 US/$24.99 CAN
Job Hunting For Dummies®	Max Messmer	1-56884-388-7	$16.99 US/$24.99 CAN
Job Interviews For Dummies®	Joyce Lain Kennedy	1-56884-859-5	$12.99 US/$17.99 CAN
Resumes For Dummies®, 2nd Edition	Joyce Lain Kennedy	0-7645-5113-2	$12.99 US/$17.99 CAN

IDG BOOKS WORLDWIDE®

For more information, or to order, call (800)762-2974

FOR DUMMIES
BESTSELLING BOOK SERIES

Dummies Books™
Bestsellers on Every Topic!

TECHNOLOGY TITLES

WEB DESIGN & PUBLISHING

Title	Author	ISBN	Price
Creating Web Pages For Dummies®, 4th Edition	Bud Smith & Arthur Bebak	0-7645-0504-1	$24.99 US/$34.99 CAN
FrontPage® 98 For Dummies®	Asha Dornfest	0-7645-0270-0	$24.99 US/$34.99 CAN
HTML 4 For Dummies®	Ed Tittel & Stephen Nelson James	0-7645-0331-6	$29.99 US/$42.99 CAN
Java™ For Dummies®, 2nd Edition	Aaron E. Walsh	0-7645-0140-2	$24.99 US/$34.99 CAN
PageMill™ 2 For Dummies®	Deke McClelland & John San Filippo	0-7645-0028-7	$24.99 US/$34.99 CAN

DESKTOP PUBLISHING GRAPHICS/MULTIMEDIA

Title	Author	ISBN	Price
CorelDRAW™ 8 For Dummies®	Deke McClelland	0-7645-0317-0	$19.99 US/$26.99 CAN
Desktop Publishing and Design For Dummies®	Roger C. Parker	1-56884-234-1	$19.99 US/$26.99 CAN
Digital Photography For Dummies®, 2nd Edition	Julie Adair King	0-7645-0431-2	$19.99 US/$28.99 CAN
Microsoft® Publisher 97 For Dummies®	Barry Sosinsky, Christopher Benz & Jim McCarter	0-7645-0148-8	$19.99 US/$26.99 CAN
Microsoft® Publisher 98 For Dummies®	Jim McCarter	0-7645-0395-2	$19.99 US/$28.99 CAN

MACINTOSH

Title	Author	ISBN	Price
Macs® For Dummies®, 6th Edition	David Pogue	0-7645-0398-7	$19.99 US/$28.99 CAN
Macs® For Teachers™, 3rd Edition	Michelle Robinette	0-7645-0226-3	$24.99 US/$34.99 CAN
The iMac For Dummies	David Pogue	0-7645-0495-9	$19.99 US/$26.99 CAN

GENERAL INTEREST TITLES

BUSINESS & PERSONAL FINANCE

Title	Author	ISBN	Price
Accounting For Dummies®	John A. Tracy, CPA	0-7645-5014-4	$19.99 US/$26.99 CAN
Business Plans For Dummies®	Paul Tiffany, Ph.D. & Steven D. Peterson, Ph.D.	1-56884-868-4	$19.99 US/$26.99 CAN
Consulting For Dummies®	Bob Nelson & Peter Economy	0-7645-5034-9	$19.99 US/$26.99 CAN
Customer Service For Dummies®	Karen Leland & Keith Bailey	1-56884-391-7	$19.99 US/$26.99 CAN
Home Buying For Dummies®	Eric Tyson, MBA & Ray Brown	1-56884-385-2	$16.99 US/$24.99 CAN
House Selling For Dummies®	Eric Tyson, MBA & Ray Brown	0-7645-5038-1	$16.99 US/$24.99 CAN
Investing For Dummies®	Eric Tyson, MBA	1-56884-393-3	$19.99 US/$26.99 CAN
Law For Dummies®	John Ventura	1-56884-860-9	$19.99 US/$26.99 CAN
Managing For Dummies®	Bob Nelson & Peter Economy	1-56884-858-7	$19.99 US/$26.99 CAN
Marketing For Dummies®	Alexander Hiam	1-56884-699-1	$19.99 US/$26.99 CAN
Mutual Funds For Dummies®, 2nd Edition	Eric Tyson, MBA	0-7645-5112-4	$19.99 US/$26.99 CAN
Negotiating For Dummies®	Michael C. Donaldson & Mimi Donaldson	1-56884-867-6	$19.99 US/$26.99 CAN
Personal Finance For Dummies®, 2nd Edition	Eric Tyson, MBA	0-7645-5013-6	$19.99 US/$26.99 CAN
Personal Finance For Dummies® For Canadians	Eric Tyson, MBA & Tony Martin	1-56884-378-X	$18.99 US/$24.99 CAN
Sales Closing For Dummies®	Tom Hopkins	0-7645-5063-2	$14.99 US/$21.99 CAN
Sales Prospecting For Dummies®	Tom Hopkins	0-7645-5066-7	$14.99 US/$21.99 CAN
Selling For Dummies®	Tom Hopkins	1-56884-389-5	$16.99 US/$24.99 CAN
Small Business For Dummies®	Eric Tyson, MBA & Jim Schell	0-7645-5094-2	$19.99 US/$26.99 CAN
Small Business Kit For Dummies®	Richard D. Harroch	0-7645-5093-4	$24.99 US/$34.99 CAN
Successful Presentations For Dummies®	Malcolm Kushner	1-56884-392-5	$16.99 US/$24.99 CAN
Time Management For Dummies®	Jeffrey J. Mayer	1-56884-360-7	$16.99 US/$24.99 CAN

AUTOMOTIVE

Title	Author	ISBN	Price
Auto Repair For Dummies®	Deanna Sclar	0-7645-5089-6	$19.99 US/$26.99 CAN
Buying A Car For Dummies®	Deanna Sclar	0-7645-5091-8	$16.99 US/$24.99 CAN
Car Care For Dummies®: The Glove Compartment Guide	Deanna Sclar	0-7645-5090-X	$9.99 US/$13.99 CAN

IDG BOOKS WORLDWIDE

For more information, or to order,
call (800)762-2974

...FOR DUMMIES™
BESTSELLING BOOK SERIES

Dummies Books™
Bestsellers on Every Topic!

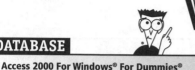

TECHNOLOGY TITLES

DATABASE

Access 2000 For Windows® For Dummies®	John Kaufeld	0-7645-0444-4	$19.99 US/$28.99 CAN
Access 97 For Windows® For Dummies®	John Kaufeld	0-7645-0048-1	$19.99 US/$26.99 CAN
Approach® 97 For Windows® For Dummies®	Deborah S. Ray & Eric J. Ray	0-7645-0001-5	$19.99 US/$26.99 CAN
Crystal Reports 7 For Dummies®	Douglas J. Wolf	0-7645-0548-3	$24.99 US/$34.99 CAN
Data Warehousing For Dummies®	Alan R. Simon	0-7645-0170-4	$24.99 US/$34.99 CAN
FileMaker® Pro 4 For Dummies®	Tom Maremaa	0-7645-0210-7	$19.99 US/$26.99 CAN
Intranet & Web Databases For Dummies®	Paul Litwin	0-7645-0221-2	$29.99 US/$42.99 CAN

NETWORKING

Building An Intranet For Dummies®	John Fronckowiak	0-7645-0276-X	$29.99 US/$42.99 CAN
cc: Mail™ For Dummies®	Victor R. Garza	0-7645-0055-4	$19.99 US/$26.99 CAN
Client/Server Computing For Dummies®, 2nd Edition	Doug Lowe	0-7645-0066-X	$24.99 US/$34.99 CAN
Lotus Notes® Release 4 For Dummies®	Stephen Londergan & Pat Freeland	1-56884-934-6	$19.99 US/$26.99 CAN
Networking For Dummies®, 4th Edition	Doug Lowe	0-7645-0498-3	$19.99 US/$28.99 CAN
Upgrading & Fixing Networks For Dummies®	Bill Camarda	0-7645-0347-2	$29.99 US/$42.99 CAN
Windows NT® Networking For Dummies®	Ed Tittel, Mary Madden, & Earl Follis	0-7645-0015-5	$24.99 US/$34.99 CAN

GENERAL INTEREST TITLES

THE ARTS

Blues For Dummies®	Lonnie Brooks, Cub Koda, & Wayne Baker Brooks	0-7645-5080-2	$24.99 US/$34.99 CAN
Classical Music For Dummies®	David Pogue & Scott Speck	0-7645-5009-8	$24.99 US/$34.99 CAN
Guitar For Dummies®	Mark Phillips & Jon Chappell of Cherry Lane Music	0-7645-5106-X	$24.99 US/$34.99 CAN
Jazz For Dummies®	Dirk Sutro	0-7645-5081-0	$24.99 US/$34.99 CAN
Opera For Dummies®	David Pogue & Scott Speck	0-7645-5010-1	$24.99 US/$34.99 CAN
Piano For Dummies®	Blake Neely of Cherry Lane Music	0-7645-5105-1	$24.99 US/$34.99 CAN

HEALTH & FITNESS

Beauty Secrets For Dummies®	Stephanie Seymour	0-7645-5078-0	$19.99 US/$26.99 CAN
Fitness For Dummies®	Suzanne Schlosberg & Liz Neporent, M.A.	1-56884-866-8	$19.99 US/$26.99 CAN
Nutrition For Dummies®	Carol Ann Rinzler	0-7645-5032-2	$19.99 US/$26.99 CAN
Sex For Dummies®	Dr. Ruth K. Westheimer	1-56884-384-4	$16.99 US/$24.99 CAN
Weight Training For Dummies®	Liz Neporent, M.A. & Suzanne Schlosberg	0-7645-5036-5	$19.99 US/$26.99 CAN

LIFESTYLE/SELF-HELP

Dating For Dummies®	Dr. Joy Browne	0-7645-5072-1	$19.99 US/$26.99 CAN
Parenting For Dummies®	Sandra H. Gookin	1-56884-383-6	$16.99 US/$24.99 CAN
Success For Dummies®	Zig Ziglar	0-7645-5061-6	$19.99 US/$26.99 CAN
Weddings For Dummies®	Marcy Blum & Laura Fisher Kaiser	0-7645-5055-1	$19.99 US/$26.99 CAN

IDG BOOKS WORLDWIDE

For more information, or to order, call (800)762-2974

BESTSELLING BOOK SERIES

Discover Dummies Online!

The Dummies Web Site is your fun and friendly online resource for the latest information about ...For Dummies® books and your favorite topics. The Web site is the place to communicate with us, exchange ideas with other ...For Dummies readers, chat with authors, and have fun!

Ten Fun and Useful Things You Can Do at www.dummies.com

1. Win free ...For Dummies books and more!
2. Register your book and be entered in a prize drawing.
3. Meet your favorite authors through the IDG Books Author Chat Series.
4. Exchange helpful information with other ...For Dummies readers.
5. Discover other great ...For Dummies books you must have!
6. Purchase Dummieswear™ exclusively from our Web site.
7. Buy ...For Dummies books online.
8. Talk to us. Make comments, ask questions, get answers!
9. Download free software.
10. Find additional useful resources from authors.

Link directly to these ten fun and useful things at
http://www.dummies.com/10useful

For other technology titles from IDG Books Worldwide, go to
www.idgbooks.com

Not on the Web yet? It's easy to get started with *Dummies 101®: The Internet For Windows®98* or *The Internet For Dummies®,* 6th Edition, at local retailers everywhere.

Find other ...*For Dummies* books on these topics:
Business • Career • Databases • Food & Beverage • Games • Gardening • Graphics • Hardware
Health & Fitness • Internet and the World Wide Web • Networking • Office Suites
Operating Systems • Personal Finance • Pets • Programming • Recreation • Sports
Spreadsheets • Teacher Resources • Test Prep • Word Processing

IDG BOOKS WORLDWIDE
BOOK REGISTRATION

We want to hear from you!

Register This Book and Win!

Visit **http://my2cents.dummies.com** to register this book and tell us how you liked it!

- ✔ Get entered in our monthly prize giveaway.

- ✔ Give us feedback about this book — tell us what you like best, what you like least, or maybe what you'd like to ask the author and us to change!

- ✔ Let us know any other ...*For Dummies*® topics that interest you.

Your feedback helps us determine what books to publish, tells us what coverage to add as we revise our books, and lets us know whether we're meeting your needs as a ...*For Dummies* reader. You're our most valuable resource, and what you have to say is important to us!

Not on the Web yet? It's easy to get started with *Dummies 101*®: *The Internet For Windows*® *98* or *The Internet For Dummies*®, 6th Edition, at local retailers everywhere.

Or let us know what you think by sending us a letter at the following address:

...*For Dummies* Book Registration
Dummies Press
7260 Shadeland Station, Suite 100
Indianapolis, IN 46256-3917
Fax 317-596-5498

...FOR DUMMIES™

BESTSELLING BOOK SERIES